Postcolonial Spaces

Also by SARA UPSTONE:

SPATIAL POLITICS IN THE POSTCOLONIAL NOVEL
BRITISH ASIAN FICTION: Twenty-First Century Voices

Also by ANDREW TEVERSON:

SALMAN RUSHDIE: Contemporary World Writers

Postcolonial Spaces

The politics of place in contemporary culture

Edited by

Andrew Teverson

and

Sara Upstone

With a Foreword by

Edward Soja

Softcover reprint of the hardcover 1st edition 2011 978-0-230-25225-7

First published 2011 by
PALGRAVE MACMILLAN

Palgrave Macmillan in the UK is an imprint of Macmillan Publishers Limited,
registered in England, company number 785998, of Houndmills, Basingstoke,
Hampshire RG21 6XS.

Palgrave Macmillan in the US is a division of St Martin's Press LLC,
175 Fifth Avenue, New York, NY 10010.

Palgrave Macmillan is the global academic imprint of the above companies
and has companies and representatives throughout the world.

Palgrave® and Macmillan® are registered trademarks in the United States,
the United Kingdom, Europe and other countries.

ISBN 978-1-349-32186-5   ISBN 978-0-230-34251-4 (eBook)
DOI 10.1057/9780230342514

This book is printed on paper suitable for recycling and made from fully
managed and sustained forest sources. Logging, pulping and manufacturing
processes are expected to conform to the environmental regulations of the
country of origin.

A catalogue record for this book is available from the British Library.

Library of Congress Cataloging-in-Publication Data
Postcolonial spaces : the politics of place in contemporary culture /
edited by Andrew Teverson, Sara Upstone.
p. cm.
Includes bibliographical references and index.

1. Commonwealth literature (English)—History and criticism. 2. Space
in literature. 3. Geography in literature. 4. Place (Philosophy) in
literature. 5. Postcolonialism—Commonwealth countries.
6. Postcolonialism in literature. I. Teverson, Andrew. II. Upstone, Sara.
PR9080.5.P72 2011
828'.9140803582—dc23   2011021383

10   9   8   7   6   5   4   3   2   1
20 19 18 17 16 15 14 13 12 11

*For Dominic and Tristan, for whom space means play (AT),
and for a wonderful mother, Christine Dailey (SU).*

Contents

Foreword

Edward Soja

As Andrew Teverson and Sara Upstone observe in their excellent editorial introduction to this collection of essays, postcolonial studies have always been spatial to some degree. This has meant that there has been a long-standing and mutually rewarding relationship between postcolonial studies and the field of human geography. These ties have become even closer given the resurgence of interest in space and spatial theory that has spread across almost every humanities and social science discipline in recent years.

At the same time, however, this so-called 'spatial turn' has raised new issues and challenges to postcolonial scholarship. In some ways, the early advantage postcolonial spatial studies have had is no longer as strong as it once was, as many other fields of study become increasingly spatialized. *Postcolonial Spaces* draws on its well-established special relationship with critical human geography but aims also to move in new directions and build more effective and synergistic bridges between the two distinctive worlds of postcolonial scholarship, one rooted in literary criticism, the other in geography.

The essays contained here are a kind of barometer indicating what has been happening in each of these postcolonial worlds, one seeking to become more spatial while the other, ostensibly more spatial to begin with, looks toward creating closer ties with literary texts and critical methods. Whether productive bridges and/or hybridities have been created in these chapters I will leave to the reader to decide. Instead, I will try briefly to give some additional perspective and background to this search for closer ties between the two worlds of postcolonial spatial studies.

Clearly at the inspirational source not just of postcolonial studies more generally but of specifically spatial versions of postcolonial criticism is the work of Edward Said. None of us, Said writes setting the spatial scene, is completely free from the *struggle over geography*, a struggle that is not just about soldiers and cannons but also about ideas, images and imaginings, about competition for land and territory and the search for fundamental and egalitarian rights to inhabit space. Struggles over real and imagined geographies are not just the leitmotif of Eurocentric orientalism and at the core of Said's explorations of culture and imperialism, they are central to nearly all postcolonial writings and provide a provocative focal point for the chapters contained here.

Postcolonial Spaces, however, is more than an extension or rebirth of Said's ideas. It is an effort to break open new ground and build upon the unprecedented diffusion of critical spatial perspectives throughout the human sciences. In nearly every chapter, for example, there is reference to a 'third space' of creative hybridity and innovative new ideas. Many of the literary scholars reaching out to geography draw on my concept of *Thirdspace* (Soja, 1996), while, somewhat counterintuitively, the three chapters written by geographers tend to refer more directly to the related but less spatially assertive conceptualization of Homi Bhabha in *The Location of Culture* (1994), referring more to notions such as the 'third cinema' and the Third World. In both concepts, the lasting interpretive power of binary logic and Big Dichotomies, such as colonizer–colonized, East and West, North and South, capitalism and socialism, is rejected in the search for alternative spaces, for *other* ways of thinking and writing about the postcolonial condition and its unending struggles over geography.

Despite these conceptually unified theorizations, however, postcolonial studies in general and postcolonial spatial studies in particular have continued to be split into two different discursive worlds. One world thrives on spatial metaphors like mapping, location, cartography, and landscape, works primarily with fictional literatures, and excels at literate textual analysis; the other often tends to sublimate its overtly spatial emphasis, eschews metaphorical flair, and strives for solid materialist exposition of real politics and oppression. These postcolonial worlds and their cultures of representation overlap but remain remarkably discrete and distinctive, especially in their paradigmatic core areas. Both worlds are represented here in *Postcolonial Spaces* although there is a concerted and creative effort to stimulate bridging and perhaps even hybridizing dialogues between them.

The existence and persistence of these two different discursive and interpretive worlds first became apparent to me, a geographer who tries to straddle both worlds, in a seminar I gave at the invitation of doctoral students in the English Department at UCLA. A few of their instructors had 'discovered' space but the students, as is often the case, were far ahead of their mentors in exploring the implications of the spatial turn for literature and criticism. They asked me to do a reading course with them. We met and I poured out my ideas about space and spatiality, while they eagerly and knowledgeably responded, introducing me not just to how the spatial turn was being perceived in English literature studies but to writings that they thought perceptively represented my ideas. Their most salient and successful recommendation led me to the brilliantly revealing and spatially infused writings of J.G. Ballard, whom I had never read before.

In the seminar, however, stylistic or, perhaps more accurately, epistemological differences emerged quite clearly. There seemed to be a formidable barrier between us, interfering with critical debate on substantive and methodological issues. Everything they were saying about spaces and spatiality revolved around textual references, around how authors they had found and read added revealing insight to spatial issues. I found it difficult to respond to their often quite vivid and elegantly phrased interpretations. Was I merely to be a kind of referee judging whether their excerpts and examinations were sufficiently spatial from my point of view? I felt I could do little else since I had not read the texts being referred to so could not think critically about what was being said, except for commenting on the style of presentation. But even this was based on their terms. I had to depend almost entirely on the judgment and interpretive skill of the student making the argument.

This made me wonder how the other English lit students who had not read the particular texts were responding. Was there some shared evaluative culture or hidden frame of reference that allowed them to follow more astutely the perambulations of their colleagues? How were the presentations appraised? Were the students just looking for rhetorical flair, or perhaps the most creative use of spatial metaphors? Setting aside these differences, we searched for some common ground. We all liked Rem Koolhaas's 'Junkspace' (2002) for its vivid descriptions (and encryptions) of the contemporary urban condition; and after I started reading Ballard with delight I discovered some wonderful links between the mysterious housing complex for super-powerful corporate moguls in his *Super-Cannes* (2000) and the economic geography literature on new industrial districts, especially the well-known high tech district on the French Riviera and its cryptic focus in the new town of Antipolis.

The students were pleased that I could find useful references for my own work but this was not surprising to them. They were confident that the world of literature could enlighten any subject, illustrate in creative prose and/or poetics every aspect of the modern world, if only they could find the right quotations. I was just a source for teaching them about using space to do their interpretive work. There was mutual learning going on but there remained an invisible barrier between the literary critic and the geographer, the former exploring fictional texts via geographical and spatial references (i.e., whatever could be found useful in the work of geographers), the latter interpreting actual geographies through the occasional and highly selective reference to particularly revealing literary texts, whether specifically spatial or not.

This brief personal excursion into the contrasting discursive worlds of postcolonial studies brings us back to what you are about to read. After an integrative and very informative editorial introduction, the 11 chapters of *Postcolonial Spaces* literally run the gamut between these quite different forms of postcolonial spatial analysis. The early chapters provide insightful textual probes into the work of Caryl Phillips on racism in the English North, Peter Carey's vividly described colonial cartographies, Jamaica Kincaid's resplendent semiotics of Caribbean gardens, and the oppressively gendered spaces that fill the novels of Anita Desai and Shashi Deshpande. Marking each is a multidisciplinary perspective and an appreciation for attachments to specific space, place, and location. Notable also is the relative absence of abstractly floating spatial metaphors.

Analysis of the micro geographies of Monica Ali's *Brick Lane* move the discussion further into concrete urban contexts, and this is developed in a series of essays on the overlapping spaces of immigrant identity, South Asian children's literature, the ideological shift from Bombay to Mumbai, the *Dirty Pretty Things* of Stephen Frears and other manifestations of immigrant diasporas and urban life. The geographers arrive in force in the last three chapters. Characteristically perhaps, they distance themselves from the presumed superficiality of textual readings and literary criticism to take the disciplinary high ground of rigorous political interpretations of actual geographical conditions. As the editors note, actual 'lived' spaces take precedence in the geographers' chapters, and suddenly it is the authors rather than someone else's texts that come to the forefront. There are discussions of the postcolonial cartographies of Ecuador, Foucault's contributions to understanding colonial urbanism, and a wide-ranging philosophical critique of postcolonial scholarship and the politics of location.

Threads of interdisciplinary dialogue and connection are woven into the 11 chapters, but the existence of two distinct worlds of postcolonial spatial studies remains prominent. The editors and a few authors attempt to use my concept of *Thirdspace* as an integrative link between the different discursive worlds of postcolonial studies, but, oddly enough, the geographers make fewer references to my work than the literary critics. Indeed, it might be said that an assertive spatial perspective, one that is explanatory and causal rather than just reflective and descriptive, is muted in these more geographical essays. Why is it that the literary critics seem to be more comfortable with giving explanatory power to postcolonial spatiality than geographers?

Part of the answer to this question has to do with the eclectic fragmentation of contemporary critical human geography as well as the tendency of many geographers to see the spatial turn and an emphasis on urban spatial causality as a combination of insult (what turn?, we have always been spatial, and we are better at it than you newcomers can ever be) and hazardous risk (edging toward the intellectual abyss of nineteenth-century abandoned geographical-cum-environmental determinism). Not subject to Geography's disciplinary structures and taboos, others experiencing the spatial turn may have far fewer inhibitions, and, I might add, greater freedoms to explore the innovative possibilities of spatial thinking.

And so, in the end, the frictions and differences between the two worlds of postcolonial spatial studies remain prominently displayed in *Postcolonial Spaces*. But rather than a weakness, this overt representation of contrasting views may be an added strength in fostering productive interdisciplinary dialogue. It points out the need to understand better the divisions that exist not just between but also *within* the two worlds of postcolonial spatial discourse. There is no singular, all-encompassing approach to postcolonial studies emanating from either geography or literary criticism. Dialogue must be opened to a wider variety of perspectives. You are all invited to contribute.

Notes on Contributors

Nicholas Dunlop is Lecturer in English Literature and Film at the University of Birmingham. He received his PhD from Queen's University Belfast, and has published numerous articles on postcolonial literature, postmodernism and contemporary British fiction. He is currently completing a monograph on postcolonial theory and representations of pedagogy in science fiction literature and film.

Shehrazade Emmambokus is currently completing her doctorial thesis entitled, 'Contemporary Adolescent Fiction from the South Asian Diaspora', at Kingston University, London. Engaging with cultural studies and sociological investigations, she applies the Overlapping Space model presented in this collection to the novels that she explores and offers readers a renewed way of understanding cultural identity development for post-diasporic individuals.

Monica Germanà is Senior Lecturer in English Literature and Creative Writing at the University of Westminster, London. Her publications include *Scottish Women's Gothic and Fantastic Writing* (Edinburgh University Press, 2010) and a special issue of *Gothic Studies* dedicated to contemporary Scottish Gothic (2011).

James Graham is a Lecturer in Communication and Culture in the Department of Media, Culture and Communication at Middlesex University. His research focuses on the relationship between identity and environment in colonial and postcolonial cultures. Alongside a monograph, *Land and Nationalism in Fictions from Southern Africa* (Routledge, 2009), he has contributed to the *Oxford Companion to Black British History* and published articles in the *Journal of Postcolonial Writing, English Studies in Africa, Transtexte(s)-Transcultures: Journal of Global Cultural Studies, Exiled Ink!*, and *Literary London*.

Caroline Herbert is Senior Lecturer in Postcolonial Literatures at Leeds Metropolitan University. She has published articles on South Asian literature and film in the *Journal of Commonwealth Literature*, the *Journal of Postcolonial Writing, Textual Practice*, and in essay collections. She is currently completing a monograph examining literary and visual representations of Bombay/Mumbai.

Elizabeth Jackson has a BA from Smith College, USA, and a PhD from Goldsmiths College, University of London. After three years of teaching colonial, postcolonial and Victorian literatures at Birkbeck College, University of London, she has recently been appointed as a lecturer in Literatures in English at the University of the West Indies, Trinidad. Her book *Feminism and Contemporary Indian Women's Writing* was published by Palgrave Macmillan in 2010.

Tariq Jazeel teaches Human Geography at the University of Sheffield, UK. His research interests include the intersections between space and the politics of difference in South Asia, especially Sri Lanka, as well as the geographies of critical and postcolonial knowledge production and responsibility.

Wendy Knepper is a Lecturer in English at Brunel University. Prior to joining Brunel, she held positions as a Visiting Research Fellow at the Institute for the Study of the Americas and a post-doctoral Social Sciences and Research Council of Canada fellowship in affiliation with Harvard University and New York University. She has contributed essays to *Small Axe* and *PMLA* as well as numerous essay collections. Currently, she is working on a book-length project about contemporary Caribbean literature in a globalizing era, editing a special issue of Brunel's *EnterText* on Andrea Levy, and co-editing a special issue of *Journal of Postcolonial Writing* on new critical approaches to the work of Wilson Harris.

Stephen Legg is an Associate Professor in the School of Geography, University of Nottingham. His research focuses on the urban politics of interwar India. His publications include *Spaces of Colonialism: Delhi's Urban Governmentalities* (2007, Wiley-Blackwell) and *Spatiality, Sovereignty and Carl Schmitt: Geographies of the Nomos* (ed. 2011, Routledge).

John McLeod is Professor of Postcolonial and Diaspora Literatures at the School of English, University of Leeds, UK. He is the author of *Postcolonial London: Rewriting the Metropolis* (Routledge, 2004) and *J. G. Farrell* (Northcote House, 2007), and he has also edited *The Revision of Englishness* (Manchester University Press, 2004) and *The Routledge Companion to Postcolonial Studies* (Routledge, 2007). A revised second edition of his best-selling book *Beginning Postcolonialism* (Manchester University Press) appeared in 2010.

Sarah A. Radcliffe is Reader in Latin American Geography at the University of Cambridge. Her research interests include postcolonial development in the Andes and the role of geography in postcolonial nation-states. A recent publication is *Indigenous Development in the Andes: Culture, Power and Transnationalism* (Duke University Press, 2009).

Andrew Teverson is Director of Studies for English Literature and Creative Writing at Kingston University, London. He is the author of *Salman Rushdie* (Manchester University Press, 2007), and has recently been writing about Rushdie's collaboration with the visual artists Tom Philips and Anish Kapoor. His current research is on folk narrative and fairy tale in postcolonial contexts, and he is completing a book on fairy tale for the Routledge New Critical Idiom series.

Sara Upstone is Principal Lecturer in English Literature at Kingston University, London. She is the author of *Spatial Politics in the Postcolonial Novel* (Ashgate, 2009) and *British Asian Fiction* (Manchester University Press, 2010) and is currently researching the role of realism in contemporary Black British writing.

Acknowledgements

Warm thanks to Lisa Hall and Brycchan Carey for their help organizing the conference from which this collection emerged. Thanks too to David Rogers, Avril Horner and Sarah Sceats for supporting the conference and offering advice on publication.

For permission to reproduce materials, thanks to Haleh Anvari for generously allowing us to reproduce a photograph from her *Chador-dadar* series (2006) for the cover of this volume, and for her permission to use the photograph that appears in Chapter 5. We are also grateful to Ana Lucía Tasiguano of the Department of Intercultural Communication of CODENPE for permission to reproduce the *Mapa de las Nacionalidades y Pueblos del Ecuador* in Chapter 9.

Finally, we would like to express our thanks for the professionalism and patience of our editors at Palgrave.

Introduction

Andrew Teverson and Sara Upstone

In his groundbreaking study, *Thirdspace* (1996), Edward Soja argues that the concept of space has often been overlooked in analyses of human experience. Locating this disregard in the privileging of history in philosophy from the Enlightenment onwards, he laments the fact that 'putting phenomena in a temporal sequence' has somehow come to be seen as 'more significant and critically revealing than putting them beside or next to each other in a spatial configuration' (1996, p. 168). Only recently, in the second half of the twentieth century, has this hierarchy been slowly and gradually challenged. What has emerged is a spatial renaissance that has recognized the importance of place and location. In the field of postcolonial studies, however, space has *always* been central. From its very beginnings, those involved in developing knowledge of colonial and postcolonial discourses have identified space in all its forms as integral to the postcolonial experience. Often cited as the seminal postcolonial critic, Edward Said's work is intimately spatial, as illustrated by two passages of his writing in particular: 'Imaginative Geography and Its Representations: Orientalizing the Oriental', in *Orientalism* ([1978] 1995, pp. 49–72), and the later devotion of the first 15 pages of *Culture and Imperialism* (1993) to the relationship between empire and geography. These interests are also encapsulated in Said's (1990) essay, 'Geography, Narrative, and Interpretation', in which he writes that studies of postcolonial literature must be rooted in the same 'concrete geography' which defines works such as Raymond Williams' *The Country and the City* (1990, p. 84). Said's work has been followed by a continued identification between matters of space and/or place in later works falling within the remit of postcolonial studies. Texts such as J.K. Noyes's *Colonial Space: Spatiality in the Discourse of German South West Africa 1884–1915* (1992) and Robert P. Marzec's *An Ecological*

1

and Postcolonial Study of Literature: From Daniel Defoe to Salman Rushdie (2007) are indicative of a corpus of spatial postcolonial works, while sections in major collections such as Iain Chambers and Lidia Curti's *The Post-colonial Question: Common Skies, Divided Horizons* (1996) and Bill Ashcroft, Gareth Griffiths and Helen Tiffin's *The Post-Colonial Studies Reader* (1994) have cemented the importance of spatial concerns in definitions of postcolonial studies as a discipline. Perhaps most notably, the influential postcolonial critic Homi Bhabha can be seen as the natural inheritor of Said's spatial perspective. Both his own concept of 'Third Space' (1999, pp. 111–32) as the location of hybridity and his focus on the nation as a site of colonial encounter (1990a, pp. 1–7; 1990b, pp. 291–322) speak to a geographical rather than historical criticism.

The metaphorical concerns of Bhabha point to a preoccupation with abstract spatiality in postcolonial criticism. Yet, equally, engagement with space is often expressed through the awareness of *location* as a factor that is profoundly important. The idea that place plays a significant role in how one defines one's own identity and, equally, how that identity is defined by others, is continually foregrounded in postcolonial studies. In particular, the colonial manipulation of national boundaries and the subsequent challenge for postcolonial states in forming cohesive identities within the terms of these inherited boundaries have made the nation a central feature in discussions of postcolonial identity. Texts such as Ian Baucom's *Out of Place: Englishness, Empire and the Locations of Identity* (1999), Timothy Brennan's *Salman Rushdie and the Third World: Myths of the Nation* (1989), Satish Deshpande's 'Hegemonic Spatial Strategies: The Nation-Space and Hindu Communalism in Twentieth-century India' (2001), Imre Szeman's *Zones of Instability: Literature, Postcolonialism, and the Nation* (2003) and Simon Gikandi's *Maps of Englishness: Writing Identity in the Culture of Colonialism* (1996) have identified the ways in which discourses of nationhood are formulated in relation to colonial and postcolonial agendas. This critical practice has been extended, in studies such as Elleke Boehmer's *Stories of Women: Gender and Narrative in the Postcolonial Nation* (2005), Sara Mills's *Gender and Colonial Space* (2005), and Sangeeta Ray's *En-Gendering India: Woman and Nation in Colonial and Postcolonial Narratives* (2000), to a concern with the gendered aspects of such national politics.

This interest in the national is supplemented with additional concern for how postcolonial identities are played out at more 'local' levels: in cities, in rural communities, in homes, in schools, and in other private and public spaces. So R.M. George's *The Politics of Home: Postcolonial Relocations and Twentieth-Century Fiction* (1996) considers how public discourses of empire are replicated on a private scale, while Joseph McLaughlin's *Writing the Urban Jungle: Reading Empire in London from Doyle to Eliot* (2000) maps the role of the urban imperial space as a model of colonial enterprise. At the same time, there has been a focus on how the postcolonial experience transcends national boundaries, including how they become intertwined in the contemporary period with discourses of globalization (During, 2000, pp. 385–404). Steve Clark's *Travel Writing and Empire* (1999), Mary Louise Pratt's *Imperial Eyes* (1992), David Spurr's *The Rhetoric of Empire: Colonial Discourse in Journalism, Travel Writing and Imperial Administration* (1993), Tim Youngs' *Travellers in Africa: British Travelogues, 1850–1900* (1994), and Syed Manzurul Islam's *The Ethics of Travel: From Marco Polo to Kafka* (1996) have drawn attention to travel as a movement through space, and have explored the implication of such movement in the production of a colonial gaze. Focus on these other scales of engagement draws attention to the pervasive impact of colonialism on the nations it conquered or settled, but also to the diverse ways in which postcolonial citizens may call into question or interrogate the roles and identities which have been the colonial legacy. Frequently, such concerns offer up multifaceted and even problematic conceptions of what it means to be 'postcolonial'. Informed – among other things – by negotiations of gender, of class, of religion, and of sexuality, the divergent politics of individual locations draws attention to the multiple registers of experience that inform how postcolonial identities develop. Equally, through concern for both private and public experience, they address the complex relationships between postcolonial individuals, families, communities, and nations and, indeed, a broader global consciousness.

As already suggested, it is Soja's work that has most effectively established a comprehensive and broad-based theoretical argument for the privileging of space in postcolonial studies. While the application of spatial theory to postcolonial studies is an original development in Soja's work, however, he also acknowledges a significant debt to the philosopher Michel Foucault whose later work exemplifies the spatialization of philosophy, and who was responsible for the prophetic and (for Soja at least) influential proclamation that 'the present epoch will perhaps be above all else the epoch of space' (Foucault, 1986, p. 22). More broadly, Soja also acknowledges the influence of the philosophical framework of French poststructuralism that undergirds Foucault's work, which has itself shown a consistent analytical concern for spatiality. Similar influences may also be seen to operate in the work of Edward Said, for whom an appreciation of space is central to the practice of colonial discourse analysis. It is already well known that Said is heavily influenced by Foucault's understanding of the notion of discourse, but it is arguably less well established that Foucault's theorization of spatiality had a direct impact on Said's understanding of colonialism. These connections are made explicit in the work of Noyes, whose own reading of colonial space draws consciously on poststructuralist terminology. His theorization of colonial space reveals a model of poststructuralist principles of *différance* and trace, as 'the increasingly rigid organization of space in colonization is constantly threatening to fragment the totality of space it seeks to create' (Noyes, 1992, p. 20). In each of these instances, the 'inherent spatiality of human life' (Soja, 1996, p. 1) is revealed as the shared concern of both postcolonial and poststructuralist thinkers alike.

This connection between postcolonial and poststructuralist theory in the realm of interest in the spatial points towards how the present study advances existing scholarship. In critiques of postcolonial theory there is often the assumption that the influence of poststructuralism on postcolonial studies has led to its detachment from 'the real world'. Aijaz Ahmad's now-famous critique of postcolonial theory's poststructuralist influences, presenting the discipline as 'debunking all efforts to speak of origins, collectivities, determinate historical projects' (1992, pp. 38, 13), has prompted a wave of similar critiques of poststructuralism's influence (Dirlik, 1994; Larsen, 2000; Chrisman, 2003; Parry, 2004). By emphasizing the shared spatiality of these two fields of study, this book instead suggests that poststructuralism is essential to making those working in postcolonial theory more, and not less, aware of the specifics of location and situation which they have sometimes under-emphasized. In the wake of the 'ethical turn' in literary studies and its reading of poststructuralism as a movement whose proponents have 'doggedly and determinedly sought to place distance between themselves and any mention of an ethical or moral perspective' (Davis and Womack, 2001, p. ix), such an assertion may be controversial. Yet it is made in acknowledgement, equally, that part of this ethical turn must be a re-evaluation of the narrow contexts in which poststructuralist theory has often been placed (Baker, 1995). Here, ironically, the issue of location is paramount: the reading of poststructuralist theory out of its French political context, and often in translation, has stripped it for many readers of the obvious associations with real-world political circumstance that the texts provide. In his appraisal of Foucault quite explicitly through events in Paris in 1968, Soja himself points towards this necessity for a spatialized reading.

Recent changes in the field of geography, in particular, can be seen to facilitate such recuperation of poststructuralist discourses. Rather than offering an alternative to the poststructuralist-influenced literary/cultural postcolonial theory, postcolonial geography has led the way in illuminating the relevance of poststructuralist theories to both the interpretation of the physical reality of colonialism, and the material struggles of postcolonial societies. Most noteworthy in this regard is the turn to Foucault, whose relevance speaks beyond Soja's project to a more generalized renaissance (Driver, 1992; Mathess, 1992; Crampton and Elden, 2008; Sharp, 2008). There has, however, also been a turn to Deleuze and Derrida (Doel, 1999; Bonta and Proveti, 2004; Buchanan and Lambert, 2005). The possibilities of this work for postcolonialism can be seen in Stephen Legg's groundbreaking essay, 'Beyond the European Province: Foucault and Postcolonialism' (2008), which documents not only Foucault's relevance to postcolonial concerns, but also the potential to make use of this knowledge in a rooted geographical framework. In doing so, geographers go some way towards realizing the 'spatial materialism' that Lawrence Grossberg (1996) sees as the culmination of a simultaneously postcolonial and poststructuralist interest in space.

In the wake of this geographical intervention, one major aim of this book is to bridge the gulf apparent in much existing postcolonial theory and criticism between textual analysis and the exciting and dynamic contributions to postcolonial thought being made in the discipline of geography. Over the past decade, academics working in the field of geography can be seen not only to have embraced postcolonial theory, but to have made an important intervention in its debates and controversies. Yet, to date, this intervention – although noted by those working in the field of postcolonial studies – has largely remained on the margins of postcolonial theory as it is presented in academic criticism, which has retained its literary and cultural bias. Geography has proved particularly important in its contribution to our understanding of material locations and domestic and urban scales. This is apparent in texts such as Alison Blunt's *Domicile and Diaspora: Anglo-Indian Women and the Spatial Politics of Home* (2005), Felix Driver and David Gilbert's *Imperial Cities: Landscape, Display and Identity* (1999), Daniel Clayton's *Islands of Truth: The Imperial Fashioning of Vancouver Island* (2000) and Jane M. Jacobs's *Edge of Empire: Postcolonialism and the City* (1996). Works such as Derek Gregory's *The Colonial Present* (2004) have also furthered scholarship on the significance of spatiality in a global context through attention to the complex spatial politics of neo-imperial discourses. Geography has also contributed significant work on the interaction between gender and imperial discourses through works such as Alison Blunt's *Travel, Gender and Imperialism: Mary Kingsley and West Africa* (1999).[1] In particular, however, these geographical interventions have foregrounded how the physical act of settlement and its textual processes – cartography and mapmaking – are the background to the textual representations focused on by many literary scholars. Studies such as Jeremy Black's *Maps and Politics* (1997) and Matthew Edney's *Mapping an Empire* (1997) illustrate the unique contribution of geography in these terms. Beginning with the turn towards critical geography in the 1970s, geography has been transformed as a discipline, with an increasing awareness of how the discourses of gender, race, and class are at work in the process of mapping, planning, and representing space. This has involved significant attention being paid to the role of geography in sustaining colonial empires, but also the ways in which global inequalities emerge in the context of the specifics of location. It has meant not just an acknowledgement of the role geography played in the colonizing enterprise, but also the need for contemporary geographical studies to 'write back' to this history of geography with a current practice that shows awareness of postcolonialism and itself resists an Orientalist positioning.[2]

Soja himself is part of this discourse: his own focus on the perspectives of Spivak and Bhabha point to the possibilities for combining textual and material practice. He is not alone here, however. Inspired explicitly by Soja's work on what they refer to as the 'geographical turn' (1994, p. 3), Anne Godlewska and Neil Smith's (1994a) edited collection *Geography and Empire* can be seen as the first major publication to emphasize the relationship between imperial discourse and geography. Here, the argument is definitively made that 'empire was ... a quintessentially geographical project' (Godlewska and Smith, 1994b, p. 3), a claim that was to be reinforced a year later with Bell *et al.*'s *Geography and Imperialism, 1820–1940* (1995). In 2002, moreover, with the publication of Alison Blunt and Cheryl McEwan's *Postcolonial Geographies*, this area of study became visibly 'postcolonial'. Making the statement that 'postcolonialism and geography are intimately linked' (2002b, p. 1), McEwan and Blunt accurately reflect the inherent spatiality of postcolonial studies. Their collection, however, did not emerge from a vacuum, but rather appears in the context of debates in geographical studies stretching back a decade prior to their own study, including Felix Driver's *Geography Militant: Cultures of Exploration and Empire* (2001), Alison Blunt and Jane Wills's 'Decolonising Geography: Postcolonial Perspectives' (2000) in their book *Dissident Geographies: An Introduction to Radical Ideas and Practice*, and Jonathan Crush's influential essay 'Post-colonialism, De-colonization, and Geography' (1994), the first to prominently argue for the reform of geographical practice to take account of postcolonial experiences.[3] In fact, McEwan and Blunt's collection can be seen as the first response to Crush's claim, eight years earlier, that 'Western geography has not, as yet, seriously engaged with the arguments of post-colonial scholars' (Crush, 1994, p. 334). Whereas Crush would claim that 'the very idea that the discipline as a whole needs de-colonizing is likely to be treated with skepticism if not derision in mainstream circles' (ibid., p. 334), the publication of McEwan and Blunt's book announces an important sea change. Perhaps most indicative in these terms is Joanne Sharp's *Geographies of Postcolonialism* (2008). An introductory text directed at geography undergraduates, it marks not just a recognized interest in postcolonial geography, but also correlative pedagogic developments.[4]

These geographical studies make it a matter of neglect to dismiss the importance not just of the abstract idea of space, but the materiality of this space, in postcolonial theory. What has been useful, in this respect, has been the positive reaction of geographers to the recognized limitations of postcolonial theory in its traditional form. Rather than distancing themselves from postcolonial theory for these reasons, geographers have increasingly foregrounded the potential improvements to the discipline that might be made by a geographical intervention. Indicative of this is the debate that has been raging in geographical studies since the late 1990s, which has become increasingly optimistic about the availability of literary and cultural postcolonialism for geographical investigation. Writing in 1997, Clive Barnett argued that social scientists' suspicion of literary and cultural theory, resulting from the perception that it is not materialist enough, could potentially reproduce institutionally sanctioned disciplinary authority through the reinforcement of reductive binary oppositions between the humanities and social sciences and the discouragement of interdisciplinary work (1997, p. 137). His review of the expressed fear of 'descent into discourse' that might be prompted by adoption of postcolonial theory – 'the implied charge that too close or too lingering attention to language, rhetoric, or textuality indicates a retreat from politically engaged, relevant research' – culminates not in an acceptance of such concerns, but rather in a recognition of the value of an intervention into postcolonial theory by geographers. His argument that '[i]nterdisciplinary appropriation by human geographers ... takes its critical distance by arguing that this sort of literary theory needs to be augmented by greater attention to material practices, actual spaces, and real politics' (ibid., p. 137), proffers a willingness to engage that has become the norm.

So for Godlewska and Smith:

> The brilliant vista of Said's work is constrained by an ambivalence towards geographies more physical than imagined, a reluctance to transgress the boundaries of discourse and to feel the tangible historical, political and cultural geographies he evokes. Yet precisely this connection of histories *of* geography with historical *geographies* is what needs to be explored.
>
> (1994b, p. 7)

It is this focus on a previously 'overlooked' (McEwan and Blunt, 2002b, p. 7) materiality which is the major contribution of geography to postcolonial studies. In their focus on 'real' space, postcolonial geographers offer postcolonial theory a potential solution: a means of going beyond what geographers see as 'cultural production' and of challenging the overly textual nature of its own practice (Sharp, 2008, p. 5). Indeed, in their introduction to *Postcolonial Geographies*, Blunt and McEwan identify this as a precise aim of their own study: 'In many ways, *Postcolonial Geographies* is a response to the criticism that greater theoretical sophistication has created greater obfuscation, and that postcolonialism is too theoretical and not rooted enough in material contexts' (2002b, p. 5).

Equally, for Sharp:

> Postcolonial theory has made very important interventions in the arts and social sciences in the last 15 to 20 years, but also has a reputation for being very difficult. It has focused in particular on the ways in which peoples can be known and how this knowledge can be communicated. It is not simply about dry academic matters though.
>
> (2008, p. 110)

In geography, therefore, one finds the answer to Ella Shohat's complaints that postcolonial theory 'collapses very different national-racial formations' to produce a 'disorienting ... dubious spatiality' (2000, pp. 129–30).

For the above reasons, the incorporation of geographical perspectives into the cultural arena of postcolonial theory does not entail a dismissal of its central tenets, or a challenge to its dominant *modus operandi*. This development is not something, that those working in postcolonial studies should be concerned about, as it has conventionally been conceived in literature and cultural studies departments. Rather, it offers an important modification of existing practice that speaks to the very concerns that have created so much unease and debate within the cultural field. It is not a rejection of the importance of texts but rather, in Driver's words, a recognition of these texts as 'articulations of practices' (2001, p. 8).[5] If one looks, for example, at the modification of the notion of hybridity by postcolonial geographers, with their critique of 'the overuse of abstract metaphors' and 'the disingenuous move of "third space" ... beyond the situated practices of place and the lived experiences of history' (Mitchell, 1997, p. 534), then one encounters the same desire for a re-balancing of emphasis in postcolonial theory that one also finds in *Postcolonial Studies: A Materialist Critique*, the work of leading postcolonial theorist Benita Parry (2004, p. 56).[6]

This appetite for dialogue between postcolonial and geographical studies has been apparent since at least the 1980s, when scholars working on the spatial contours of the postcolonial experience began to express the desire for a more specific theorization of their discipline. It is, for instance, evident in works such as Peter Hulme's *Colonial Encounters: Europe and the Native Caribbean, 1492–1797* (1986), in which Hulme's discussion of literary texts such as *Robinson Crusoe* and *The Tempest* is framed by a focus on 'particular geographical and ideological terrain (1986, p. 2). More recently, Tim Youngs' discussion in *Travellers of Africa* of Soja, and his claim to be 'more historicist' (1994, pp. 4–5) than Bhabha, equally foregrounds such a connection.

That this dialogue is a two-way exchange, furthermore, is evident not just in the way that postcolonial geographers have adopted, with modification, the poststructuralist frameworks of literary or cultural postcolonial theory, but also in the range of sources postcolonial geographers use. That 'the very root meaning of the word "geography" is literally "earth writing"' (Barnes and Duncan, 1992, p. 1) points to the textuality that is always part of the geographical endeavour. Examine, for example, Sharp's *Geographies of Postcolonialism*, and one encounters, among the maps and case studies, literary texts, travel narratives, autobiography, film, and art. Both Sharp and Blunt and McEwan begin their books with reference to Said's *Out of Place* and, indeed, Said's influence is felt in a number of geographical criticisms.[7] Godlewska and Smith begin with Conrad; Driver has written about Conrad and Mackinder (1992); Neil Smith (1994) has framed his arguments elsewhere in terms of both Said and the work of literary scholar Mary Louise Pratt; Blunt and Wills include sections on the significance of Said, Bhabha and Spivak. While Sharp announces the importance of practice, the notion of geographies as not just real, but also imagined, is central to her geographical postcolonialism (2008, p. 17), a continued focus which can be seen to reflect not just the importance of Soja's influence, but also an interest in textuality – the writing of space in its broadest terms – that is shared by both cultural and geographical scholars. Indeed, Sharp has been the most significant contributor to the fusion of geographical and literary perspectives from within the former discipline: her essay 'Locating Imaginary Homelands: Literature, Geography, and Salman Rushdie' (1996) argues that geographers 'have not made sufficient use of literary sources in their work' as an 'alternative account of processes that they are seeking to describe and explain' (ibid., p. 119). Her focus on Rushdie's 'geo-graphing' and 'self-consciously spatial texts' with their 'territorial forms of identification' (ibid., p. 124) is a model of interdisciplinary enquiry that this book seeks to replicate.

In this sense, the opposition between geographical and literary practice is increasingly a false one, since they have been brought together by the acknowledgement of a 'simultaneously "real and imagined"' (Soja, 1996, p. 239) space in colonial and postcolonial discourses. That Bhabha and Soja share a 'third space' indicates this confluence – but also the important differences of emphasis – between the two disciplines. While Soja's thirdspace is primarily real – located in Los Angeles – and secondarily is imagined through its inhabitants, Bhabha's third space, in contrast, is primarily imagined – a metaphor for the hybrid postcolonial encounter – and only secondarily rooted in a material geography. That the two fields are so similar and yet coterminously so different in their approach speaks to how each enriches the other: pointing geography towards its textuality, and literary studies towards the importance of the material.

Coming, as it does, in the wake of such critical developments, *Postcolonial Spaces* is a truly interdisciplinary project. Other studies have also begun to explore this terrain. Graham Huggan's *Interdisciplinary Measures: Literature and the Future of Postcolonial Studies* (2008), for instance, is equally forceful in its affirmation that the fusion of geography and literature is at the centre of interdisciplinarity in postcolonial studies. That Huggan devotes one-third of his book to literature and geography speaks to the relevance of such connections for the future of postcolonial theory as an interdisciplinary field of enquiry. What this collection of essays does which Huggan's monograph does not, however, is to incorporate interdisciplinary perspectives directly, by representing the work of both geographers *and* literary and cultural critics. Moreover, *Postcolonial Spaces* – although rooted predominantly in geography and literature – also aims to draw more generally upon the possibilities of this dynamic cross-over which, again, Huggan has done much to emphasize.[8]

Beyond the concern for cultural studies and geography, postcolonial spatiality has drawn contributions from a wide number of fields, including history, as is evident from David Philip Miller and Peter Hans Reill's *Visions of Empire* (1996), Simon Ryan's *The Cartographic Eye: How Explorers Saw Australia* (1996), and D. Graham Burnett's *Masters of All They Surveyed: Explorations, Geography, and a British El Dorado* (2000), and sociology, as attested by Anthony King's *Global Cities: Post-Imperialism and the Internationalization of London* (1990) or – most indicatively – Paul Carter's self-confessed interdisciplinary work *The Road to Botany Bay: An Essay in Spatial History* (1987).

Including contributions from geographers, literature specialists, those working in film studies, and media and cultural studies specialists, the chapters here cover the fields of literature, film, art, geography, and media studies. Many of them emerged from a conference held at Kingston University, London, in 2007, which brought together academics in all of these fields, and from countries including Britain, the USA, Israel, Hong Kong, Sweden, Portugal, Slovakia, Istanbul, Singapore, Taiwan, South Africa, India, and Egypt: a global delegation that may be seen as indicative of the broad, international concern with issues of postcolonial spatiality.

Overview of the book

Perhaps more importantly, all of the chapters in this book can be seen to be documents that attest to the significance of the lessons offered by interdisciplinary dialogue. While products of their own disciplines, each chapter speaks to the coterminously textual and material nature of postcolonial spatiality. The opening four chapters of this book present what might be considered to be conventional 'literary' discourses of postcolonial spatiality. Yet, in each of these cases, the authors have engaged with the specifics of geographical location that replaces the abstraction of earlier postcolonial theory with rooted engagements that are deeply aware of the material struggles underlying the imaginative representations they focus on. In Chapter 1, John McLeod re-centres postcolonial theory's frequent reading of London as a synecdoche for England by considering Caryl Phillips's representation of the English North. In doing so, he asks important questions about the imagining of diasporic spaces, and those locations which may not comfortably fit conventional models of multicultural transformation. This interrogation of concepts of mappable space continues in Chapter 2, in which Nicholas Dunlop reads Peter Carey's early short story 'Do You Love Me?'

(1994) in relation to colonial cartography. Arguing for a productive relationship between postmodernism and postcolonialism, Dunlop speaks directly to concerns about the influence of western philosophy on postcolonialism, exemplifying the possibilities offered when such approaches are fused with an explicit concern for materiality.

This emphasis on spatial diversity continues in Chapters 3 and 4, with Wendy Knepper's focus on the garden in the work of Jamaica Kincaid as a site of both postcolonial contestation and renewal, and with Elizabeth Jackson's discussion of the domestic settings of the novels of Anita Desai and Shashi Deshpande. For Knepper and Jackson, these small scales exemplify the pervasiveness of colonial ideologies but also the very unique ways in which resistance to these ideologies may be developed, away from national politics, and particularly by women.

The second half of the book involves a shift of emphasis, presenting chapters originating from the fields of cultural studies and geography. Linking these two sections are Chapters 5 and 6, which both focus on the simultaneously textual and material nature of postcolonial spatialities. In Chapter 5, Monica Germanà takes up the gendered concerns of Knepper and Jackson with work on both the real-world politics of clothing in Muslim communities and its fictional representation – here embodied in Monica Ali's controversial novel *Brick Lane* (2003) – which reflects the interdisciplinary work of scholars engaging in postcolonial spatiality and the cross-over between literary and sociological perspectives. Chapter 6, Shehrazade Emmambokus's essay on the negotiation of diasporic identity as presented in South Asian diasporic children's literature, is likewise strongly engaged with the real-world experience of second-generation South Asian diasporic individuals. In Chapters 7 and 8, this imaginative dialogue with material space is picked up by Caroline Herbert and James Graham in their studies of, respectively, Milan Luthria's *Taxi 9 2 11* (2006) and Stephen Frears's *Dirty Pretty Things* (2002). Through engaging with the metropolitan centre, respectively Mumbai and London, Graham and Herbert consider how the city both reinforces and diverges from national ideologies and how the cinematic portrayals of these spaces offer engagement with issues of urban inequality, globalization, and the connection between 'lived' and 'imagined' geographies.

These 'lived' geographies take precedence in the book's final three chapters. In Chapter 9, Sarah Radcliffe's study of map-making in Ecuador offers a perfect example of the contribution of geographers to postcolonial spatialities, broadening the focus from the South Asian case studies which often dominate literary criticism to offer an insightful reading of the politics of location in South America. Then, in Chapter 10, Stephen Legg addresses how Foucault's work – already, as discussed above, of great relevance to postcolonial scholars – might be made use of in the study of a 'colonial urbanism', expanding upon his early ground-breaking work on Foucault in a postcolonial context. Finally, in Chapter 11, Tariq Jazeel considers the geography of postcolonial knowledge itself, emphasizing the idea that postcolonial scholarship cannot be read outside a politics of location. In moving from the literary, to the material, to the disciplinary, we aim to emphasize how connected these seemingly 'different' perspectives are; and to show that a concern for postcolonial spatiality can be neither entirely rooted in the material nor in the imaginary but, rather, must acknowledge the incessant interweaving of these discourses in how space is lived, represented, and studied.

Notes

1. See also Gowans (2001).
2. For an early intervention in this area, see Hudson (1977).
3. Blunt and McEwan's book emerged from a conference at the University of Southampton in 1998.
4. Sharp's book is the result of a course she taught in the Geography department at the University of Glasgow for ten years. See also Clayton (2003).
5. See also Sharp (2008, p. 6), which echoes this sentiment.
6. For Parry, 'the implications of rewriting a historical project of invasion, expropriation and exploitation in the indeterminate and always deferred terms Bhabha proposes and implements are immense, and for me immensely troubling' (2004, p. 56).
7. See, for example, Rogers (1992).
8. See, for example, Huggan (2002).

1
English somewheres
Caryl Phillips and the English North

John McLeod

> The fact that [*Dancing in the Dark*] is set in America
> doesn't really matter. It's about the same basic process:
> being vigilant about one's history and suspicious of the
> narrative that is presented to me as the narrative of the
> people, as the narrative of the region, as the narrative of
> the town, as the narrative of the country, I'm suspicious
> of it all. And therefore I'm going in and occasionally
> trying to do a little historical repair work. The impulse
> comes from having grown up in Leeds – in England.
>
> (Phillips, cited in McLeod, 2009, p. 148)

It is only relatively recently that Yorkshire's arguably most successful
contemporary novelist, Caryl Phillips, has become explicitly concerned
with the English North in his writing. It is a surprising preoccupation,
perhaps, given Phillips's long-standing literary disavowal of the specifics of historical place as part of his attempt to explore wider questions
of culture and identity untethered to more solipsistic concerns of race,
locale or biography. Prior to 2000, the North hardly figured in his writing. Of his early plays and novels which feature British settings, only
one seems to include a northern location: the 'Somewhere in England'
section of *Crossing the River* (1993), which includes subtle references to
an unspecified region not dissimilar to South Yorkshire and Sheffield.
Since 2000, Phillips has published two novels, *A Distant Shore* (2003)
and *In the Falling Snow* (2009), in which the North is prominent; a
work of non-fiction, *The Atlantic Sound* (2000), part of which concerns
Liverpool's role in the Atlantic slave trade; a short autobiographical story
'Growing Pains' (2005); and a generically challenging work of fiction,
Foreigners: Three English Lives (2007), which includes a long, powerful

section entitled 'Northern Lights' concerning the death in Leeds in 1969 of the Nigerian migrant David Oluwale and the culpability of two officers from the now-defunct Leeds City Police Force. Intriguingly, among this variable and rich body of recent work Phillips has developed a distinct discursive envisioning of the North. This chapter is concerned with exploring briefly Phillips's North, especially its bifocal character, as a tentative heterotopia which holds out the possibility of postcolonial transformation within a grimly prejudicial region.

As is well known, Phillips arrived in the northern English city of Leeds in 1958, only a few weeks after his birth in St Kitts, and he was to spend the vast majority of his young life there until going up to Queen's College, Oxford University, in 1976 (see Jaggi, 2000, pp. 159–60). In his essays and interviews he has called attention to the often racist and inhospitable nature of Leeds which forever corrupted the extent to which it could be thought of as his home. In the Introduction to his collection of his essays *A New World Order* (2001), Phillips recalls, as a 7-year-old, kissing a white girl outside his school: 'A cluster of parents stand by and look on with horror. I am aware of the girl's sudden surprise, of the parents' outrage, but I walk past the parents. My sooty touch on their tiny Desdemona in the working-class streets of Leeds' (Phillips, 2001, p. 3). Yet Phillips has by no means turned his back on his first city, nor allowed the prejudices of others to invalidate his rights of tenure in, or sense of connection to, the city of Leeds. His celebrated passion for Leeds United Football Club is crucial in this respect, as it is through his sporting affiliation that he first realized the possibility of there being a different Leeds. While the racism prevalent at English football grounds certainly complicated his following Leeds United as a teenager, his avid support for the club alongside friends and family epitomized another way of being in Leeds where the horror of race could be at least momentarily suspended – significantly, his enthusiasm for the city's football team was clinched early in life when his white babysitter took him to watch Leeds United play Leicester City at Elland Road in the 1960s.

In his 1998 essay, 'Leeds United and Me', while confessing that he accepts or rejects invitations to speak in Britain based upon Leeds United's league fixtures, Phillips reflects upon supporting Leeds United as vital conjunction or crossing point where his first city, the emotional life of his diasporic family and his early convivial relationships with white Britons were significantly conjoined:

Leeds United reminds me of my father. Leeds United reminds me of my best friend, John. Leeds United reminds me of the moment my mother caught me crying as a teenager because in 1972 Leeds had lost the game that would have given them the double [the league title and FA Cup triumph]. Leeds United reminds me of who I am. All together now, 'We are Leeds, We are Leeds, We are Leeds'.

(ibid., p. 301)

If Leeds has been the space of postwar British racial prejudice, Phillips has also thought of other Leeds spaces where tactical and at times transgressive relationships have been built in difficult times, across generations and races. These forge – albeit fleetingly – alternative accommodating connections signified by the togetherness of the football crowd's plural pronoun in that chant of 'We are Leeds' (and promised, too, in the challenging innocence of sharing a playground kiss). As Phillips has stated on another occasion, sport is 'tribal. Tribes are not always made up of people who look the same, they're not always made up of people who necessarily speak the same language' (Clingman, 2009, p. 117); and he comments in the same interview of the propensity of sports supporters to embrace each other when celebrating success. While Phillips's memories of following Leeds United do not forget the bigotry of football crowds in the 1960s and 1970s, his remarks about supporting the city's football team unveil a vista on another kind of North where the recreational may suggest re-creation – of a way of dwelling where the prejudices of race are challenged by the 'surprised' encounters happening in Leeds's playgrounds or on the football terraces.

My brief exploration of Phillips's writing about the North will focus on three brief textual examples of Phillips's bifocal envisioning of Leeds as bleakly prejudicial yet clinching alternative postcolonial possibilities which can be mined amidst the North's unhappy history of intolerance. The fact that Phillips rarely specifies the locations of his northern fictions suggests that he is concerned with the region generally, and with regional behaviours which we might call northern, rather than with the city of Leeds in particular or *in toto*. His writing negotiates between, on the one hand, a revisionary encounter with Northern England in which the region's history of discrimination is laid bare; and, on the other, the tentative confecting of a postcolonial northern heterotopia, both accommodating and embracing, which is set against the North's intolerance and chauvinism. This second, sportingly 'tribal' North is discovered in fleeting moments in the region's past and is often dwarfed by the grave and indeed fatal historical context in which it is discerned. While leaving his readers in no doubt of the North's shameful history of inhospitality, especially in 'Northern Lights', Phillips amplifies this alternative

North in his writing partly as a way of embracing a possible new future based on the region's submerged postcolonial past. Hence, the North which emerges from Phillips's writing exists somewhere between the experiential and the noumenal, the concrete and the imagined – or, to borrow from the aforementioned section heading from *Crossing the River*, between the tangible historical specifics of the North and an uncertain, unreached imagined community that temporarily happens 'somewhere'. As we shall see, Phillips's North is both familiar and revisionary, recognizable and redefined: an English 'somewhere' that is hinged to, not held by, the prejudicial particulars of localized place.

'Somewhere in England' is Phillips's first fictional representation of the North, and its key elements anticipate the more developed and sustained imagining of the region in his twenty-first-century writing. A central matter is its demythologizing challenge to received images of the North familiar from literary and popular cultures, especially those which eulogize the North as sociable and accommodating. As Dave Russell has argued, while the role of Northern England in the national imagination has been historically variable, several recurring claims about it have contributed to its discursive legacy. These include a nostalgic sense of community and collectivity associated with northern folk (conjured, for example, in the paintings of L. S. Lowry) which contrasts with the more individuated and isolating pursuits of modern life in the English South; the '"strong" or "dominant" woman, those who hold together families and wider social networks in the face of poverty and personal tragedy' (Russell, 2004, p. 92); and the perception that there resides in the North 'a supposed authenticity believed to be lacking elsewhere in English culture' (ibid., p. 278) which may be contrasted with the bourgeois cosmopolitan sophistry of London and the Home Counties. Phillips's writing about the North accesses these and other northern topoi, but always in a vigilant, revisionary mode. In 'Somewhere in England', which is set predominantly during the years of the Second World War, Phillips engages with the fiction of the 'strong' Northern female in the figure of the white female narrator, Joyce, and rejects the confection of kinship and community often associated with the North as distinctly friendly and welcoming – a space of *Gemeinschaft* collectivity distinct from the self-interested *Gesellschaft* locales of the South. Joyce conveys life during wartime through a series of dated vignettes which disobey chronological unfolding and instead cross unexpectedly back and forth across time, from which there gradually emerges a sobering vision of the region. In articulating the story of Joyce's relationship with a black American soldier, Travis, who is stationed in Joyce's village in the early 1940s and with whom she conceives a mixed-race child, Phillips interrupts the predominant 'narrative of the region' and unearths an often unseen, alternative northern dwelling embodied by the emotional and physical embrace between a white English woman and a black American man.

The North of 'Somewhere in England' is never named, but Phillips drops several hints that the story may be set in a rural location in the vicinity of the South Yorkshire city of Sheffield. The unnamed village where Joyce lives unhappily with her husband Len is situated to the south of Joshua Tetley's brewery (in Leeds), while Sam Smith's brewery (located in Tadcaster, near York) is mentioned as to the 'east' (Phillips, 1993, p. 168). When Joyce visits a nearby bombed-out town to learn of her mother's death in an air raid, she provides a litany of Sheffield's famous steel industry: 'Everybody knew [the German bombers] were after the steelworks. Firth Brown & Co., J. Arthur Balfour and Co., Vickers. All of them' (ibid., p. 177). These hints deftly secure the narrative in a knowable region of England; yet Phillips's general reluctance to name the town or the village where Joyce lives, preferring the vagueness of 'Somewhere', deliberately keeps the focus of the text on the generalized conception of the North as an idea or mode of being. Bleakly perhaps, for much of the narrative, the northern community of 'Somewhere in England' appears as a masculine closed collective which does not welcome intrusion from the outside, and Phillips makes much of the insularity and small-mindedness of the region's men. When a group of evacuated children arrive in the village, Joyce records her husband's response: 'I looked across at Len, who firmly shook his head. Not even one of them, he said. They can bloody well go back to where they came from' (ibid., p. 144). The arrival of the black American soldiers in June 1942 affords other such unwelcoming displays, this time mixed with the prejudices of race. The brutality of this masculine northern environment is epitomized in Len's behaviour on his release from prison in 1943, where he had been serving a short sentence for profiteering on the black market during wartime. Cognisant that Joyce has been seeing Travis socially, Len refuses to acknowledge that his behaviour bears responsibility for Joyce's loss of feelings for him and instead he reasserts his authority by striking out at Travis's race and Joyce's gender:

> He pushed his finger into my face. He jabbed at me to punctuate his sentences. You won't see him, or any of 'em. You won't go to town, to the pub, have them in here, talk to them, nothing, as long as

I'm here. I'd never have married you, or taken you out of that bloody slum, if I'd known you were going to behave like a slut.

(ibid., p. 214)

Focalized through the figure of Len is Phillips's deeply critical envisioning of northern life in keen opposition to the well-established *topoi*: closed not convivial, hostile rather than hospitable, lacking the kind of communal togetherness which, as Russell argued, has so frequently been associated with the ruddy-faced bonhomie of northern living.

Faced with the antipathy and dishonesty of those around her, Phillips's Joyce may appear a familiar example of the strong, resourceful northern female who remains undaunted in the face of hardship. But Phillips is careful to free her from the enclosure of cliché via a number of bold and telling manoeuvres. Significantly, Joyce is an inauthentic villager – in her own words, an 'uninvited outsider' (ibid., p. 129). Her strained relationship with Len does little to endear her to her neighbours. When Len is imprisoned, Joyce steadfastly refuses to support him: 'I returned to the village alone. To face their accusing eyes. I had not "stuck by him". It was important for me to abandon any vanity' (ibid., p. 199). In contrast to the cliché, Joyce's strong temperament is evidenced precisely by her fortitude in *not* bowing to the sacrificial demands of kin or keeping the domestic realm of the family together at all costs. She refuses to allow her enduring mother's hostility to her wedding to Len to deflect her from her purpose, which effectively ends their relationship; and she comes to reject her marriage after suffering Len's verbal and physical abuse and witnessing the perpetual bloody-mindedness of his fellow male villagers.

Joyce's female strength, then, is decisively not typically 'northern'; contrariwise, it manifests itself in her willingness to enter into relationships which take her beyond the authentic northern realm of hearth and home. A clear link is suggested between Joyce's openness to difference and her own sense of dislocatedness, so that when the black American soldiers arrive, the possibility for her empathetic connection with the new arrivals is high. On first seeing them, Joyce intriguingly 'wanted to warn them' (ibid., p. 129), almost as if she is keen to protect them from the prejudicial eyes of the villagers that instantly turn towards her once the soldiers have repaired to their barracks. Joyce's romance and subsequent wedding to Travis best encapsulate her fortitude, of course, and in the story of their relationship Phillips points to the hidden history of another version of the North based on transgressive encounter and bold embrace – one that recalls Phillips's brigandly kiss outside his school, perhaps. As Stephen Clingman argues, Phillips has often been concerned with 'all those asymmetrically marginalized and excluded people of whatever origins whose paths cross in ways that shift from the complex and the complimentary to the jagged, tangential and disjunctive' (Clingman, 2007, p. 46). 'Somewhere in England' anticipates Phillips's twenty-first-century writing by recreating the North as a place of crossed paths. Appropriately, this other North is embodied by an embrace at a junction: specifically that between Joyce and Travis which takes place at a railway station on New Year's Day 1945, when Travis returns briefly to the region on leave to marry his pregnant fiancée:

> He let his bag fall to the platform. Joyce. That was all he said. Just, Joyce. I could see now, the gap in the middle of his teeth. At the bottom. And then he reached out and pulled me towards him. I couldn't believe it. He'd come back to me. He really wanted me. That day, crying on the platform, safe in Travis's arms.
>
> (Phillips, 1993, pp. 225–6)

This safe refuge of reciprocity holds the potential to dismantle the disjunctive propensity of northern life as both Joyce and Travis experience it, but it is short-lived. Travis is killed in action not long afterwards, and Joyce is forced to surrender for adoption their child, Greer, to an anonymous 'lady with the blue coat' that entreats Joyce to 'be sensible'. Shortly afterwards she leaves the village and moves back to the town, where 'For weeks afterwards, I wandered around the park looking at women pushing their prams' (ibid., p. 230).

The termination of Joyce and Travis's relationship, as well as Joyce's attenuated motherhood, underlines the mortal fragility of the novel's postcolonial northern vista and mode of being from being sentimentalized or idealized. In many ways the cruel, brutal North of Len wins out in the end; Joyce, Travis and Greer are ultimately denied the right to settle in the village. Yet their brief encounter unromantically challenges the North's 'regional narrative' of collectivity and conviviality by exposing the tryst with race and gender on which it often depends. The relationship between Joyce and Travis, then, beckons another story of the North glimpsed in those temporary embraces that transport people beyond the confines of their proper place. Their relationship, despite its brevity and proximity to pain, offers a discursive revisioning of the region which offers to take us to somewhere else.

In his post-2000 writing, this glimpse of an alternative North comes more substantially into view. His 2003 novel, *A Distant Shore* is also set in an unspecified North and also features a short affair between a white woman and black man, newly arrived in the region: a retired school-teacher, Dorothy, and an African refugee formally called Gabriel who is now known as Solomon. They live in Stoneleigh, a new development atop a hill in the fictional village of Weston which 'divide[s] into two' (Phillips, 2003, p. 4). Again, the novel's northern setting is conjured vaguely rather than through the identification of concrete locations. Dorothy tells us that 'the biggest thing that had ever happened in Weston was Mrs Thatcher closing the pits, and that was over twenty years ago' (ibid., p. 4) – a reference to the miners strikes of the early 1980s and the Conservative Government's winding down of Britain's coal industry which impacted particularly on Yorkshire and the English North. When Gabriel/Solomon is destitute in London, he is told by his solicitor Katherine to hitch a ride out of the city: 'Just remember you want to go north' (ibid., p. 182). Yet the promise of North as a potential place of safety from the exploitative hardships of the metropolis for refugees is cruelly denied in the novel, as Gabriel/Solomon's murder in Weston confirms. For those deemed foreign in contemporary England, there is no significant North/South divide.

The queasiness with strangers and cultural difference which characterized the village of 'Somewhere in England' is much more marked in *A Distant Shore* which thematizes the issue of foreignness in its opening sentences: 'England has changed. These days it's difficult to tell who's from around here and who's not. Who belongs and who's a stranger. It's disturbing. It doesn't feel right' (ibid., p.3). The murderous consequences of these disturbed feelings are dispiritingly exposed in the death of Gabriel/Solomon, dumped in Weston's canal by a gang of racist youths. Just after his death, Dorothy is told by the landlord of a pub near the canal that the death must have been an accident as 'folks like these' (ibid., p. 48) would not be capable of killing:

> If you've lived here as long as I have, love, and you've grown up with folks like these, you'd understand that there's not one among them capable of harming anybody. That's just how they are. Decent folk committed to their families and their community. We don't have murderers here. A few villains, some with light fingers, and a few who are quick with their fists, but that's about it. Nothing more than this.
>
> (ibid., p. 48–9)

The landlord's determined delineation of northern 'decent folk' as stalwarts of goodness despite their brusque temperament recalls the

indulgent boisterousness of the working-class northern souls familiar from the pages of Alan Sillitoe and John Braine, and echoes the
'defensive nature of much northern regional ideology' (Russell, 2004,
p. 93) which Russell detects in a range of northern writing throughout
the twentieth century. In focalizing the culpability of 'folks like these'
in acts of prejudicial intolerance, *A Distant Shore* directly challenges
the landlord's banal confection of northern kinship and decency. The
anonymous 'love letters' (Phillips, 2001, p. 42) which Gabriel/Solomon
receives – racist missives, some of which enfold razor blades – suggests
a provincial environment much more brutal where the cutting senti-
ments of racial hatred are all-too-readily literalized.

In a penetrating and articulate reading of *A Distant Shore*, Andrew Warnes
argues that Solomon's bleak fortunes suggest that the 'postcolonial fantasy
of a raceless and democratic future has died on the green fields, amid the
outstanding bigotry, of provincial England' (2007, p. 43); while the deathly
shadow which his murder casts over the novel signifies the troubling 'crisis of social identification' (ibid., p. 43) at large in present-day Yorkshire in
which its inhabitants are fenced off by, and entrenched within, declared
difference of class, race and culture. While the novel's austerity and gloom
are undeniable, the 'postcolonial fantasy' of another North – embodied
in the sporting or loving embrace, as we have seen – persists in *A Distant
Shore*, and suggests that Phillips is not yet ready to relinquish the other
North which he has known. Threaded through the complex narrative
tapestry of the novel – like 'Somewhere in England' it is characterized by
unexpected transitions between time, place, and, additionally, narrators –
is a slim yet significant narrative strand of brief, fragile encounters, often
featuring Gabriel/Solomon's survival in England.

Gabriel/Solomon manages to secure a job as a night-watchman in
Weston and at last find a place to live due to the brave kindness of three
people. A young girl, Denise, whom he befriends while sleeping in a
derelict house, eventually refuses to support her racist father's claims
that Gabriel/Solomon has mistreated her (the accusation initially lands
him in prison); his solicitor Katherine helps him avoid living rough in
London by helping him hitch a ride in a lorry to the North; and the lorry
driver, Mike, introduces him to his family and helps Gabriel/Solomon
find his feet. Each of these accommodating, temporary and short-lived
relationships is marked by a seemingly innocuous gesture or embrace.
As Gabriel/Solomon talks to a tearful Denise about her abusive father
in the derelict house, he comes to understand that she, too, is seeking
a place of safety in a cruel country. This understanding is signified by
their distinctly non-sexual embrace of rapport: '[Gabriel/Solomon] puts

his arms around her and holds her. There is something comforting about her young weight on his body, and Gabriel decides to stay in this position until she calms down' (Phillips, 2003, p. 188). Before Katherine drives away from the rain-soaked road, 'she leans over and blows Gabriel a kiss' (ibid., p. 182). At Mike's funeral, his mother Mrs. Anderson offers a kindly embrace to Gabriel/Solomon:

> Mum reaches up and touches my face with her fingertips. I was much caressed by this family, and my attachment and gratitude to them are very great. She is a small thin woman, but this gesture feels strong. Mum holds me in her spell. And then she places the palms of her cold hands against my cheeks and pulls my head down towards her. She kisses me at the point where my wet hair meets my wet skin. And then she releases me.
>
> (ibid., p. 271)

A clasp, a kiss – in such elementary gestures, Gabriel/Solomon is here transported to somewhere other than the rain-soaked cemetery, where his African past and the English present are meaningfully crossed. If a spell can be defined as transformative gesture with the mystical power to impact upon one's fortune, then this small moment of warmth crucially releases that 'postcolonial fantasy' which Warnes assumes has died. Indeed, the fact that Mrs. Anderson's 'spell' takes place at a burial site underscores Phillips's attempt in the novel to protect such postcolonial possibilities from termination amidst the prevailing prejudices of the English North.

These fleeting possibilities stubbornly suggest another way of dwelling in the North: a glimpse of 'somewhere' else that rivals the landlord's hollow fiction of a benign 'here'. Phillips absolutely does not romanticize or proffer such gestures as winning out over the kind of racism that leaves Gabriel/Solomon dead in the local canal. But as in 'Somewhere in England', a representation of the North as Phillips has known it would be incomplete without them. If the North is to be a democratic postcolonial space beyond race and discrimination, then depicting this vernacular micro-history of seemingly ordinary, innocuous and often brief attachment provides a crucial discursive resource that might stimulate something which Paul Gilroy believes is vital to any transformative postcolonial project: 'that diminishing and invaluable commodity: hope' (Gilroy, 2004, p. 58).

Gabriel/Solomon's fate, beaten to death and dumped in a canal, grimly recalls one of the North's most notorious racist killings: the hounding of a Nigerian migrant, David Oluwale, by the Leeds City Police Force. Oluwale's body was fished out of the city's River Aire in May 1969; he was last seen alive being chased by the Leeds police. Arriving in the North in 1949 as stowaway from Lagos, Nigeria, Oluwale's life in Leeds was abruptly altered in 1953 when he was arrested and sent to Menston Asylum for eight years. On his release in 1961, and permanently affected by his treatment in Menston (electric shock therapy was not uncommon for inmates), Oluwale often lived rough in Leeds, sleeping in shop doorways. He became the target for two police officers, Inspector Geoff Elleker and Sergeant Ken Kitching, who abused him terribly and are widely believed to have been responsible for his death. In November 1971, both men were found guilty of abusing Oluwale, although charges of manslaughter were dismissed by the judge, Mr. Justice Hinchliffe. Each officer was imprisoned. Oluwale's killing is a shameful episode in the history of Leeds, one which, as Kester Aspden argues, the city has been keen to forget: 'There was shame that such a thing could happen on the streets of Leeds, right under the noses of its citizens. Blacks ending up face down dead in rivers was the kind of thing that happened in the Deep South, not Leeds' (Aspden, 2007, p. 227). Such amnesia remains; today, attempts to erect a memorial to Oluwale in the city have received a cool reception in some civic quarters (see Farrar, 2009). Caryl Phillips has been an important figure in these efforts, and not least because his most powerful work on the North, 'Northern Lights', directly concerns Oluwale's killing. Featuring a number of narratorial voices, and modulating between memoir, essay, historiography and fiction, Phillips's telling of the vile treatment of Oluwale is also the occasion where Phillips's postcolonial re-envisioning of the North is most effectively clinched.

As is made clear in both Kester Aspden's book *Nationality: Wog: The Hounding of David Oluwale* and Phillips's 'Northern Lights', the police made great sport of seizing Oluwale while he slept rough in Leeds, driving him out of the city and depositing him miles from habitation. The cruelty of this is vividly conjured by one of the narrators of 'Northern Lights': 'Middleton Woods. South Leeds. Beyond Hunslet and Beeston. Close to Belle Isle. David was dropped in a wilderness and found himself surrounded by dark, inhospitable nature ... Go back to nature, black boy from Lagos. Go back to the jungle' (Phillips, 2007, p. 249). For the police, banishing Oluwale from Leeds was paramount; but as Phillips underlines, Oluwale would repeatedly return to Leeds in open defiance of those who would deny his presence there. As one narrator puts it: 'It was as though he was challenging them to remove him from the city.

They would beat him and arrest him, but his attitude was clear: "I'll just do what I want to do and I won't disappear"' (ibid., p. 219).

While 'Northern Lights' grimly unearths the prejudice and racism of Leeds, arguably its primary task is to accommodate and admit Oluwale to a revisioned metropolitan space in which his presence appears as typical rather than foreign. This involves positing a history of the city which prioritizes some of the key elements of Oluwale's life, primarily his migrancy, as a way of breaking up for good the narrow northern chauvinism explored in 'Somewhere in England' and *A Distant Shore*. Woven into Oluwale's story in 'Northern Lights' is a substantial account of the history of Leeds from its earliest beginnings. As the narrator points out, the city owes its fortunes to a river crossing: namely, the bridge built by the Romans across the River Aire to enable a road link between Manchester and York. Leeds begins at, and as, a conjunction, where movement and passage are facilitated across water. From this originary moment of the Romans 'crossing the river', the narrator traces the many other peoples who have arrived in the region, sometimes settling there and altering its fortunes: the conquering Normans; Jews from nineteenth-century Germany, Russia and Poland; Catholic Irish migrants; postwar settlers from Africa and the Caribbean. This migratory history of Leeds is offered not as marginal to but definitive of the city's fortunes and perpetual recreation. If the North has been linked to notions of national authenticity as Dave Russell argues, then Phillips uproots any sense of 'native' Yorkshire space by effectively declaring that all who reside there are ancestrally linked to migrants, to the extent that the cleft between native and foreigner effectively ceases. Those seeking to defend Leeds from foreigners, such as the 1960s Leeds City Police Force, are effectively subscribing to a proprietorial understanding of local space which the history of the region utterly undermines.

In writing a refocused history of Leeds in 'Northern Lights', therefore, Phillips proffers a transformed vision of northern space that runs counter to the racialized chauvinistic localism of the region. This matter is clinched at the level of form. In his complex and compelling interweaving of voices, narrators and perspectives, Phillips pursues a discursive reckoning with the North which admits the different kinds of citizens of Leeds into a shared aesthetic space. His text moves between those who remember Oluwale with affection (black and white), accounts of court proceedings, recollections of police officers, documents from mortuary and welfare services, and more besides. On a handful of occasions Phillips too appears, as a silent witness to the landscapes of Oluwale's life and death, visiting Oluwale's lodgings near the University of Leeds and at one point standing outside the current home of former Inspector Elleker in the suburb of Horsforth.

Significantly, the narrative begins with a Caribbean migrant woman remembering with affection her brief encounters with Oluwale as they passed on the street:

> I always acknowledged David and he'd just say, 'Take care, behave yourself'. That's all. 'Take care, behave yourself.' But it happened regularly enough so that we sort of got to know each other ... I remember crying when I heard that he'd died. I felt it hard. Like I'd lost a true friend.
>
> (Phillips, 2007, pp. 167, 169)

The weight of these small moments of compassion and exchange is measured a few pages later, when a white friend of Oluwale's remembers talking to him at the Jubilee Hall where David would go to dance. As the narrative gathers propensity, a constellation of such memories, reciprocities and affection is illuminated, and is clinched at the level of form by the lexical embrace of the multiple narrators' collective polyvocality. Set against the racism of Leeds, therefore, is a newly brokered discursive space that functions as a tentative northern heterotopia recovered from the past and projected towards the future. In this alternative North, Oluwale exists not as the infrahuman foreigner of the police officer's charge sheet but as a fully human citizen of Leeds: recognized, remembered, critiqued, loved, and missed. In the text's final sentences, Phillips assumes the mantle of narrator and movingly declares Oluwale's rights of tenure in this reconfigured northern heterotopia while contemplating the site of his grave in Killingbeck Cemetery:

> In death you have fulfilled a promise made at birth. Here at Killingbeck Cemetery there is no more land for graves. Soon there will be no more burials in this place. Everybody can rest peacefully. You have achieved a summit, David. Climbed to the top of a hill, and from here you can look down. You are still in Leeds. Forever in Leeds.
>
> (ibid., p. 260)

In the northern space brokered by Phillips's text, Oluwale defies once and for all the police's crass attempts to banish him from the city forever. He appears as an eternal, not erased, citizen of Leeds whom 'Northern Lights' situates like the city's founding bridge at the heart of the city's history, and whom the text recalls in order to embrace the North's unvanquished accommodating possibilities. The challenge for Phillips's northern readers is to make concrete this tentatively re-envisioned North which admits to the realities of difference and so-called foreigners in its historical origins and contemporary milieu.

Caryl Phillips's English North is the toll of two landscapes: the first, chauvinistic, divisive and deathly; the second, reciprocal, embracing and fertile. The northern 'English somewheres' towards which his work travels are never idealized or glibly celebrated, but articulated in order to secure a postcolonial discourse of the North, in contradistinction to the usual clichés – one which suggests the tactics needed for a transformed future for the region. It is an imagined heterotopia at once local and cosmopolitan; where, in the words of Kwame Anthony Appiah, 'we have obligations to others, obligations that stretch beyond those to whom we are related by the ties of kith and kin, or even the more formal ties of a shared citizenship' (2006, p. xiii). Phillips's north emerges as something more than the 'little repair work' he modestly claims when reflecting upon the focus of much of his writing. In its cosmopolitan collectivity – hymned by that sporting invitation to chant '[a]ltogether now' – it demands the dismissal of those assumptions about the North and its formulaic representations into which so many northern folk are still rarely admitted.

2

A few words about the role of the Cartographers

Mapping and postcolonial resistance in Peter Carey's 'Do You Love Me?'

Nicholas Dunlop

In the context of the settler colonization of what Stephen Slemon has usefully termed the 'second world' (1990, p. 30), the map and concomitant appropriative strategies devised and implemented by the colonizing agency tend to embody those cartographic constructions which Graham Huggan characterizes as 'inevitably distortive ... they can neither contain nor explain the reality that they purport to represent' (1996, p. 34). The maps of the colonizer, although 'invested with the generative power of originary myth' (ibid., p. 34), are incapable of dispersing the sense of inauthenticity and inappropriateness of the settler enterprise. Huggan sees the postcolonial involvement with mapping as rejecting 'cartographic enclosure and the imposed cultural limits that notion implies' (1990, p. 131). By contesting the authority of the map – by exposing the brutality and arbitrariness of the processes by which it is constructed, and by rejecting the appropriative strategy of (re-)naming space – there is an increasing tendency within postcolonial writing to resist the enclosed, static and hierarchized perspective of the colonial agency and instead look towards the transformational possibilities of hybridity, a new discourse which, in Huggan's terms:

> emphasises the provisionality of all cultures and which celebrates the particular diversity of formerly colonised cultures ... The reassessment of cartography ... indicates a shift of emphasis away from the desire for homogeneity towards an acceptance of diversity reflected in the interpretation of the map, not as a means of spatial containment or systematic organisation, but as a medium of spatial perception which allows for the formulation of links both between and within cultures.
>
> (ibid., p. 132)

The authoritative appearance of the map is a recurring trope in the fiction of Peter Carey, from his earliest unpublished work up to and including 2009's *Parrott and Olivier in America*. Carey's work has consistently articulated a resistant scepticism to hegemonic epistemologies as a means of ideological control. Carey often deploys an interrogative approach to colonial cartography as a means of reinscribing the postcolonial experience, and his speculative early short story, 'Do You Love Me?' (1994) offers a heuristic insight into how Carey conflates the postcolonial and the postmodern in order to articulate the propensity towards semiotic instability and connotative discontinuity in the mapping and naming of colonial space. In 'Do You Love Me?', Carey recalibrates his cartographic critique to fit the speculative mode; as in his later novel *The Unusual Life of Tristan Smith* (1994), the articulation of a fantastic imaginary space permits the text to extend the imperial impulse to map and name to its (il)logical conclusion. Carey's satirical reading of the socio-political role of scientific interpretations of reality, and their complicity in the construction of perceptions of nationhood, emphasizes what Huggan terms 'the ironic tension ... between the slipperiness of the sign and the apparent fixity of the structure or system in which that sign is placed' (1996, p. 35). It is this provisional and arbitrary relationship which lies at the heart of the postcolonial interrogation of the map in 'Do You Love Me?'

The inhabitants of the society in 'Do You Love Me?' are obsessed with knowing 'always, exactly where we stand ... We have a passion for lists' (1994, p. 1). The people possess an all-encompassing rage for order, a desire to inscribe in tangible form the underlying structures and rules upon which their society is based, and by extension to textualize their own spatial and temporal reality. They attempt to gain this knowledge by participating in an ongoing process of charting both landscape and inhabitants in terms of two separate, but overlapping, scientific forms: the map and the census. The undertaking of such a project, and the motives and perceptions behind it, not only gesture towards the sense of rootlessness, inauthenticity and alienation so prevalent in postcolonial cultures, but also imply an ironic inversion of the realities of the purportedly civilizing processes of the colonial project, where new landscapes and indigenous peoples were forcibly subjected to the scientific rigours of the European colonizer in an attempt to incorporate their Otherness within a secure and rigid set of discourses.

As a consequence of the importance accorded to their task, the society's mapmakers are granted the status of scientist-priests, an elite social grouping who are 'well paid, admired, and [have] no small opinion of themselves' (ibid., p. 2). The Cartographers are employed to trace and reinscribe the spatial boundaries of the landscape, and their annual report is intimately associated with an occult festival, which will determine the prosperity of the coming year. Mark Monmonier notes that real cartographers are assigned a similarly mystical status as those in Carey's tale, asserting:

> [The public] as with many things beyond their full understanding ... readily entrust map-making to a priesthood of technically competent designers and drafters working for government agencies and commercial firms ... Map users seldom, if ever, question these authorities, and they often fail to appreciate the map's power as a tool of deliberate falsification or subtle propaganda.
>
> (Monmonier, 1991, p. 1)

The structures of the society are also subject to the same scientific scrutiny; an inventory is taken of the material possessions of each inhabitant on the night of the Festival of the Corn, as each family moves their belongings into the street 'so that the census officials may the more easily check the inventory of each household' (Carey, 1994, p. 1). The national conception of self is intimately connected with these rigorous scientific analyses of cartography and census, with each inhabitant's social and physical position accounted for within what Benedict Anderson terms the 'totalising classification' of the overlapping scientific modes (Anderson, 1991, p. 173). These processes are not undertaken with the aim of consolidating the authority of a hegemonic agency, or for other explicitly exploitative purposes; rather, they constitute a self-conscious attempt to construct a stable and distinct national identity, based on empirical spatial awareness and detailed categorization of social and cultural structures. The knowledge of space and its boundaries is the crucial factor in supporting the flimsy structure of nationhood, as

> our people crave, more than anything else, to know the extent of the nation, to know, exactly, the shape of the coastline, to hear what land may have been lost to the sea, to know what has been reclaimed and what is still in doubt.
>
> (Carey, 1994, p. 2)

The provisionality of such a conception of nationhood is apparent when the Cartographers' report is unfavourable: 'If the Cartographers' report is good, the Festival of the Corn will be a good Festival. If the report is bad, one can always sense ... a feeling of nervousness and apprehension in the revellers, a certain desperation' (ibid., p. 2).

Given the flimsy ideological foundation upon which this sense of nationhood is constructed, the oscillation of the inhabitants between arrogance and panic is unsurprising. The necessity for the yearly drawing and redrawing of the map reveals a paradoxical awareness of the provisional and ephemeral nature of the cartographic mode of representation. The myth of the map as an authoritative and totalizing structure is exploded and replaced with the realization of the map as a palimpsest, continually inscribed and re-inscribed as the landscape swells and shifts spatially along a temporal axis. Because of this continuous movement, the inhabitants can never know exactly where they stand. The Cartographers' efforts must ultimately be in vain, as they attempt to incorporate the shifting reality of the landscape within modes of scientific discourse which, by their nature, can encompass only static forms.

The inadequacy of the figure of the map in 'Do You Love Me?' may be decoded as an interrogation of the weaknesses and ideological fractures in the totalizing structures of colonial discourse in its entirety. The 'cultural cringe' experienced by the inhabitants of the society is directly analogous to that suggested by A. A. Phillips in relation to the fragility of Australian formulations of national identity, which are also intimately bound up with notions of incorporating space and landscape within a fixed set of scientific modes of representation.[1] As Huggan explains in 'Decolonising the Map', however, the inherent weaknesses in these discursive systems mean that such attempts at mimetic representations of reality must be regarded with suspicion. The overwhelming desire of the society in 'Do You Love Me?' is for rigid delineation of social and spatial boundaries, a fixed set of rules and structures upon which a sense of nationhood may be constructed. The concept of such a structure, operating from a fixed centre, is, as Derrida points out in 'Structure, Sign and Play', 'contradictorily coherent' (Derrida, 1978, p. 279): the point from which the structure derives its authority cannot itself be guaranteed. Therefore any conception of fixity or stability must be provisional, and treated as such. Huggan asserts that 'the exemplary structuralist activity involved in the production of the map (the demarcation of boundaries, allocation of points and connection of lines within an enclosed, self-sufficient unit) traces back to a point of presence whose stability cannot be guaranteed' (Huggan, 1990, p. 128). This lack of stability is clearly revealed in 'Do You Love Me?' when the territory itself begins to dematerialize, exposing the cartographic image as having laid 'false claim to the fixity of its own origins and to the coherence of the system it orients and organises' (ibid., p. 128). Consequently, the claims of the map to be authoritative are undermined by the inherent weaknesses of mimetic modes of representation; by asserting a totalizing authority, they serve also to reveal the fissures within. These weaknesses invoke Homi Bhabha's interpretation of all modes of colonial discourse as inherently ambivalent, oscillating between the assumption of power and the awareness of its absence. The fissures in meaning between the reality of the landscape and the approximate reading of it offered by the map illustrate the split between colonial discourse's 'appearance as original and authoritative and its articulation as repetition and difference' (Bhabha, 1994, p. 107). The figure of the map in 'Do You Love Me?', in attempting to assert the originality and authority of the scientific mode, neatly illustrates the ambivalence of the discursive system, in that it initially enacts the kind of threatening mimicry which is, in Bhabha's term, 'at once resemblance and menace' (ibid., p. 86), simultaneously reinforcing and undermining the authority of the classifying structure. Instead of being a perfectly realized and authoritative copy, the mimetic representation highlights its own sense of difference: the map is a subjective reading of the landscape which is 'almost the same, but not quite' (ibid., p. 86). The progression from mimicry to mockery, which is potentially present in all forms of mimicry, occurs when the territory continues to dissolve at such a rate as to render the map's claims to objectivity and authority ludicrous. The dissolution of the territory implies a rejection of that aspect of colonial discourse characterized by Said as 'synchronic essentialism' ([1978] 1995, p. 240). The diachronic nature of the territory's disintegration exerts a 'constant pressure' upon the panoptic and static vision of space embodied by the cartographic image. Said proposes that:

> the source of pressure is narrative, in that if any Oriental detail can be shown to move, or develop, diachrony is introduced into the system. What seemed stable – and the Orient is synonymous with stability and unchanging eternality – now appears unstable.
>
> (ibid., p. 240)

In occupying an interstitial space between the synchronic and diachronic impulses, the fluctuating correspondence between map and territory in 'Do You Love Me?' articulates the tension which constructs mimicry as an ironic and threatening compromise which implicitly critiques the monolithic nature of colonial discourse (Bhabha, 1994, pp. 85–6).

The ultimate disintegration of the fragile society in 'Do You Love Me?' is precipitated by the steady dematerialization of the territory. Initially, the phenomenon is scarcely remarked upon, since those regions which are becoming 'less and less real' (Carey, 1994, p. 2) are on the geographical margins. They are 'invariably uninhabited, unused for agriculture or industry', while 'long pieces of coastline ... had begun to disappear like the image on an improperly fixed photograph' (ibid., p. 2). The narrator's father, himself a Cartographer of some standing, observes:

> The nether regions were among the first to disappear, and this in itself is significant. These regions ... are seldom visited by men and only then by people like me whose sole job is to make sure that they're still there. We had no use for these areas, these deserts, swamps and coastlines which is why, of course, they disappeared. They were merely possessions of ours, and if they had any use at all it was as symbols for our poets, writers and film makers. They were used as symbols of alienation, lovelessness, loneliness, uselessness and so on.
>
> (ibid., p. 7)

This passage offers a knowing and satirical reading of that wide-ranging set of cultural, political and social circumstances which has been identified as the postcolonial condition. Like Australia and other appropriated territories incorporated within the imperial project, the 'nether regions' are assigned value by the hegemonic forces of the metropolis in purely economic terms. It is indeed significant that the dissolution of these peripheral territories – these 'mere possessions' – is initially regarded with little more than mild alarm, as the threat seems to lie in the resistance of the landscape to the authority of the Cartographers, as opposed to the loss of the land itself. The disruption of this authority therefore operates at a discursive – as opposed to empirical – level.

The reduction of landscape to poetic symbol also lends itself to a postcolonial reading. The range of symbolic usages cited is revealing in terms of how marginal spaces are perceived and constructed by those wielding power from the centre, and how those outlying lands are defined in terms of simplistic Manichean oppositions. These binary constructions serve to perpetuate the dominance of hegemony, and provide moral justification for the exploitation of the inferior member of the binary relationship. The marginal lands are expendable, as their uselessness is contrasted with the utility of the centre, their alienation juxtaposed with the metropolis's incorporation into the cultural and socio-political structures from which assignations of value emanate.

Carey's ironic assertion – that marginal territories can be said to possess value only in terms of their usefulness to metropolitan sites of cultural production – suggests another possible reading. The passage above may be decoded as a subtle postcolonial response to those very modes of cultural production which seek to negate the intrinsic value of those areas on the periphery, while re-stating the privileged position at the centre. Carey may be seen to be interrogating the practices of those novelists of Empire who fashionably made use of Britain's colonial outposts as symbols and narrative devices in their work. As Leon Litvack observes, very often the colonies functioned in Victorian texts of Empire as little more than a 'theatrical "green room"' (1999, p. 25), a theoretically empty space to which characters could be dispatched when their function had been fulfilled, or from which they could be retrieved, having undergone some suitably dramatic transformation. In either case, the significant narrative events remain firmly situated in the metropolis. Carey, in focusing attention on the hegemonic motivations behind such narrative practices, attempts to reassign some sense of value to these neglected and exploited spaces. By doing so, 'Do You Love Me?' makes its own contribution to the ongoing and necessary strategy of 'writing back', the phrase and process popularized by Ashcroft *et al.* in *The Empire Writes Back* (1989).

Returning to the trope of the map, 'Do You Love Me?' traces the process of decay in the semiotic status of the Cartographers' map, its decline from an approximation of reality to a meaningless formation of codes and symbols which bears no relation whatsoever to the territory it claims to represent. In 'Breaking the Chain', Ian Adam contends that the disappearance of the land and the consequent obsolescence of the map constitute a 'crisis of the sign', a referent set adrift from its stylized signifier (1990, p. 84). The progressive gulf in meaning between sign and signified may also, however, be traced in terms of Baudrillard's definition of the simulation. Before progressing to a more detailed exploration of this concept, a brief discussion of the story's most obvious intertextual reference may be appropriate.

'Do You Love Me?' enacts an ironic and knowing inversion of Jorge Luis Borges's short fable, 'On Exactitude in Science' (1946). In Borges's tale, the Cartographers' Guilds construct a map of the Empire 'whose size was that of the Empire and which coincided point for point with it', covering the entire territory ([1946] 1998, p. 325). With the decline of the Empire, however, the map is exposed to the elements, and slowly decays until only 'Tattered Ruins' remain in the desert, 'inhabited by Animals and Beggars; in all the Land there is no other relic of the Disciplines of

Geography' (ibid., p. 325). Baudrillard, in his essay on 'Simulacra and Simulations', begins his analysis with an allegorical reading of this tale, focusing his attention on 'the metaphysical beauty of this ruined abstraction, bearing witness to an imperial pride and rotting like a carcass, returning to the substance of the soil, rather as an aging double ends up being confused with the real thing' (1992, p. 166). He goes on to assert, however, that allegorical readings of the fable are now useless, as the relationship between sign and referent has come undone. The cartographic image exists in a vacuum in which it alludes only to itself, and correspondence between the real and the representation ceases to exist:

> Abstraction today is no longer that of the map, the double, the mirror or the concept. Simulation is no longer that of a territory, a referential being or a substance. It is the generation by models of a real without origin or reality: a hyperreal. The territory no longer precedes the map, nor survives it. Henceforth, it is the map which precedes the territory – *precession of simulacra* – it is the map which engenders the territory and if we were to revive the fable today, it would be the territory whose shreds are slowly rotting across the map. It is the real, and not the map, whose vestiges subsist here and there, in the deserts which are no longer those of the Empire, but our own.
>
> (ibid., p. 166, emphasis original)

This extract serves to illustrate how Carey's own fable enacts precisely the type of inversions of meaning to which Baudrillard refers. As the territory decays, the society in 'Do You Love Me?' shifts into the hinterland of the *'desert of the real itself'* (Baudrillard, 1992, p. 166, emphasis original).

As the landscape dissolves, the cartographic image can be interpreted as progressing through the successive stages of semiotic failure proposed by Baudrillard. As the story opens, the image possesses the innate authority of an authentic representation, and functions as the fixed centre upon which the superstructure of a coherent national identity is constructed. This recalls Baudrillard's definition of the first stage of simulation, when the representation (the concept of which is itself rooted in the belief that 'the sign and the real are equivalent') operates as the authentic 'reflection of a basic reality ... The image is a *good* appearance: the representation is of the order of sacrament' (ibid., p. 170, emphasis original). In this phase, the discursive system succeeds in masking entirely its own internal fractures, and perceptions of a communal nationhood are able to assume their own contradictory coherence.

As the territory continues to disintegrate, the image enters the second phase of simulation, in which it 'masks and perverts a basic reality ... it is an *evil* appearance: of the order of malefice' (ibid., p. 170, emphasis original). The perversion and manipulation of reality are facilitated by the introduction of the Fischerscope, a piece of scientific apparatus which is 'able to detect the presence of any object, no matter how dematerialized or insubstantial. In this way the Cartographers were still able to map the questionable pairs of the nether regions' (Carey, 1994, pp. 2–3). The Cartographers thus manipulate the scientific process to fashion a new and false image of reality, incorporating territory which hovers threateningly between existence and oblivion. The necessity for such a fiction is intimately connected with the provisional nature of the fragile structures of nationhood: 'To have returned with blanks on the maps would have created such public anxiety that no one dared think what it might do to the stability of our society' (ibid., p. 3). An ironic nod to Australia's own dubious cartographic history may also be detected in this statement, which displays an awareness of the creative liberties taken by those mapmakers of the French School who used imagination to fill in the gaps in their empirical experience.

The territory, at this stage, retains its reality, albeit in a provisional sense, and the cartographic image may still lay claim to some fragile form of 'ideal coextensivity between the map and the territory' (Baudrillard, 1992, p. 167). Eventually, however, entire regions disappear 'so completely that even the Fischerscope could not detect them' (Carey, 1994, p. 3). The response of the discursive system is immediate and drastic; the Cartographers, 'acting under political pressure, used old maps to fake in the missing sections' (ibid., p. 3). The map now serves to disguise the extent of the disintegration, and by doing so the cartographic image enters the third phase of simulation – its purpose to mask the '*absence* of a basic reality' (Baudrillard, 1992, p. 170, emphasis original). The inability of scientific discourse to capture the temporal and spatial aspects of a reality which now shifts along both axes is juxtaposed with the Cartographers' attempt to conceal this failure (and, perhaps, to halt or stall the process of disintegration) by reference to older, more stable representations. The fear of blank spaces has become all-encompassing, and the cartographic image may now be decoded as what Horrocks and Jevtic term 'a panic-stricken production of the real' (1999, p. 110).

The process of dematerialization continues apace as the narrative unfolds. Eventually, buildings begin to disappear. The ambivalence of the colonial subject is evident in the reactions to the disappearance of those buildings belonging to multinational corporations, who have enacted their own mode of economic imperialism in this society. The dematerialization of the ICI headquarters causes the panicked inhabitants to storm angrily into 'the Shell building next door' (Carey, 1994, p. 5) and ransack it: the local press remarks upon 'the great number of weeping men and women who hurled typewriters from windows and scattered files through crowds of frightened office workers' (ibid., p. 5). The problematic nature of postcolonial responses to the colonizing agency is addressed in terms of the oscillation between such nationalistic self-determination and the paradoxical awareness of the colonized subject's own complicity in these manifestations of imperialism, since 'five days later they displayed similar anger when the Shell building itself disappeared' (ibid., p. 5). This ambivalence shares definite characteristics with Bhabha's analysis, in *The Location of Culture* (1994), of the problematic nature of the relationship between colonizer and colonized, characterized by the provisionality and instability of their interdependent and intersecting positions.

The cartographic image enters the final phase of simulation when material objects, and ultimately the inhabitants themselves, begin to dematerialize. The system of signs has, in the final analysis, broken down irreparably; in Baudrillard's terms, the map 'bears no resemblance to any reality whatever: it is its own pure simulacrum' (1992, p. 170). The assertion by Horrocks and Jevtic that the image 'threatens the real by simulating it' (1999, p. 110), again invites comparison with Bhabha's proposed discourse of mimicry, which itself embodies a constant potential threat to the authority of the discourse of colonialism, by continually producing 'its slippage, its excess, its difference' (Bhabha, 1994, p. 86). The concepts of simulation and mimicry, although obviously differing in many ways, nonetheless share the defining characteristics which undermine the assumed authority of the cartographic representation of the real. In exposing the fractures within the discursive systems by which such mimetic abstractions are produced, an awareness of the provisionality and ambivalence of such structures is generated. Despite the best efforts of the Cartographers, the cartographic image is ultimately rendered meaningless.

It is ironically implied at one point, as theories are proposed concerning the nature of the phenomenon, that the Cartographers literally possess the power to construct reality based on their maps and charts. One of the 'Theories That Arose At the Time' suggests the possibility that, in this society, the map may indeed precede the territory:

The fact that the world is disappearing has been caused by the sloppy work of the Cartographers and census takers. Those who had filled out their census forms incorrectly would lose those items they had neglected to describe. People overlooked in the census by impatient officials would also disappear.

(Carey, 1994, p. 6)

The implication being, of course, that in this society, to have one's details recorded and have one's physical position marked on a chart is to confirm one's existence. The acknowledgement of the hegemony determines not only conceptions of self, including fragile perceptions of national identity, but also authenticates physical existence within a spatial reality. This idea suggests a postcolonial reading which intersects neatly with the settler perception (frequently alluded to in writing from the colonies of the 'second world') of alienation from the cultural centre of the metropolis, and a desire for acknowledgement and assignation of value from the colonial agency. Carey's approach, in a manner typical of his fiction, pushes this concept past the point of ridiculousness for satirical purpose, implying that since for one reason or another these places and people have strayed beyond the realms of scientific/colonial discourse, their existence must necessarily be regarded as provisional.

'Do You Love Me?' analyzes, interrogates and deconstructs the cartographic image in such a way as to expose the dangerously ambiguous role which such models play in the creation and maintenance of social forms, including the production of a distinct national identity. The narrator's father believes that 'if humanity doesn't need something it will disappear. People who are not loved will disappear. Everything that is not loved will disappear from the face of the earth' (ibid., p. 6). It is the fragility of the emotional connection between humanity and the landscape which is blamed for the dematerializations. This society, in placing its faith purely in the rigours of cartographic method, has severed the visceral link between man and land. Although Anthony Hassall's assertion that 'perhaps if it is not loved by an occupying people, the land is not there in any worthwhile sense' (Hassall, 1994, p. 34) is possibly an overly simplistic reading, it nonetheless highlights the correlation between this imaginary society and those actual settler colonies who still feel this sense of dislocation from the landscape. This preoccupation with the failure of modes of discourse – whether cartographic or linguistic – to provide a sense of connectedness with the territory is a recurring motif in much Australian fiction.

Carey's story argues that readings of space and subsequent assignations of value are arbitrary and misleading at best, and deliberately disingenuous at worst. The process of mapping is laden with inherent flaws, in terms of both the false assumptions of objectivity and authority which the cartographic model adopts, and of the social and cultural ideologies behind their construction. The narrator's father asserts:

> the world needs Cartographers ... because if they didn't have Cartographers the fools wouldn't know where they were. They wouldn't know if they were up themselves if they didn't have a Cartographer to tell them what's happening.
>
> (Carey, 1994, p. 9)

It is apparent, however, that in such a society the desire for order and spatial awareness leads only to corruption and decay, which are both rooted in the disproportionate power wielded by the cartographic symbol. The world may well need Cartographers, as the narrator's father believes; however, when the relationship between the model and the real dissolves into the realm of pure simulation, the society collapses in on itself. The fragile structures upon which national identity is founded also dissolve, and anarchy is the consequence. The map's descent into meaninglessness reveals 'the cartographer's mad project' (Baudrillard, 1992, p. 167) to be just that: the map is ultimately a transparent and two-dimensional construct, a jumble of meaningless codes and symbols, unable to contain or explain the reality to which it refers, with obviously subversive ramifications for the monolithic assumption of authority embedded within colonial discourse.

Note

1. Phillips defines the cultural cringe as the acceptance within settler colonies that 'the domestic cultural product will be worse than the imported article' (1950, p. 299).

3

'How does your garden grow?' or Jamaica Kincaid's spatial praxis in *My Garden (Book):* and *Among Flowers: A Walk in the Himalaya*

Wendy Knepper

Jamaica Kincaid's recent books on gardening and collecting seeds, *My Garden (Book):* (2000) and *Among Flowers: A Walk in the Himalaya* (2005), present the garden as a space of rumination and regenerative resistance: a place where she might critique imperialism(s) and seed new relations to the world. While *My Garden (Book):* reflects Kincaid's ongoing interest in the ways in which imperial practices and global discourses, such as conquest and botany, have served both to displace and reconstruct a sense of locality, *Among Flowers* turns to a post-9/11 world where a sense of home is now fraught by anxieties about 'distant proximities' among various places in the world and often conflicting spatial orders. In considering Kincaid's approach to spatiality, I begin by outlining the ways in which the garden incarnates a complex ecology for spatial reproduction and then turn to an analysis of how these dynamics infuse the relational spatial poetics at work in *My Garden (Book):*, which offers a meditation on the garden as dwelling place. Turning to *Among Flowers*, I situate Kincaid's spatial politics of the garden in light of debates about negotiating multiple, often overlapping, and disjunctive spatialities in a globalizing world, particularly in the post-9/11 era. Finally, I consider the ways in which Kincaid's approach to the garden discloses new horizons for spatial relations in a global context. She shows that the world cannot be left out of the garden at the same time that she demonstrates her garden is a place in and through which worldly relations are negotiated. Concerns about spatial reproduction, which are central to the activities of garden design, seeding, planting and weeding, take root in Kincaid's garden so that its very beds and the selection of plants come to signify as politically meaningful events in the world. Consequently, the garden emerges as a vital site where worldly relations are regenerated through often ambivalent dialogues with other places and spatial orders.

The garden as living text in *My Garden (Book)*:

Generally speaking, the garden represents a remarkably fecund terrain for explorations of relational spatial praxes. Mark Francis and Randolph T. Hester, Jr. observe that '[t]he power of the garden, lies in its *simultaneous* existence as an idea, a place and an action' (1990, p. 7) and call for a holistic approach to understanding the meaning, function, and possibilities of the garden:

> One cannot examine a garden as a physical place without probing the ideas that generated the selection of its materials and the making of its geometry. One cannot fully understand the idea of the garden without knowing something about the process that created it. Also in the act of gardening reside both ideology and a desire to create a physical order. The garden exists not only as an idea or a place or an action but as a complex ecology of spatial reality, cognitive practice, and real work.
>
> (ibid., p. 7)

The garden invites its creator(s) and visitors to enter into a spatial relation that corresponds to what Edward Soja terms 'thirdspace', placing emphasis on space as simultaneously lived, conceived, and perceived; this framework is particularly helpful when considering the ways in which prevailing, emergent, and alternative spatial imaginaries, often uneasily, co-exist and sometimes come into conflict (Soja, 1996, p. 74). Specifically, this approach to the garden invites a critique of its ideological formation and the labour required to create and sustain it. Indeed, any garden embodies a particular kind of spatial praxis: 'the transformation of (spatial) knowledge into (spatial) action in a field of unevenly developed (spatial) power' (ibid., p. 31). In ontological and epistemological terms, the garden grows in living relation to a changing world order. Potentially, the organic spatial praxis of gardening can tell us something about the shifting relations among ideologies, powers, and actions in the world.

In the context of the Caribbean, the complex ecology of the garden as a spatial reality and praxis is shaped by the imperial flows of commodities, capital, peoples, ideas, practices, and discourses (DeLoughrey *et al.*, 2005; Campbell and Somerville, 2007). While colonizers perceived the Caribbean to be a new Eden, the plantation, with its related practices of slavery and indenture, depended on the exploitation of peoples and natural resources (Tiffin, 2000, pp. 149–63; O'Brien, 2002, pp. 167–84; DeLoughrey, 2004, pp. 298–310). Caribbean literature often reflects an uneasy awareness of the garden as a space of imperial desire, a place of conquest and a site of resistance (Rhys, 1982; Mootoo, 1996; Lamming, [1953] 2003). Kincaid's writing on gardening attests to the uneven dynamics at work in the Caribbean garden when she notes that her garden becomes 'a way of getting to the past that is my own (the Caribbean Sea) and the past as it is indirectly related to me (the conquest of Mexico and its surroundings)' (2000: p. xiv). Specifically, she explores various intersecting and co-existing paradigms for the garden, including the pre-Columbian garden of the Aztecs, the colonial conception of the New World as Eden, the global garden of botany and empire, the plantation, and the Creole garden of the yard.[1] Thus, the place of the garden comes to represent various, shifting paradigms and practices of Caribbean spatiality in the context of local and personal struggles for self-articulation as well as through dislocation and the flows of empire.

The very title of Kincaid's work, *My Garden (Book):*, calls attention to the garden as an organic text of self-inscription. The parenthetical inclusion of the word 'book' reminds the reader that the garden is a text while the presence of a colon indicates that this garden/text is a precursor to an explanation that remains to be planted/written. In this context, Wilson Harris's description of the landscape as a living text might be applied to Kincaid's garden/text:

> The landscape is alive, it is a text in itself, it is a living text. And the question is, how can one find, as an imaginative writer, another kind of living text which corresponds to that living text. There is a dialogue there between one's internal being, one's psyche, and the nature of place, the landscape. There has to be some sort of bridge, which allows one to see all sorts of relationships which one tends to eclipse, which one tends not to see at all.
>
> (Harris, quoted in Maes-Jelinek, 1991, p. 33)

For Harris, language provides a bridge between space as a lived and imagined experience because it is a resource from within oneself and without, embodied in nature as well as the persons and cultures inhabiting the land (ibid., p. 33). Through language, one grasps unconscious, subconscious and conscious connections to the natural environment (ibid., p.33). Likewise, for Kincaid, 'the garden … is so bound up with words about the garden, with words themselves, that any set idea about the garden, any set picture, is a provocation' (2000, p. xiii).

Kincaid's initial recognition of the garden as living text begins with reading about the world of plants and gardens related to the 'discovery' and conquest of the New World:

> That is how my garden began; then again, it would not be at all false to say that just at that moment I was reading a book and that book (written by the historian William Prescott) happened to be about the conquest of Mexico, or New Spain, as it was then called, and I came upon the flower called marigold, and the flower called dahlia and the flower called zinnia, and after that the garden was to me more than the garden as I used to think of it. After that the garden was something else.
>
> (ibid., p. xiii)

In this passage, Kincaid resists the impulse to 'conquer her subject': the colonial history of the Caribbean. Instead, her evasive rhetoric and circuitous uses of language (exemplified by phrases such as 'it would not be at all false to say' and 'it came about') are at odds with her ostensible subject: a knowable history of the conquest of 'New Spain'. She rewrites 'discovery' as a happening (indicated by phrases such as 'happened to be about' and 'came upon'). Her spatial rhetoric thus shifts attention from the history of colonial 'discovery' to the moment of postcolonial encounter. Kincaid discloses a living relationship to garden/text, which she seeks to renew through her creative rewriting/seeding of the garden as 'a complex ecology of spatial reality, cognitive practice, and real work' (Francis and Hester, Jr., 1990, p. 7).

While many critics stress the impact of empire on the Caribbean garden, Kincaid also alludes to the ways local practices were folded into empire and dispersed. Notably, Kincaid reclaims local meaning when she refers to the history of the *cocoxohitl*, which was renamed dahlia in the colonial era (2000, pp. 87–8): she alludes to the power of flowers, which had sacred, ritual, and festive meaning for the Aztec who engaged in the flower wars in order to make the required human sacrifices to the gods. After conquest, she says, no colonial subject would have been inspired to commit a criminal act at the sight of a dahlia (ibid., p. 88). This is because the significance of the *cocoxohitl* in Aztec culture and the significance of flowers more generally would have been effaced through the processes of colonial intervention. Thus, Kincaid's living text serves to re-route imperial histories of the Caribbean garden(text): through a history that predates Western conquest.

Kincaid interrogates the notion of the garden as a space of conquest through her subversive, often opaque, scrutiny of her own spatial praxes as a gardener. She acknowledges that the act of gardening is fraught with the desire for conquest: 'But this desire to pin one's garden down, to conquer it, and leave your own imprint, it's so vain, so unavoidable' (Balutansky and Kincaid, 2002, p. 794). Given such assertions, it is not surprising that some critics see Kincaid's relation to the garden as taking the form of a quest for spatial control (D'Amore, 2005, p. 153). Jeanne C. Ewert observes that Kincaid's 'passionate acts of collection and appropriation' embody the alterity and hybridity of the author whose 'voice of the colonized inside herself speaks in the tones of the colonizer' (2007, p. 125). However, I would point out that Kincaid finds happiness in the garden because it is a locale that resists her intentions, designs, and impulses to create a certain kind of order:

> Nothing works just the way I thought it would, nothing works just the way I had imagined it, and when sometimes it does look like what I had imagined (and this, thank God is rare) I am startled that my imagination is so ordinary.
>
> (2000, p. 6)

The spontaneity of life in the garden defies efforts to conquer space. Thus, Kincaid recuperates the delight of the pre-Columbian garden where 'things were planted for no other reason than the sheer joy of it' (ibid., p. 87). At the same time, the allusion to Aztec histories of ritual sacrifice suggests a profound awareness of the contradiction that 'perhaps every good thing that stands before us comes at a great cost to someone else' (ibid., p. 113). In her living text, the power of the 'garden(text):' lies in its potential to highlight the disjunctive ecologies of spatial desire, knowledge, and labour practices through time.

The garden enables Kincaid to discover new way of dwelling in the world. In the chapter entitled 'The House', she explains that her house in Vermont mimics that of her childhood home where the distinction between inside and outside was blurred (ibid., p. 31). As a child, she grew up in the yard and her sense of domestic space was defined by relations to family members, cooking outside, and living relations to plants and trees, such as the soursop and breadfruit. Similarly, her garden is a place where vegetables are grown, providing nourishment. Books such as *Mrs. Beeton's Guide to Household Management* and Elizabeth David's cookbooks reinforce the sense that the garden is a way of transforming a house into a home that nourishes its inhabitants (ibid., p. 23). Kincaid, likewise, sees the garden as a place that fosters the space of domesticity in which 'anyone might feel comfortable expelling any bodily fluid' (ibid., p. 23): the garden is part of a domestic ecosystem where food is produced, prepared, ingested, nourishes, and is expelled. It is affiliated with the small events of everyday domestic life, but, at the same time, Kincaid asserts that '[t]he world turns on the small event' (ibid., p. 24). In fracturing the distinction between inner/outer, the domestic sphere and the world, a new way of understanding the power of the garden is offered, which presents its simultaneous existence as an idea, act, and place that links home and world. As such, Kincaid's garden corresponds to Harris's definition of a living text as one that opens up a dialogue between one's internal being, one's psyche, and the nature of place, allowing one to see all sorts of relationships that might otherwise go unnoticed. In seeing the garden as part of her home and the world, Kincaid bridges the distance between the small event of gardening and the ethics of dwelling in the world. This is especially evident when we consider that her definition of home implies an ethics of being in the world:

> a home being the place in which the mystical way of maneuvering through the world in an ethical way, a way universally understood to be honorable and universally understood to be ecstatic and universally understood to be the way that we would all want it to be, carefully balanced between our own needs and the needs of other people, people we do not know and can never like, but people all the same who must be considered with utmost seriousness, the same seriousness with which we consider our own lives.
>
> (ibid., p. 33)

Through her personal experience of the domestic Caribbean garden, Kincaid comes to appreciate a new kind of globalism, which differs considerably from botanical models of coercive forms of knowledge, action, and power. Thus, the garden serves as a site of differential spatial expression, enabling her to express new ways of being in the world.

Seeding the garden: distant proximities in *Among Flowers*

In *Among Flowers*, Kincaid's quest for new seeds to plant takes her to the Himalayas where she explores connections between the garden as a small place and other places and spaces in the world (Kincaid, 2005, p. 189). In Nepal, her quest brings her into contact with Maoists, prompting discussion of issues such as terrorism and (global) citizenship. Kincaid's encounter is situated in light of the global affiliations of gardening and guerrilla activities; discourses that have been linked through Third World solidarity movements, particularly as articulated by Ernesto Che Guevara and Maoist doctrine (Reynolds, 2008). Claims to the land, demands for self-government, and discourses about the earth as a space of seeding and planting are revisited through a series of uneasy encounters between the gardener-trekkers and the Maoists. Rather than propose a revolutionary mode of resistance, Kincaid offers a complicated vision of the resistant and contested spatialities in the global order, particularly in light of the post-9/11 context for this work. Kincaid notes that she had first planned to go looking for seeds in 2001, but the events of 9/11 intervened and the journey was postponed for a year. In calling attention to the meaning of this event, Kincaid signals her awareness of the shifting spatial relations which shape *Among Flowers*: "How grateful I am to the uniquely American capability for reducing many things to an abbreviation, for in writing these words, *The Events of September 11*, I need not offer a proper explanation, a detailed explanation of why I made this journey one year later" (Kincaid, 2005, p. 5). Her approach to space, often in an oblique fashion, shows the many ways in which the shifting global order inflects her relations to the garden and the world.

In a globalizing world, particularly following 9/11, concerns about spatiality and a global sense of place have taken on a new urgency. Soja notes that in recent years we have seen a spatial turn, characterized by various efforts 'to think of the *spatiality* of human life in much the same way that we have persistently approached ... its *historicality* and *sociality*' (1996, p. 2).[2] For Anthony Giddens, globalization itself entails 'the intensification of worldwide social relations which link distant localities in such a way that local happenings are shaped by events occurring many miles away and vice versa' (1990, p. 64). James Rosenau observes that we live in a world of 'distant proximities in which the forces pressing for greater globalization and those inducing greater localization interactively play themselves out' (2003, p. 2). Rosenau suggests that distance might be defined as follows:

> Distance is not measured only in miles across land and sea; it can also involve less tangible spaces, more abstract conceptions in which distance is assessed across organizations, hierarchies, event sequences, social strata, market relationships, migration patterns, and a host of other nonterritorial spaces.
>
> (ibid., p. 6)

He observes that there is 'no self-evident line that divides the distant from the proximate' (ibid., p. 6). In the post-9/11 world, the sense of a barrier to the world outside has been destroyed for many Americans, enabling some to perceive interdependencies which have long been evident to marginalized peoples. Rosenau sees evidence of a world undergoing 'fragmegration', which suggests 'the pervasive interaction between fragmenting and interacting dynamics unfolding at every level of community' (ibid., p. 11). The presence of disjunctive, often incommensurate, spatial practices and paradigms has profoundly destabilized a sense of borders and distance.

An awareness of distant proximities and anxieties about the fragmenting and integrating aspects of trans-local spaces in the (post)colonial and globalizing world infuses Kincaid's work. For instance, Kincaid's description of the spatial relations of her garden shows how multiple, seemingly distant locations come together:

> Eden is never far from the gardener's mind. It is The Garden to which we all refer, whether we know it or not. And it is forever out of reach. As I walked up and down the terrain in the foothills of the Himalaya looking for plants appropriate for growing in my garden I am now (even now, for the garden is ongoing, and a stop to it means death) making in Vermont, the strangeness of my situation was not lost to me. Vermont, all by itself, should be Eden and gardenworthy enough. But apparently, I do not find it so. I seem to believe that I will find my idyll more a true ideal, only if I can populate it with plants from another side of the world.
>
> (Kincaid, 2005, p. 189)

Through gathering seeds from distant parts of the world and planting them, Kincaid forges connections with other garden zones. Instead of the botanical perspective of a global system of rationalized plants – that Enlightenment sensibility that informs the post/colonial garden – Kincaid engages in distancing and approximating dynamics. Eden is both out of reach and potentially nearby. Vermont and the Himalayas are linked through the material relations of the plants. Indeed, upon her return, Kincaid's sense of spatiality is profoundly trans-located; she compares the mountains in Vermont (particularly Mount Antony) to the Himalayan mountains she has traversed. The attempt to locate the garden leads to a sense of distant proximities in which various conceptions of spatiality converge and diverge.

A sense of dislocation and 'fragmegration' pervades *Among Flowers*. Locally, in Nepal, the theme of terror arises through the presence of the Maoist guerrillas:

> What was I doing in a world in which the king and the Maoists were in mortal conflict? The irony of me getting into the local spirit of things was not lost on me, but this feeling of estrangement was soon replaced altogether with a sense of being lost in amazement and wonder and awe.
>
> (ibid., p. 20)

Kincaid comes to feel there is 'no border between myself and what I was seeing before me, no border between myself and my day-to-day existence' (ibid., p. 20). Between the political and the personal, the physical and the ideological, the near and far worlds of Vermont and the Himalayas, Kincaid engages in a new kind of spatial orientation to the world, which reflects post-9/11 sensibilities that borders can be easily transgressed. Distant proximities are embodied as the land and the peoples, local and distant, are seen in disruptive spatial relations. Camouflage uniforms are intended to establish a borderless relationship between the self and natural horizons. By blending into the landscape, the individual gains the power to engage in surprise attacks on the enemy. For Kincaid, the Maoists' blue camouflage uniforms are linked to a sense of spatial derangement:

> Why blue, and not green (for forest) or brown (for desert), did not remain a mystery for too long. In Nepal, the sky is part of your consciousness, you look up as much as you look down. As much as I looked down to see where I should place my feet, I looked up to see the sky because so much of what happened up there determined the earth on which I stood. The sky everywhere is on the whole blue; from time to time, it deviates from that; in Nepal it deviated from that more often than I was used to, and it often did so with a quickness that brought to my mind a deranged personality, or just ordinary mental instability.
>
> (ibid., p. 23)

This disorderly spatiality affects not only her apprehension of the physical world but also of the people she encounters through this living textuality. Kincaid's body becomes a marker of distant proximities when a local woman admires her plaited hair and wants to learn how to make her hair look like the author's. Kincaid remarks that she did not know how to tell the woman that 'my hairdo, which she liked so much, was made possible by weaving into my own hair the real hair of a woman from a part of the world that was quite like her own' (ibid., p. 46). The familiar African-American weave hairstyle, conveying a certain socio-cultural aesthetic, is subject to defamiliarization through its relation to the local Asian world context. Trans-local encounters and disruptions in the spatial order reflect anxieties about the ways identities are located and resituated in everyday life, whether in Nepal or America.

Local and global acts of terror are brought into dialogue as Kincaid accounts for her journeys to and through Nepal. While the initial trip was delayed by 9/11, the American government had already issued warnings about the risks associated with travel in Nepal due to the Maoists (whom the American government also deems to be terrorists).[3] Kincaid was aware of the possible dangers before she left. At the same time, she recognizes that the traversal of spatial boundaries can also have moral implications: when a person kills another, eventually a line is eradicated and other people are also killed (ibid., p. 62). Nonetheless, her desire for garden-worldly relations outweighs her fear of being hurt:

> Still, the thought of the garden and to see growing things in it that I had seen in their natural habitat, to see the surface of the earth stilled, far away from where I am from, perhaps I would be lucky and see only the writings of the Maoists, perhaps I would never, ever see them at all.
>
> (ibid., p. 62)

The inevitable encounter with the Maoists is coupled with the encounter with the threatening aspects of the natural world in the form of leeches. Literally, this is because their course is diverted and they have to camp in places where leeches exist. Symbolically, the Maoists' demands for payments of thousands of rupees underscore the relations between the 'leeching' of the eco-tourist as he/she comes to terms with transnational spatialities, which are not merely a site of privileged self-fulfilment. Eventually, Kincaid observes that the Maoists and leeches became indistinguishable to her (ibid., p. 90). She asks, 'How to explain to a leech that we did not like President Powell? How to tell a Maoist that Powell wasn't even the President?' (ibid., p. 90). Kincaid is attentive to a global economy where citizens are made 'to pay for' the actions of the nation to which they belong. The travellers sense they must disavow affiliations with imperial powers in order to survive the trek through the Himalaya. As a result of the Maoist encounter, the travellers are forced to change their course both literally and symbolically as they take a new direction through the mountains and feel compelled to adopt new identities: 'Sue and Bleddyn became Welsh and Dan and I became Canadians' (ibid., p. 73). This renegotiation of identity in light of global-local relations shows the extent to which the political and the personal converge; Colin Powell's visit to the region, during which he denounced the Maoists as terrorists, transforms the local encounter into a symbolic encounter with the global order. The difficulties of negotiating a strange, sometimes perilous, natural terrain become commensurate with (nearly) insurmountable difficulties of overcoming differences in language, culture, and politics, whether at home or in the world.

Disjunctive spatial relations are evident in Kincaid's writing. While Kincaid expresses concern about AIDS in Nepal when speaking about local health issues (ibid., p. 29) and shares certain opinions with the Maoists because she too 'had her own reasons to be angry with President Powell' (ibid., p. 74), these moments of potential solidarity are sometimes overshadowed by a sense of (American) entitlement. Kincaid's inclusion of a photograph of a porter bent down under the weight of the goods he is carrying through the mountains carries the caption 'Porters loads can exceed one hundred pounds' (ibid., p. 83). Kincaid's prose reflects the tensions between the tourist's pleasures and the local labourer's (the porter) roles in the global economy:

> What had they been doing when we were exploring the landscape, looking for things that would grow in our garden, things that would give us pleasure, not only in their growing, but also with the satisfaction with which we could see them growing and remember seeing them alive in their place of origin, a mountainside, a small village, a not easily accessible place in the large (still) world?
>
> (ibid., p. 83)

This querulous question reflects a particular privileged, narcissistic view of one's place in the global order; the garden becomes a site to be planted with souvenirs that attest to 'the luxury of the conqueror' (Simmons, 1994, p. 22) as someone who freely collects and transplants specimens from distant areas of the world. With this encounter, Kincaid offers a highly ambivalent representation of her role as a global gardener: her actions in the world and her garden are never removed from the inequities of power in the global economy.

Derek Walcott notes that Kincaid's writing constantly 'heads towards its own contradiction' as if each sentence is 'discovering itself, discovering how it feels' (1990, p. 80). Stylistically, lexical repetition and rewording convey a sense of doubling back (anadiplosis) that calls attention to differing spatial relations of return: the porters (physical labour), the trekkers (pleasure and anticipation) and the gardener (memory as return). This ironic critique of disjunctures in the global order takes on hyperbolic proportions when Kincaid describes how the Maoists' sense of injustice is comparable to and yet differs from that of the trekking gardeners:

> The Maoists were right, I felt in particular: life itself was perfectly fair, people had created many injustices; it was the created injustices that led to me being here, dependent on Sherpas, for without this original injustice, I would not be in Nepal and the Sherpas would be doing something not related to me. And then again, the Maoists were wrong, the porters should be fired; they were not being good porters. They should bend to our demands, among which was to be made comfortable when we wanted to be comfortable. We were very used to being comfortable ... when we were not comfortable, we did our best to rid ourselves of the people who were not making us comfortable.
>
> (Kincaid, 2005, p. 84)

Kincaid introduces an uneasy awareness of competing perceptions of space and territoriality where the meaning of justice and injustice is subject to the fragmenting and integrating potential of the global order. The repetition of the words 'injustice' and 'comfortable' continues the pattern of textual return, reinforcing the sense of a local-global spatial order where the comforts of some depend on injustice to others.[4]

Ultimately, the garden is experienced as a site seeded with the perils and aspirations of the global encounter. At times, natural spaces represent a harmonious set of relations to the plants of the world: poinsettia and *Datura*, 'plants that are native to Mexico', are seen in bloom with 'trunks as thick as maple trees in Vermont' (ibid., p. 171). In other instances, the promise of an idyllic garden space is disrupted. When the travellers arrive in Donje, they unpack some five hundred packets of seeds and set up camp only to be confronted by Maoists (who had already driven out the Nepalese authority at gunpoint). Kincaid describes the moment of Maoist-gardener encounter as 'one of the many that holds in it a metaphor of the very idea of the garden itself' (ibid., p. 168):

> We had in our possession seeds that, if properly germinated, would produce some of the most beautiful and desirable flowering plants to

appear in a garden situated in the temperate zone; at the very same time we were in danger of being killed and our dream of the garden in the temperate zone, the place in which we lived, would die with us also. At the very moment we were projecting ourselves into an ideal idyll we were in between life and death.

(ibid., pp. 168–9)

Along with other tourists, Kincaid boards 'an airplane, the kind that is always pictured in fatal accidents involving people from rich countries in the process of experiencing the world as spectacle' (ibid., pp. 185–6). Seen through the windows of the plane, the mountain peaks of Nepal are captured from a spectral perspective, appearing as the kind of image found in a calendar designed for the export market: the mountains become a reference point for the viewer, becoming 'a backdrop against which time passing is marked off' (ibid., p. 186). The illusion of time-less spatiality is soon disrupted when days later, Kincaid learns that the airport at which she had camped has been attacked by Maoists and some people killed. Her wonder and amazement at the beauty of the landscape and spaces of Nepal are resituated in relation to the distant proximities of peoples, plants, and political beliefs in the 'fragmegrated' global order. To sum up, Kincaid's multifarious, epiphanic approach to spatial poetics is indicative of anxieties about a sense of one's place in a world order where relations among various spatial paradigms are increasingly porous and disjunctive.

The garden as the place of spaces: the gardener and the world

In closing, I want to consider Kincaid's approach to a relational sense of place, which might be defined in opposition to Manuel Castells's notions of a 'space of places' and a 'space of flows' (Castells, 2000, pp. 453–60). While Castells defines a 'space of places' as 'a locale whose form, function, and meaning are self-contained within the boundaries of physical contiguity' (ibid., p. 453), Kincaid shows that the garden is a locale whose form, function, and meaning are ever-changing because it is a living, growing text. Through the activities of seeding, transplant-ing, and growing the garden, the gardener not only imagines but shapes a particular place in the world. Rooted though the garden may be, it does not represent a fixed place for Kincaid, but an active space of rumi-nation and connection. Though she travels far and wide and introduces plants from around the world, Kincaid's garden cannot be described as 'a space of flows' or 'the material organization of time-sharing social practices that work through flows' (ibid., p. 442). By showing us how the plants come to be in the garden, Kincaid brings to life the perils, and possibilities of the garden as a place that allows her to negotiate a relationship to different spatial orders. The garden as spatial praxis entails confrontations of a very profound nature with the environment, culture, transplanted identities, shifting power relations, and mutable constructs of identity.

Through actual and imagined acts of gathering seeds and planting, Kincaid discovers new cognitive, affective, and bodily relations to the world. In her analysis of the practices (acts) of gardening/writing, Isabel Hoving sees Kincaid's garden as a disruption of 'unity and coherence, and the soothing certitude of imagined space' (Hoving, 2002, p. 133). The garden is a place of encounter where new relations to the world might be negotiated:

> I was making this trip with the garden in mind to begin with; so everything I saw, I thought, How would this look in the garden? This was not the last time I came to realize that the garden itself was a way of accommodating and making acceptable, comfortable, familiar, the wild, the strange.
>
> (Kincaid, 2005, p. 44)

Like Hoving, I see Kincaid's garden as a material space, shaped by the political, and a frame for agency, which allows for 'a diverse, yet concrete set of critical and rebellious acts' (Hoving, 2002, p. 132). Kincaid's garden texts persistently return to the borders of the apolitical and political; she investigates how the borders of the garden represent a way of constructing the imagined and lived borders of the political in everyday life. For instance, as a gardener, Kincaid is keenly aware of her position as an American citizen, someone who has 'crossed a line' and 'joined the conquering class' (Kincaid, 2000, p. 92) in a country often seen as an imperial and/or neo-colonial power. In *My Garden (Book):*, her garden is a visible reminder of the fact that her 'feet are (so to speak) in two worlds' (ibid., p. 92) and in *Among Flowers*, she states that her true ideal is to create a garden populated with plants from another side of the world (2005, p. 189). As such, her garden is a place where identity and relations are also inscribed through interactions with other places

Organic ways of conceiving, perceiving, living, and imagining relations to the world come to life in Kincaid's garden. While the Edenic story deals with the desire for knowledge in the form of an apple that can be consumed, Kincaid's garden story unfolds as a meditative space of inquiry and wonder. For example, when asked about the odd shapes and arrangement of her flower beds, she realizes that she is not quite sure what she is trying to accomplish. Eventually, she intuits her spatial purpose: the 'garden I was making (and am still making and will always be making) resembled a map of the Caribbean and the sea that surrounds it' (Kincaid, 2000, p. xiv). Gardening becomes an exercise in imagined cartography, reworking geographic boundaries and transplanting the Caribbean imaginary. Through the garden, she navigates a way through the places that shape her identity in the world: Vermont, the Caribbean, England, and China, among other places. In the concluding chapter to *My Garden (Book):*, entitled 'The Garden in Eden', Kincaid locates her own identity in relation to 'the plants for which I have no immediate use and grow only for an interest that is peculiar to me, and so this is the part of the garden which carries me to the world' (ibid., p. 171). As a 'contact zone', where social cultures meet and clash (Pratt, M. L., 1992, p. 4), the garden offers a locale for the writer/gardener to address otherness, uneven power dynamics, and regional inequities.

The practices of spatial reproduction – such as the activities of design, digging, seeding, and planting – can both displace and disclose 'the relation between the source[s] of the world and ourselves' (Cooper, 2006, p. 150). Gardening becomes a meaningful form of spatial action because the activities of creating borders, recounting the histories of plants, ordering plants from afar, and planting them are seen as directly related and indirect ways of relating to other people and places in the world through time. Rachel Azima notes that Kincaid discovers 'a model of place-connection that allows for relationships to multiple places and takes into account the persistent interaction of these place-relationships with one another' (2006–07, p. 102) while Melanie Murray observes that Kincaid's garden serves as a 'a site of negotiation' among shifting identities and locations (2001, pp. 118, 124). Through accounts of 'small events', Kincaid demonstrates that there are powerful links between the garden and social relations in the world. For example, after making a racist remark about blacks in the military, a labourer in the garden tries to apologize to Kincaid by giving her bulbs to plant, but she throws them in the rubbish bin (Kincaid, 2000, p. 49). When she catches a raccoon, who threatens her garden, she wants to kill it, but the 'three whining pacifists' in her family convince her to free the animal instead (ibid., p. 34). These small events also include accounts of her readerly encounters with Vita Sackville-West,[5] Linnaeus, Tsitsi Dangarembga, and others who have played a significant role in shaping or writing about the spatial history of the garden. While she rejects Sackville-West's garden aesthetics because there is 'no mention of the sad weight of the world' in her garden texts (ibid., p. 59), Dangarembga is identified as a kindred spirit who recognizes that there is form of liberation at 'the sight of things growing just for the sheer joy of it' (ibid., p. 86). These and other real and imagined 'small events', involving guests, fellow gardeners, labourers, family, friends, botanists, and animals, enable her to dramatize encounters with racial identities, the cultivation of borders, cultural difference, delight, and acts of violence through time and place. For Kincaid, gardening as spatial praxis not only constantly tests ethical relations to the wider world but also elicits an alternative spatial order.

To plant a garden is to enter into a living relation to the world. Hoving observes that the inscription of the Caribbean landscape suggests an 'as yet undefined, interrelated global imaginative space, where it [the landscape] receives new meaning and vitality' (2005, p. 167). The same might be said of Kincaid's garden, except that sense of vitality is accompanied by an awareness of conflict and struggle. This relationship is characterized by a sense of expectancy (of things to come) and dissatisfaction (in relation to the ideal). Kincaid sees the act of gardening as an attempt to 'bring in from the wild as many things as can be appreciated, as many things as it is possible for a gardener to give meaning to, as many things as it is possible for the gardener to understand' (Kincaid, 2000, p. 175). Kincaid's garden thus occupies an open relation to the world: the garden functions as a connective site of relational potential because 'the world cannot be left out of the garden' (ibid., p. 59). Critique of the spatial imaginary takes the form of a radical/radicle living textuality via the garden as a site of open, unresolved tensions where she negotiates competing notions of place and various, often conflicting, global spatial paradigms. The garden's simultaneous existence as an idea, place, and action gives way to shifting discourses, a relational sense of place, and a space of rumination where organic inscription enables new spatial relations to be seeded.

To conclude, the garden enables Kincaid to navigate a sense of place in the world. Through the garden as spatial praxis, Kincaid engages in trans-local exchanges that enable her to negotiate affective, remembered, lived, and imagined relations to imperialisms past and present, looking back to the age of discovery, encounter, and conquest not in order to account for a chronology of the garden, but rather to understand the horizons of contemporary practices and material realities of places in the world. If, as Castells suggests, there is a need to build cultural, political, and physical bridges between the space of flows (globalization) and the space of places (localization) (Castells, 2000, pp. 458–9), Kincaid offers a meditation on how this sensibility and sense of agency might be achieved in the everyday practice of gardening as a form of vernacular globalism or a local expression of global relations. A living text with worldly affiliations, the garden offers a place where rumination, regenerative resistance, and relation to a changing world order take seed and grow. The garden is a place where one might come to be at home among the various spatialities of the changing world order.

Notes

1. As many critics have noted, Kincaid's writing about the garden explores 'the myriad ways in which gardening and botany are inextricably linked to empire' (Scott, 2006, p. 58; see also Soto-Crespo (2002, p. 352) and Fidecaro (2006b, pp. 250–1), such as through the desire for territorial control (Kincaid, 2000, pp. 86–8), the power to name (Fidecaro, 2006a, pp. 73–92), colonial hierarchies (Kincaid, 2000, p. 99), cartography (ibid., p. xiv), and the conquest of space (ibid., pp. 89–90, 98).
2. For example, this critical vocabulary includes terms such as heterotopia, spatial hybridity, borderlands, rhizomes, the Poetics of Relation, the planetary, and the '-scapes' of globality (see Bhabha, 1994, p. 38; Appadurai, 1996, pp. 31–3; Soja, 1996, pp. 157–63; Glissant, 1997, pp. 11–12; Anzaldúa, 1999, pp. 34, p. 99; Spivak, 2003, p. 71ff; Gilroy, 2005, p. xv).
3. From 1996 to 2006, the Nepalese Civil War (called the People's War by the Maoists) entailed conflicts between government forces and Maoists. A Comprehensive Peace Agreement signed on 21 November 2006 is now monitored by the United Nations Mission in Nepal. According to some experts, more than 12,000 people were killed during the war and an estimated 100,000 to 150,000 were displaced as a result of the conflict. The Maoists controlled many rural areas, including the mountainous terrain through which Kincaid and her companions journeyed. The United States and the EU were among those who provided money in support of the Nepalese government as part of the global war on terrorism and in an effort to avoid destabilization in the area. In 2002, when Kincaid was in Nepal, King Gyanendra deposed Prime Minister Deuba and the entire Council of Ministers, assumed executive power, and cancelled the planned elections; he then appointed Lokendra Bahadur Chand as Prime Minister.
4. In an interview with Marina Warner, Kincaid spoke openly about the uneven power and economic dynamics that underpin the eco-touristic encounter where the porters 'are exploited, no question and anything that you can do for them, do' (Warner, 2006, p. 56).
5. Anne Collett offers an interesting reading of Kincaid's relation to Sackville-West. See Collett (2006, pp. 59–62).

4
Gender and space in postcolonial fiction
South Asian novelists re-imagining women's spatial boundaries

Elizabeth Jackson

Being positioned on the margin of the dominant discourse seems to express itself in a preoccupation with boundaries and space. The notion of a border giving physical presence to a state of marginality is recurrent in both women's and postcolonial writing. So too are notions of invisible boundaries and spatial segregation based on gender, ethnicity, social class and other categories of identity. However, contestation and renegotiation of the meaning of spaces are always possible, so that the remaking of spaces is central to much feminist and postcolonial work. In this chapter I want to discuss the notion of gendered space in the postcolonial context before going on to investigate some of the ways in which postcolonial novelists seek to re-imagine women's spatial boundaries, focusing particularly on the fictional writings of South Asian women from India and Britain.

The centre needs its margin; hence the paradox that the 'others' in terms of gender and cultural identity are marginalized but also given their own places: the slum, the ghetto, the zenana, the harem, the colony, the closet, the Third World, the private. Moreover, space and behaviour are intimately and intricately related. Aside from physical and geographical borders, other, invisible boundaries affect human behaviour and keep individuals in place, such as the boundaries enclosing ghettoes and ethnically segregated areas but also the glass ceilings placed above professional women. There are also the insidiously powerful boundaries which often lie within the female psyche as a result of women's socialization. Indeed, femininity itself has been defined as 'a tradition of imposed limitations' (Brownmiller, 1984, p. 14).

Western feminisms have always been concerned with the spatial politics of difference, and feminists have seen space as central both to masculinist power and to feminist resistance. They have argued that the social construction of gender difference establishes some (private) spaces as women's, and other (public) spaces as men's, and that those constructions serve to reinforce the power relations of gendered identity. Certainly, many of the struggles of western feminism can be seen as a diverse array of challenges to the distinction between the public and the private and to the comparative value accorded to them. There have been attempts to build domestic spaces that do not rely on the privatized domestic labour of women; there have been many struggles to reconstitute the public so that women have a right to occupy its spaces and participate in its activities; there have been attempts to give a higher status to the domestic sphere, as well as struggles to erase the distinction entirely.

Much recent feminist scholarship suggests, however, that the distinction between public and private space is more important in some women's lives than in others, and that it varies according to class, race, culture, generation and ethnicity. Alison Blunt concludes that 'the geography of the public/private division should be seen as mostly relevant to white, middle-class feminism' (Blunt and Rose, 1994, p. 4), but others note its application to a wider range of cultural contexts. Many women all over the world have been relegated to spaces separate from those of men. Spatial segregation in terms of gender is not universal, but in the many cultures in which it occurs, it is associated with lower status for women, the negative association being the greatest when segregation reduces women's access to knowledge highly valued in the public realm. That spatial segregation usually equals lower status for women is borne out in many examples, and feminist geographers have found that women's status is lowest in societies with highly differentiated public and private spheres. The very division into public and private spheres has been seen as a tool for upholding patriarchy itself, with one sphere seen as an expansive male territory and the other a domain of female constriction.

In South Asia, both Hindu and Muslim women have historically been subjected to various forms of purdah. Purdah practices have varied over time and between regions, ranging from minor restrictions on women's mobility to total incarceration within the home. All forms of purdah have been displays of class privilege, the implication being that families who keep 'their' women in purdah can afford to forgo the income from their labour outside the home. While few women in contemporary India are subjected to the more restrictive forms of purdah, Indian feminists have drawn attention to the fact that women's mobility in public spaces is still curtailed by ideologies of respectability, as well as the apparently widespread practice of sexual harassment (or 'eve teasing' as it is called in India). In addition to the danger of sexual aggression (both actual and perceived), Kalpana Viswanath has pointed out that the cultural ideology of purity and pollution plays an important role in controlling women's behaviour and the spaces they can occupy. She explains:

> Purity and pollution are central categories that determine social relationships in Hindu society. Within the caste hierarchy, there are certain castes which are considered inherently more or less pure ... Within the context of women's lives, purity and pollution take on a further dimension as these are closely linked to their sexuality and fertility. Women's bodily experiences of menstruation, childbirth, lactation are also seen to define them as polluting or impure.
>
> (1997, p. 315)

South Asian feminist writers have been challenging traditional restrictions on women's mobility and the spaces they are allowed to occupy, in ways that can be illustrated by comparing the approaches of two prominent Indian novelists: Anita Desai and Shashi Deshpande. Born within a year of each other during the 1930s, both Desai and Deshpande witnessed revolutionary changes in gender ideology within India during their lifetimes. Arguably they are also agents of such change, in the sense that their fiction challenges traditional Hindu conceptions of women's 'place' in the physical world and in the social order. Desai, who began publishing novels during the 1960s, has progressively expanded the geographical settings of her novels, gradually giving her female protagonists more space – more physical space, more psychological space, more space to move and think freely. She does not consider herself a feminist, but much feminist criticism is implied in her fiction. Deshpande, by contrast, is a self-proclaimed feminist who began publishing novels during the early 1980s – a time when the women's movement in India was gathering momentum. While her novels are not polemical, they consistently feature female protagonists who actively challenge traditional customs and taboos regarding the spaces which they as women are allowed to occupy.

Social change, of course, is never monolithic. On the contrary, it is always uneven, always debated and contested. The concept of feminism has been particularly controversial in India and other developing nations for a number of reasons. On the one hand, traditionalists argue that it alienates women from their culture, religion and family responsibilities; while some on the left see it as a diversion from the more important class struggle or the struggle against western cultural and economic imperialism. Underlying both views is the assumption that feminism is an essentially western ideology. However, I hope to show that the fiction of these two novelists, and their re-imagining of women's spatial boundaries, are a direct response to the particular problems and needs of *Indian* women, and not simply a western ideological import, as some anti-feminists would like to suggest.

In terms of physical and psychological space, Desai's earlier novels explore the claustrophobia of family-bound Indian women. She is aware of the gendered nature of her earlier artistic vision, having explained her views of the differences between male and female writers in a 1983 interview:

> [Women] live mostly in such confined spaces and therefore their field of observation is at the same time more restricted and more intense. This leads to their placing their emphases differently from men, on having a very different set of values. Whereas a man is more concerned with action, experience and achievement, a woman writer is more concerned with thought, emotion and sensation. At least, so one would think, but this is by no means always so.
>
> (Ram, 1983, p. 32)

This concurs with Virginia Woolf's argument in *A Room of One's Own* (1929), and yet Desai's later novels suggest a more complicated relationship between gender, physical space, emotional space and artistic vision. Although the field of spatial vision in her novels has progressively widened over time, all of her works, no matter how expansive the geographical settings, focus on the individual subjective experience of intensely introspective protagonists. Conversely, limited physical spaces are no barrier to extensive imaginative reach in her fiction.

Let me illustrate these ideas with some concrete examples. Desai's first novel, *Cry, the Peacock* (1963) is intensely focused on the troubled psyche of its protagonist, Maya, whose spatial world is limited to her home, her garden and the homes of a few friends. The restrictions to which she is subjected contribute to Maya's emotional deterioration, and the narrative movingly portrays her gradual slide into insanity. Sita in *Where Shall We Go This Summer?* (1975) ventures away from her home in Bombay to an island which may be nearby geographically but is vastly far away in terms of her experience. Her journey to the island of Manori is not a holiday but literally a process of running away from her domestic life in Bombay. In this sense, she undertakes not just a journey to another physical space but also an emotional journey which can be interpreted in various ways. Some critics see her journey as a retreat from the world of the masculine values of competitiveness and aggression, and her final decision to return to her husband and children in Bombay as a defeat, a failure to achieve selfhood and autonomy. Others see her journey as one of self-discovery which leads to her recognition of 'reality' and her decision to return to the world of social responsibility which she cannot, in any case, escape.

The conflict between the need to withdraw for self-preservation and the need to be involved in the painful process of life continues in *Fire on the Mountain* (1977), in which the elderly protagonist has retreated to a hill station, hoping to spend the rest of her life in isolation. There is an expansive sense of space in this novel, involving panoramic views and large areas over which a troubled young girl wanders. The narrative, however, is focused on the thoughts, perceptions and conversations of the main characters. There is no authorial comment, no contextualization, no description except through the perspectives of the experiencing characters. The same is true of *Clear Light of Day* (1980), which is set in a particular neighbourhood in Delhi while ranging far afield in terms of feelings and memories. The perspectives of the two Das sisters, Bim and Tara, are presented and compared in such a way that we are left with a feeling of having traversed long distances – not in space but in time, through their memories, conversations and emotional experiences. Desai's next three novels – *In Custody* (1984), *Baumgartner's Bombay* (1988) and *Journey to Ithaca* (1995) – feature progressively wider geographical settings, but again the perspective is insistently subjective. Finally, in *Fasting, Feasting* (1999), space is envisioned as equally constraining for a timid young man compelled by his family to travel to America for his university education as it is for his homebound sister back in India. Here the common element is lack of choice over the space one occupies, whether it's the young man who experiences his male privilege as a burden or the woman who suffers intensely from emotional and physical claustrophobia. Both are constrained in different ways by gendered expectations which, in effect, ignore their individual needs and desires.

While Desai's protagonists seek to expand their range of emotional and intellectual experience, Deshpande's protagonists actively struggle against gendered spatial boundaries. In particular, they challenge spatial restrictions arising from orthodox Hindu conceptions of women as 'impure' or 'polluting', as well as patriarchal constraints on their thought and behaviour. For example, many of her protagonists express resentment against the Brahmin taboos imposed on them during

menstruation. Saru, in *The Dark Holds No Terrors* (1980), recalls her adolescent horror at these restrictions:

> It was torture ... the three days when I couldn't enter the kitchen or
> the puja room ... the sleeping on a straw mat covered with a thin
> sheet ... the feeling of being a pariah, with my special cup and plate
> by my side in which I was served from a distance, for my touch was,
> it seemed, pollution.
>
> (1980, p. 62)

Indu in *Roots and Shadows* (1983) expresses a similarly resentful reaction to the injunction that: 'For four days now, you are unclean. You
can't touch anyone or anything.' And that, she observes, 'had been my
introduction to the beautiful world of being a woman. I was unclean'
(ibid., p. 115).

Not surprisingly, the heroines of these novels actively rebel against
their traditional upbringings, refusing to be confined to the gendered
spaces allotted to them. Rejecting arranged marriages and caste customs,
both of them choose their own husbands and train as professionals in
order to escape the domestic servility and economic dependence which
characterizes the lives of their mothers and other female relatives. Sadly,
they later find that their professional success cannot bring them the
power and privileges reserved for men in India.

The difference between these two novels, published in the early 1980s,
and *Small Remedies*, published in 2000, illustrates the rapid rate of social
change within India during the past few decades. In *Small Remedies*, the
spatial restrictions that an older woman confronted during her youth
are presented as outdated conventions of a bygone era which surprise
the younger generation. An accomplished musician, Savitribai overcame
overwhelming obstacles to learn music. In particular, she had to confront the gendered restrictions of the spaces which she as a woman had
been allowed to occupy. For example, in her youth she was passionately
fond of music but the only performances she was allowed to attend
were in private houses, and even there the women often had to sit in
another room, away from where the performer and male audience were
sitting. When she finally persuaded a professional musician to take her
on as a pupil, she had to live ten miles away from him:

> She regrets ... the fact that she can't live near the temple like his
> other students, the male pupils. They, being on the spot, can listen to
> him doing his *riaz*, they have the benefit of the classes he suddenly

decides to take on the spur of the moment, hours which are, she hears with envy, much more rewarding, illuminating sometimes, than the scheduled classes.

(Deshpande, 2000, p. 132)

But Savitribai succeeds as a musician, against the odds, though she pays a high price in the process, having to sacrifice her family life and her respectability to pursue her dream.

Gendered restrictions in India, then, have been intricately tied up with those of other hierarchies, particularly those of caste, religion and social class. The protagonists of these novels are elite women, subject to very strict controls on their physical boundaries and behaviour in order to maintain family respectability. Poorer women, by contrast, have always needed to venture outside their homes for employment because their income is essential for family survival. Their greater mobility, however, is accompanied by greater vulnerability to exploitation, abuse and victimization. In Deshpande's novels the fear of sexual assault seems to be strongly felt by lower-class women, like the character in *The Binding Vine* (1993) who says to her more privileged counterpart: 'Women like you will never understand what it is like for us. We have to keep to our places, we can never step out. There are always people wanting to throw stones at us, our own people first of all' (Deshpande, 1993, p. 47).

Although the element of feminist protest is sharper and more direct in the novels of Deshpande than in those of Desai, it is not simply a matter of westernization because, unlike Desai, Deshpande does not engage with the West in her fiction. Whereas in Desai's narratives any consideration of women's needs or rights is perceived by the more conservative characters as an aping of western ways, conflicts around gender ideology in Deshpande's narratives make no reference to the West. Instead they centre on generation, caste, social class and religion. The automatic labelling of feminist ideas as 'western' or 'un-Indian' ignores these other factors and therefore does not do justice to the rich diversity and heterogeneity of India itself.

A consideration of 'diaspora fiction', such as Monica Ali's novel *Brick Lane* (2003), suggests that the relationship between gender, cultural identity and space may be even more complex for South Asian women living in the West. In this particular novel, one of the complexities is associated with the ambiguity of Brick Lane as a space. Situated in the heart of London, side by side with the financial centre of the city, the geographical area around Brick Lane is nevertheless still conceived as a segregated space for the underprivileged. For over 200 years it has been a home for refugees, housing the Huguenots escaping French persecution, followed by East European Jews fleeing the pogroms during the late nineteenth and early twentieth centuries, and immigrants from Bangladesh, Malta, Cyprus, the Caribbean and Somalia have been settling there for many years. The Bangladeshi community is currently by far the largest of these groups, in part due to an influx of migrant workers who arrived from Dhaka in the late 1960s in the hope of finding work in the textile factories. As the area has become more and more densely populated by Bangladeshis, and as these seemingly transient migrants become a more settled and permanent population, Brick Lane has also become a site of cultural conflict, and the number of racist attacks has continued to grow. In addition, the area has seen a sharp rise in radical Islam, as the community seeks its own identity in an attempt to fight back against discrimination and prejudice. Brick Lane has also been affected by rising (exoticist) consumerism, so that it is increasingly perceived as a tourist attraction, but it is still associated with social deprivation and poorly maintained housing estates.

Women in the diaspora are subjected to conflicts and experiences markedly different from those of men; experiences which are increasingly being reflected in their writing. Some arrive as university students and stay on. But for others the element of choice in the fact of migration is limited. They often arrive in the West as appendages of the men in their lives, as wives, daughters or mothers. Educational levels may be different and there may be language barriers, so that diasporic situations can sometimes intensify the idea of men as negotiators with the external world and women as custodians of traditional culture within the home.

In *Brick Lane*, the narrator concentrates in minute detail on the intricacies of the everyday life of the protagonist, Nazneen, a Bangladeshi immigrant who arrives in London as a bride in an arranged marriage. Overturning the popular western perception of 'Third World women' – particularly Muslim women – as repressed and secluded in their countries of origin, Nazneen is actually far more enclosed in her domestic setting within the London housing estate than she ever was in Bangladesh. While her childhood in Bangladesh is never idealized in the narrative, it is her married life in London that is portrayed as more restricted in space, in opportunity, in freedom to make decisions of her own. Nazneen's space is metaphorically as well as literally constricted during her first years in London, and the narrative intricately traces her reactions to her experiences and environment, noting for example how, after looking around the room and observing the flaws in the flat's decor, 'she looked and she saw that she was trapped inside this body, inside this room, inside this flat, inside this concrete slab of entombed humanity' (Ali, 2003, p. 61). The narrator continues to elaborate minutely on the material contents and physical attributes of this domestic interior because it constitutes Nazneen's world, and her neighbourhood seems to have an invisible boundary which she rarely crosses because the world outside this boundary is so alien to her.

While Nazneen is effectively in purdah in London, her sister Hasina works outside the home in Bangladesh, a situation in keeping with recent studies which have shown that

> In Bangladesh, a country ... [with] strong norms of purdah ... women appeared to have abandoned old norms in response to new opportunities ... By contrast, in Britain ... Bangladeshi women were largely found working from home, in apparent conformity with purdah norms.
>
> (Kabeer, 2000, p. viii)

However, there is a sense in which purdah traditions can be carried into feminized work spaces, as for example in *Brick Lane* where the situation of women in Bangladesh going out to work merits protest by local mullahs and by husbands who urge their 'garment girls' to wear burkhas inside the factory. Current theorists have shown that in the West too, even in the twenty-first century, there is a sense in which working women are largely restricted to a new 'private sphere' operating within the public sphere itself. That is, women tend to opt for the types of roles in the public sphere that they were conventionally allocated within the private sphere.

Brick Lane also overturns the popular perception of paid employment outside the home being necessarily liberating or empowering for women. Although Hasina reports at first that 'working is like [a] cure' (ibid., p. 107), because it gives her a new sense of identity and self-worth, she is increasingly exploited by successive employers. On one level, this supports Kerstin Shands's suggestion that it is mainly 'white, middle-class and career-oriented feminists' who find the home static and suffocating (1999, p. 68). She argues that 'women refugees or expatriates might have completely different perceptions and ideals, as may many Third World women who are requesting the right to remain in the home' (ibid.). However, while Hasina does not relish the concept of domestic confinement, whether by choice or by 'right', her exploitation in the workplace is clearly linked to her gender and her social class. Whereas the home has conventionally been seen as a place of rest and refuge for the privileged (mainly men), it is rarely a place of rest for people who work there (mainly women). Constructions of the home as a place of safety are also challenged by statistics on domestic violence. While *Brick Lane* ends optimistically with Nazneen gaining a sense of physical – and hence psychic – freedom, Deshpande's novels suggest that expanding women's physical boundaries is necessary but not sufficient for challenging the social customs which disempower them.

Several conclusions emerge from this comparison of the re-imagining of women's spatial boundaries in the fictional writings of these postcolonial novelists from India and Britain. We note a number of recurring themes, including the sense of enclosure and entrapment of family-bound women in Monica Ali's *Brick Lane,* which is also prominent in Desai's earlier novels. Pervading all of these texts is a sense of women's lack of choice over the spaces they are allowed (or feel free) to occupy, whether this lack of choice is based on Hindu ideologies of female 'impurity' (as in Deshpande's novels), explicit patriarchal control (as in Desai's *Fasting, Feasting*), economic disadvantage (Hasina's situation in *Brick Lane*), or the sense of displacement and powerlessness of a migrant wife in an alien culture and society (Nazneen's status in *Brick Lane*). Theorists have emphasized the relationship between gender, social class and ethnicity in spatial restrictions, and in these novels, at least, this relationship always seems to work to women's disadvantage. For example, while Desai's and Deshpande's protagonists are elite women subjected to strict controls on their physical boundaries and behaviour in order to maintain family respectability, Nazneen's lack of mobility in *Brick Lane* is based on her *lower* status as a dependent wife in an economically disadvantaged ethnic minority family. It is significant that Nazneen begins to perceive possibilities for taking control of her own life only when she begins to re-imagine her spatial boundaries which have been shaped by both her gender and her cultural identity as a Bangladeshi immigrant. By transgressing those boundaries, she is effectively renegotiating them because, as Sara Mills has pointed out, 'social structures should not be seen as necessarily determining particular spatial relations; indeed it is much more of a two-way process' (2005, p. 25). This implies that women and men negotiate their positions in space though their interrogations of their respective social positions, and these spaces and positions can always be renegotiated, in the postcolonial context as well as in the context of gender.

5
From *hijab* to sweatshops
Segregated bodies and contested space in Monica Ali's *Brick Lane*

Monica Germanà

> Colonial discourse of the body relies upon this con-
> tradiction, a body at once intensely visible, but at the
> same time unrecognised: nothing because it has only
> one form but also, for this very same reason, strongly
> defined.
>
> (Upstone, 2009, p. 151)

In her insightful analysis of postcolonial spaces, Sara Upstone discusses the body as the ultimate frontier of the politics that shape postcolonial spaces. The body is the contested site of apparently conflicting discourses: in resisting colonial order and discipline, the colonized body does not nevertheless fall back on Cartesian dualism, which would reject the body in order to privilege anti-corporeal discourses. On the contrary, and this is particularly visible in the postcolonial novels of Toni Morrison, Salman Rushdie and Wilson Harris that Upstone considers, the colonized body can in fact be reclaimed 'not in terms of the stereotype that denigrated it, but in terms of a celebratory discourse that will celebrate' (Upstone, 2009, p. 174).

This chapter will focus on the politics of postcolonial space in relation to the negotiations that occur through and on the female body and its sartorial appearance. In particular, the first part of this chapter will seek to analyse the complex spatial issues that emerge from the practice of veiling and the ideological implications of female Muslim dress. Within the Muslim context, the main questions will refer to notions of spatial segregation, which the veil, or *hijab*, is associated with; within the postcolonial and diasporic contexts of migration, dress becomes an even more problematic hub of intersecting questions of identity, involving trajectories of integration and assimilation, or resistance to either process.

These questions will be explored with particular reference to Monica Ali's *Brick Lane* (2003); after some theoretical considerations on the significance of the *hijab*, I will argue that the notion of segregation performs a crucial function in the complex politics of identity negotiation within the new space of postcolonial migration and that this use of clothing becomes particularly relevant in relation to Muslim dress. To support my argument, I will also integrate references to aesthetic and political responses to the *hijab* across a range of media. In the last section of this chapter, the notion of segregation will be discussed in relation to the contested space of the garment factory, articulating an interrogation of the power dynamics and structures of oppression that the sweatshop economy presents at the threshold between twentieth and twenty-first centuries.

In her seminal work on gender politics in Muslim societies, Fatima Mernissi observed that: 'Muslim sexuality is territorial: its regulatory mechanisms consists primarily in a strict allocation of space to each sex and an elaborate ritual for resolving the contradictions arising from the inevitable intersections of spaces' (1975, p. 489). Mernissi's argument stresses the relevance of sexuality in the link between power and the spatial boundaries of Muslim society: such division results, traditionally, and particularly in the upper levels of society, in the strict division of the *Umma* – the men's (public) space – and the *family* – the women's (private) space. More specifically, the segregation of women was traditionally facilitated, as is well known, in the regulated space of the *harem* or *harim*, which, Sarah Graham-Brown remarked, 'in Arabic means a sacred, inviolable place, and it also means the female members of the family' (1988, p. 503). Graham-Brown sees a direct link between female oppression and the segregated space of the *harem*, which she associates, indiscriminately perhaps, with other practices such as polygamy and repudiation (ibid., p. 503). While recognizing on one hand, the permeability of the *harem* to the external worlds of other communities of women and its hierarchical structure, which empowered older women in particular, the *harem* remained symbolic of female oppression through the practice of segregation that extended to other spaces of social interaction:

> Sexual segregation and seclusion did not mean simply the creation of a boundary between public and private space but the control of women's movements and visibility whether they were at home, at work in the fields or walking in the street. Control of the physical space in which women moved took many forms: the segregation of

the home into men's and women's quarters; the designation of separate spaces for women in public places and on public transport.

(ibid., pp. 515–16)

More problems arise, of course, with 'desegregation', that is the contested
space created by various social and economic circumstances, including
labour work and migration, which prise open the social boundaries pre-
scribed by religion, allowing the (disrupting) presence of female bodies
within the *Umma*. Additionally, Mernissi suggests, the very notion of
segregation is accompanied by an increased aura of transgression, which
is bound to the idea of trespassing such boundaries (1975, p. 491). In this
respect, the practice of veiling performs an ambiguous function, drawing
attention to that which is meant to remain unseen: 'The veil means that
the woman is present in the men's world, but invisible; she has no right
to be in the street' (ibid., p. 493). The particularly colourful designs of
Muslim dress produced by women in some parts of the world underpin
such ambiguity: the active role undertaken by women in the production
of such attractive garments in the Hormozgan region in Iran elicits an
ambiguous response to the questions of enforced invisibility that such
garments as the *niqab* are associated with (Fakhri, 2008). The function
of the veil is, in theory at least, to prevent the disruptive action that the
intrusion of a female body within a male space would have, if entirely
visible: 'A woman has no right to use male spaces. If she enters them,
she is upsetting the male's order and his peace of mind' (Mernissi, 1975,
p. 494). Such a threat is linked to a subversive view of female sexuality,
and the Muslim woman's identification with '*fitna*, chaos, and with the
anti-divine and anti-social forces of the universe' (ibid., p. 496). It is an
important notion of chaos that Upstone also uses to theorize the subversive role of the colonized body within the problematic space delineated
by the postcolonial novel. Although colonialism imposes ideological
order and structure on the 'natural' fluidity of the colonized space, traces
of the underlying chaos emerge in various cultural forms of resistance,
including the postcolonial novel: 'The trace of chaos is ever-present, in
all spaces' (Upstone, 2009, p. 11).

Aesthetic responses to the *hijab* reveal significant links to shared
notions of disarray and disruption across different discourses. In 1998,
the Turkish-Cypriot fashion designer Hussein Chalayan launched a controversial Autumn/Winter collection, which pivoted around the *chador*
as a symbol of Muslim patriarchal oppression: the collection consisted of
chadors revealing the female bodies underneath them in varying degrees,
starting from a mask covering a naked model's face to a full-length

chador. Chalayan, who does not practise any belief, commented on the controversies generated by the collection, explaining his intention in terms of the negotiations of personal space, which, in his view, Muslim dress oppresses: 'It was about defining your space structurally and graphically. It wasn't really supposed to be offensive. It was supposed to illustrate a particular kind of position. This was about the cultural loss of self' (White, 1998).

While Chalayan's collection offered a stark critique of the traditional *chador* and the function it performs in the negotiation of the Muslim woman's body, other aesthetic approaches to the garment offer more complex responses. Iranian-based photographers Shadi Ghadirian and Haleh Anvari, like Chalayan, have explored the significance of Muslim dress in their works. Selected works from two of Ghadirian's collections, the 'Ghajar Series' and 'Like Everyday Life', displayed at the Saatchi Gallery in London in 2008, interrogate the role of Muslim women in relation to their position in traditional marriages; in doing so, Ghadirian's work respects the conventions of Shariah law and does not to expose the flesh of her models. In one set of images, taken from the 'Ghajar Series', the models, who occupy a central position in her photographs, wear the traditional Iranian dress, their bodies juxtaposed to objects representative of 'modern' technology (telephone, vacuum cleaner, stereo, etc.). In others, the domesticity of the women's universe takes on a more satirical turn, as models are replaced by faceless silhouettes clad in *chadors* with the addition of domestic tools (iron, cleaver, colander, washing-up glove, etc.) in place of their faces: the surreal humour of these images may suggest a subtext of female oppression, though I would argue that here the absurd comedy of these images also serves to perform a form of subversive resistance, particularly visible in the juxtaposition of the fluid texture of the *chador* against, for example, the sharp blade of the meat cleaver: the clichéd passivity of the oppressed female body is assertively re-addressed by the potential aggressiveness implicit in the knife.

Haleh Anvari, like Ghadirian, frequently uses the *chador* as a central image in her depiction of (Iranian) women. Space, only implicitly addressed in Ghadirian's work, becomes crucial in Anvari's images, which explore the interaction between different cultures and the responses to the Iranian dress, which appears in bright colours and attractive patterns in her collection *Chador-Dadar*: 'The black chador is such an unforgiving garment,' Anvari says in interview, 'Even when you photograph it, it has no nuances: there is no shade, no light play. It's just solid, static' (Hanman, 2008). In her installation *The Power of Cliché* (Figure 5.1),

Figure 5.1   The Farsi graffiti in the background can be translated 'My sister, the light of God shines in the blackness of your chador' (trans. Haleh Anvari)
Source: Photograph by Haleh Anvari, 2005.

Anvari's concern is with the clichéd image of Iranian women constructed by Western media, which becomes an instrumental metonymy to justify aggressive foreign policy; in her words: 'Why is it that every time there is news transmitted from/about Iran, the accompanying image is of a woman in a black chador. How did this traditional garment become the shorthand for a nation?' (Anvari website). In *Chador-Dadar*, the shots, taken in various iconic locations around the world, produce multiple critical functions: subverting the notion of anonymous invisibility that the black *chador* may hold, these images capture the unrestrained fluidity of the coloured *chador*, which, simultaneously, disrupts the fixed architecture of Piccadilly Circus, the Louvre (featured on the cover of this volume) and the Taj Mahal, among other places; as Anvari explains:

> If the chador is the icon for Iran, let it meet the icons for some other nations. *Chador-dadar* became a live installation in every city it was photographed and ultimately revealed as much about the nature of the people it visited than it did about itself. We made it to Dubai, to Taj Mahal, the Amber Fort in Jaipur, we went to London and joined a

peace protest, we visited Big Ben, then onto Paris, the Louvre, where we were thrown out because the Hejab is a hot button issue and to Istanbul where the only model I could find wouldn't wear the Chador because she was a secularist, so in Istanbul I became a model and she photographed!

(Anvari, website)

With its deliberate focus on spatial negotiation, *Chador-Dadar* exposes the ambiguous fluidity that the Muslim dress embodies: drawing attention to that which is not to be seen, the collection also launches a process of inverse colonization, where the chaos brought in by the Other disruptively possesses the controlled spaces of past Empires.

I will now to turn to a detailed analysis of Ali's *Brick Lane*, a novel that, as the controversies about the film adaptation suggested in 2006, exposes problematic issues of body/identity negotiation within the multicultural space of East London. As the theoretical and aesthetic discourses discussed in the previous section have demonstrated, the treatment of Muslim dress is a powerful tool of identity negotiation particularly in texts such as *Brick Lane*, concerned, as Yasmin Hussain observes, with 'a discourse of locality, a sense of place which embraces networks of families and friends and signifies a specific space, both geographically and psychologically, that is experienced in terms of neighbourhood' (2005, p. 97). Despite the numerous attacks on Ali's novel for its lack of authenticity, the novel succeeds in resisting the tendency to homogenize ethnicity and attitudes towards Islam: on the contrary, the novel presents varying approaches to Muslim faith and practice, and does not rest on essentialist positions with regard to the three paradigms of identity – religion, gender and race – that it seeks to explore. The outspoken Mrs Azad, Dr Azad's wife, for instance, overtly criticizes the view, purported by Chanu, Nazneen's husband, that the female immigrant's identity must be tied to traditional customs and practices, including clothing. In her words:

> Listen, when I'm in Bangladesh I put on a sari and cover my head and all that. But here I go out to work. I work with white girls and I'm just one of them. If I want to come home and eat curry, that's my business. Some women spend ten, twenty years here and they only learn two words of English ... They go around covered from head to toe, in their little walking prisons, and when someone calls to them in the street they are upset. The society is racist. The society

is all wrong. Everything should change for them. They don't have to change one thing. That ... is the tragedy.

(Ali, 2003, p. 114)

The sartorial appearance of the doctor's wife embodies her politics of uncompromising assimilation: her Westernized style matches her essentialist critique of Muslim dress. Significantly, her views, however, point to a schizoid inside/outside, private/public divide, though one which is controlled by the individual's own choices.

If Mrs Azad's Westernized fashion and emancipated femininity embody the performance of assimilated identity, the sartorial appearance of Nazneen's friend Razia incarnates the migrant's in-between space, positioned on the borderlands of gender and national hybridity: 'The folds were never right: too bunched, too loose, too far to the side, too low or too high' and Nazneen thinks 'Razia would look better in overalls', because 'Overalls would match her big shoes' (ibid., p. 49): Razia's disarrayed sari signifies resistance to order and an uneasy relationship with her cultural background, while her 'big shoes', like Western women's heels, are symbolic of her struggle for power: 'Her shoes were big as trucks and battered by untold collisions' (ibid., p. 69); Razia's body is the site of conflict and untold battles. Moreover, Razia, Chanu notes, 'cuts her hair like a tramp' (ibid., p. 83), thus progressively transforming her looks and fashioning her body to represent her acquired emancipation and status: 'Now that she wore trousers she sat like a man' (ibid., p. 123); in relation to gender, the masculine quality of Razia's looks, in Nazneen's view, implicates Razia's emancipation from her previous role as Bengali woman/wife. But it is in terms of national identity that Razia, who, after acquiring British citizenship, wears 'the Union Jack over salwaar pants' (ibid., p. 228), and truly represents the in-between status of the first-generation migrant. A similar hybrid outfit is described by Tarquin Hall in *Salaam Brick Lane: A Year in the New East End*:

Mr Ali's choice of clothing was as much a reflection of his mixed cultural identity as his accent. He wore a long, collarless salwar, but in place of the usual matching baggy pants and sandals or slip-on shoes, he'd opted for a pair of Levis and alligator cowboy boots. His white prayer cap, although in need of a wash, suggested a man of faith, but was at odds with the whiff of booze on his breath, and helped complete the impression of a person of contradictions.

(2005, p. 2)

Hall, like Ali, documents the layered structure that the migrant's body, almost by default, develops as a result of the process of identity negotiation within the postcolonial space of contemporary London. The ideology behind the migrant's identity – be it national, religious or ethnic – is indissolubly tied to dress, and *Brick Lane*, like other postcolonial texts, brings these issues to the forefront. In Diran Adebayo's *Some Kind of Black* (1996), a novel that, as its title suggests, interrogates racial and cultural parameters of identity, the main character, Dele, self-consciously exposes the complex discourse of self-representation for second generation Black African people and the intricate patterns of cross-fertilization that exist between different ethnic groups in the postcolonial metropolis. Such concerns not only affect contemporary British fiction; the importance of wearing the right kind of clothes to establish a sense of belonging emerges, for instance, in the earlier narrative of Sam Selvon's *The Lonely Londoners*, where

> Galahad feel like a king living in London. The first time he take a craft out, he dress up good, for one of the first things he do after he get a work was to stock up with clothes like stupidness, as if to make up for all the hard times when he didn't have nice things to wear.
>
> ([1956] 2006, p. 73)

With both these novels, *Brick Lane* shares, on one hand, the problematic quest for identity of immigrants, and, on the other, the appreciation of the profound implications of clothing for the purposes of integration within the postcolonial space of migration. Like Razia and Mrs Azad, Nazneen's daughter, Shahana, offers a critical resistance to traditional modes of self-representation. Shahana resists the enforced Bengali education Chanu tries to impose on his family; she expresses her dislike of Bengali classical music and is unable to write in her parents' native language. Her rebelliousness and desire to assimilate are shown within the novel's fashion discourse: 'She wanted to wear jeans. She hated her kameez and spoiled her entire wardrobe by pouring paint on them' (Ali 2003, p. 180). She wants her lip pierced and a tattoo and argues 'It's my body' (ibid., p. 292); she also asks for moisturizer, shampoo and dangly earrings. When Nazneen suffers a nervous breakdown, she takes advantage of Chanu's distraction and wears her tight jeans (ibid., p. 327). Similar concerns surface, too, in Hanif Kureishi's *The Buddha of Suburbia* and Zadie Smith's *White Teeth* (2000), novels that document the problematic negotiation of the liminal spaces occupied by second-generation immigrants and the mixed-raced children of first-generation immigrants through sub-cultural trends.

In the confused post-9/11 climate, more than ever, Brick Lane becomes the contested site of clashing views over Islam, dislocated identities and territorial politics. The Islamic veil becomes particularly problematic, anticipating in a sense the 'veil controversy' in October 2006, two months after the Campaign Against Monica Ali's Film *Brick Lane* in July of the same year. In October 2006, Jack Straw's statement that he 'would prefer women not to wear the veil at all' stirred a heated controversy and debate over the Islamic woman's need to integrate and maintain her own identity through the wearing of the veil. It should be noted here that Straw did not object to women's wearing headscarves, but had asked constituents to remove, if they would, the *niqab*, which covers the whole face, leaving only a narrow slit open for the eyes (Browne, 2006, p. 6). Among others, Salman Rushdie defended Straw's position against the *niqab*, claiming that 'veils suck' and adding that 'the veil is a way of taking power away from women', in an interview on BBC Radio 4 (Butt, 2006).

The veil controversy had been foreshadowed a few months earlier when, on 26 July 2006, plans to shoot the film adaptation of Monica Ali's *Brick Lane* in the original settings were abandoned due to protests from local businesses in the Bangladeshi community. Against Ali's portrayal of their community as '[u]neducated. Illiterate. Close-minded', the spokesman for the Campaign, Abdul Salique, defended the right of the community to burn the book: '[If] she has the right to freedom of speech, we have the right to burn books' (Lewis, 2006). As Dominic Head has noted, 'despite threats of blockades, violence and book-burning, the low-key protest featured the symbolic "binning", rather than burning, of the novel, a considered gesture that was a far cry from the irrationality of the anti-Rushdie campaign of the late 1980s' (2008, p. 77). Significantly, however, the controversy surrounding Ali's novel re-ignited old disputes within the British literary scene. Germaine Greer backed the campaign, accusing Ali's novel of lacking authenticity – 'Brick Lane is a real place; there was no need for Monica Ali to reinvent it' – and of building her narrative around a 'pre-existing stereotype', ultimately playing a disloyal trick on Bangladeshi Britons, whom Greer urged to abstain from reading the novel and watching the movie (Greer, 2006). Rushdie's response to Greer's article showed polemic tones in a letter published in *The Guardian* five days later: 'To suit Greer, the British-Bangladeshi Ali is denied her heritage and belittled for her Britishness, while her British-Bangladeshi critics are denied that same Britishness, which most of them would certainly insist was theirs by right' (Rushdie, 2006).

The controversy, arguably more a media than racial/religious affair, displayed a profound, though interesting, misreading of the novel, which – if sometimes over-relying on 'types' (Head, 2008, p. 81), makes a point of presenting a range of voices within the Muslim community of Brick Lane. After 9/11, however, the Islamic Bangladeshi community in *Brick Lane* became the centre of racial and religious tensions, which in turn, accentuate certain radical positions: these manifestly emerge in the novel's references to the *hijab*. As remarked by Hussain, 'the appearance of traditional dress, the attraction to brotherhood and sisterhood cannot be understood by only looking for internal causes. They are the obvious consequences of inter-ethnic relations and symbols of separatism which serve to distinguish the "us" from "them" (2005, p. 103). In the postcolonial space of twenty-first-century London, the meeting point of migration from the East and the globalized economy of the West, clothing is seldom clear of political charge. When Nazneen first meets Karim, 'the middle-man' with whom she shares a passionate affair, 'He wore his jeans tight and his shirtsleeves rolled up to the elbow' (Ali, 2003, p. 210); after his involvement with the Bengal Tigers intensifies, Karim grows a beard (ibid., p. 302) and later develops what Nazneen identifies as a 'new style' (ibid., p. 376). Karim's views of women accordingly reflect his radicalized appearance: 'you've got two types', he explains to Nazneen, 'There's your westernized girl, wears what she likes, all the make-up going on, short skirts and that soon as she's out of her father's sight ... Then there's your religious girl, wears the scarf or even the burkha' (ibid., p. 385).

Nazneen, who struggles to see which type she may fit in, is in Karim's words 'the real thing' (ibid., p. 385), as the novel appears in fact to repudiate any reductive readings of the ways in which women choose to live their Muslim faith and adopt the *hijab*. The first time Nazneen attends the Bengal Tigers meeting, she notes 'Two girls in hijab' (ibid., p. 236); they ask for 'Sex education for girls' (ibid., p. 240); at the following meeting, the girls 'had upgraded to burkhas' (ibid., p. 279) and speak 'as one voice' (ibid., p. 285), complaining that 'We get called names' (ibid., p. 285). The immigrant woman's dress becomes a powerful ideological symbol and one that is subject to change in response to local as well as global politics. Against either form of radicalism, Chanu's response is nevertheless charged with politics, when he changes his daughters' dress code to suit the political message he wants to divulge: 'If he had a Lion Hearts leaflet in his hand, he wanted his daughters covered' (ibid., p. 265), but 'if he saw some girls go by in hijab he became agitated at this display of peasant ignorance. Then the girls went out in skirts' (ibid., p. 265). But it's a no-win situation; after 9/11, women in Islamic dress 'had [their] hijab pulled off', whereas 'Razia wore her Union Jack sweatshirt and it was spat on' (ibid., p. 368).

Religion is only one of the layers that inform the sartorial references in the novel. From a cultural point of view, the novel focuses, as already seen in relation to Razia's appearance, specifically on South Asian dress, a metaphor for the country of origin, which the migrant's experience never abandons completely: '[t]he novel', Hussain observes of *Brick Lane*, 'focuses on the reconstitution of a cultural base in the diaspora which corresponds to the continuous reinterpretation of a "traditional" cultural form that existed for centuries in the country of origin' (2005, p. 102); but the cultural associations that the South Asian *sari* bears are not without problems, as Nazneen remembers that when Amma takes her life by throwing herself over a sharp spike, 'she was wearing her best sari' (Ali, 2003, p. 46). This thought seems to haunt Nazneen, because the *sari* represents, among other ideas, that notion of feminine endurance of Fate, she, as a child, has longed to embrace:

> She looked forward to that day. She longed to be enriched by this hardship, to cast off her childish baggy pants and long shirt and begin to wear this suffering that was rich and layered and deeply coloured as the saris which enfolded Amma's troubled bones.
>
> (ibid., p. 103)

Its association with Amma's suicide suggests that the *sari* is also representative of the particular space of female entrapment occupied by Amma. Walking around Whitechapel in London, Nazneen's *sari* is simultaneously a protective shield and a cumbersome cage, and Nazneen becomes aware of being 'Without coat, without a suit, without a white face, without a destination' (ibid., p. 56). The *sari* also functions as *hijab*, as Nazneen will 'pull the end of her sari over her hair' when she goes out, but alone with Karim, she reviews her understanding of *purdah* and 'forgets' to cover her head. Yet to Karim she clearly represents the archetypal Bengali woman, as he overtly admits: 'That sari ... My mother had one. Same material I mean' (ibid., p. 212). The beginning of the affair with Karim is also marked by a conscious ceremony involving a special sari (ibid., p. 277). As well as catalyzing her sensuality, the sari is also the paradoxical bondage obstructing Nazneen's freedom: 'The sari, which seconds ago had felt light as air, became heavy chains' (ibid., p. 277). Only at the end, when Razia and her daughters finally take her ice-skating and her husband has gone back to Bangladesh alone, is the *sari* no longer an impediment. On the contrary, as long as your body is ideologically liberated, the novel seems to suggest, traditional clothing cannot *per se* constitute an impediment:

> 'But you can't skate in a sari' ...
> 'This is England, ... You can do whatever you like!'

(ibid., p. 492)

Despite its relatively happy ending, the novel's portrayal of the garment industry both in London and Dhaka is ambiguously placed within the tradition of migrant sweatshop stories, discussed, for instance, in Laura Hapke's study of 'sweatshop' nostalgia, narratives in which the hardship experienced by workers in the textile and garment industry came to represent an important step in the fulfilment of the migrant's dream of success. At the end of the novel, Ali acknowledges Naila Kabeer's study of the garment industry *The Power to Choose* (2000), a work that informs Ali's understanding of the complex dynamics between the exploitation of female labour and the spaces of garment production in London and Dhaka, which Ali represents through the parallel experiences of Nazneen and her sister, Hasina. References to clothing production relate the novel to the history of the textile industry and sweatshops in Whitechapel, as well as the larger globalization of the garment industry of the past twenty years. As Ethel C. Brookes notes, 'the dual identity of garment production – fashion and clothing – have relied on women as producers, consumers, retailers, and models' (2007, p. xiv). Following Nazneen's and Hasina's parallel paths, Ali explores women's roles in relation to garment production and the female condition: the dual focus of the novel addresses the complex issues underlying women's labour in Bangladesh, on one hand, and the opportunities offered to the female migrant on the other.

At the beginning of the twentieth century, campaigners in favour of industrialization used the sweatshop as the negative pole of a moral dichotomy: 'Where the factory was sanitary', Daniel E. Bender notes, 'the sweatshop bred disease' (2004, p. 9). Moral concerns derived from the fact that in early twentieth-century America, sweatshops, including the one turned into the Lower Eastside Tenement House Museum in New York, as well as in Britain, were domestic workshops overcrowded with (unwanted) immigrants, often living in the premises with poor sanitation. Promiscuity, squalor and disease were therefore attached to the idea of the sweatshop, fuelling the already high levels of xenophobia. In the late twentieth-century, while campaigns against sweatshops continue to disclose a similar paternalistic and conservative ideology, simultaneously, they also articulate more seemingly progressive positions, including the emphatic question of sustainability. In this context female emancipation becomes a thorny issue. While on one hand the garment industry allows women to earn money, on the other, the prejudice attached to the factory workers may undermine their positions, particularly when it upsets accepted patriarchal norms and gender roles with regard to segregation. In *Brick Lane*, Mrs Islam makes an interesting remark about the dangerous space of the garment factory:

> Mixing with all sorts: Turkish, English, Jewish. All sorts. I am not old-fashioned ... I don't wear burkha. I keep purdah in my mind, which is the most important thing. Plus I have cardigans and anoraks and a scarf for my head. But if you mix with all these people, even if these are good people, you have to give up your culture to accept theirs.
>
> (Ali, 2003, p. 29)

Significantly, from an ethnic and cultural point of view, the garment factory is identified as a hybrid space, one that threatens to dilute one migrant's cultural identity, on one hand, and defies traditional rules about gender segregation, on the other. Tied to the notion of family honour on one hand, and the shame that women may bring on their kin, on the other, 'Purdah literally means "veil" or "curtain" and expresses the symbolic, physical and economic demarcation of the universe along gender lines' (Kabeer, 2000, p. 34). *Purdah* therefore refers not only to the actual practice to cover the female body, but also to the appropriate practices of gender segregation outside the home, including the workplace, to maintain this notion of moral propriety. Though it has often been argued otherwise, *purdah* reflects the patriarchal order and in particular, the rules of patrilineal descent' (ibid., p. 34). Similar concerns emerge in Dhaka, where Hasina works as a machinist. Hasina's description of the Bangladeshi factory reveals its segregated structure: 'It [the factory] have three room around courtyard all new solid concrete. One place is for machine. I go there. Another for cutting and finishing. Men go there' (Ali, 2003, pp. 149–50). The most skilled jobs – and no doubt the highest paid jobs – are exclusively given to male workers: 'They [men] make pattern and cut cloth these are difficult job', Hasina explains, 'Also they iron. That job too dangerous for woman we do not understand electricity' (ibid., p. 152). Even with the rigid gender division of jobs, the female factory worker still suffers moral prejudice; such prejudice is fuelled by proactive campaigners: 'Here come the garment girls. Choose the one you like ... They say it sinful for men and women working together' (ibid., p. 152). Though providing a valuable source of income to its female workers, the garment industry may also become a space of patriarchal entrapment, exploiting women as consumers as well as producers of clothes. In some instances, the two can also converge as is the case with another of Hasina's colleagues, rewarded for her productivity with a new *sari*: 'They give a sari and for this sari she take beating' (ibid., p. 157). Eventually it is Hasina's turn to suffer the prejudice. Accused of 'lewd' behaviour, she is dismissed and is forced to admit that 'This factory have ruin me' (ibid., p. 169): prostitution and extreme poverty are what Hasina is left with after her factory.

Clashing with Hasina's account from Bangladesh, in Britain, Chanu's idealism and national pride provide the historical background to the history of the textile industry in Bangladesh. His ideas are infused with the nostalgic notion of a long-lost past; when he buys Nazneen a sewing machine, he talks of the 'honourable craft of tailoring' (ibid., p. 208), failing to see that Nazneen is in fact going to be exploited according to the logic of the contracting system, or sweated labour: 'If she worked fast, if she didn't make mistakes', Nazneen reflects, 'she could earn as much as three pounds fifty pence in one hour' (ibid., p. 213): this incidentally reflects the level of exploitation which workers such as Nazneen would face in London: in 2001, the minimum wage was fixed at £3.70. Chanu's observations, however, serve the purpose of introducing the notion of colonial exploitation, which links with the global garment industry Hasina becomes involved in: 'It was the British, of course, who destroyed our textile industry' (ibid., p. 316) and that 'The Dhaka looms were sacrificed ... so that the mills of Manchester could be born' (ibid., p. 317). His claim that 'the British cut the fingers off Bengali weavers' relates to the exploitation still suffered, under the veiled pretence of fair labour, by workers such as Hasina, who notes 'my back is killing. Sewing all day and all day' (ibid., p. 188) and later informs Nazneen that 'another woman who see job advertising in newspaper and go to Malaysia. She sew clothes from eight in the morning to ten in the evening seven days out of seven' (ibid., p. 338).

Hasina's letters further reveal the ambivalent function and manifestations of the fashion industry in Bangladesh. Rescued by a rich woman, who calls herself 'Lovely', Hasina gets a different perspective on the glamour scene of Bangladesh. Lovely exploits Hasina for her own image: to take 'a destitute woman' in her own house raises her profile as beautiful rich philanthropist. Lovely herself is representative of a class of privileged women whose fashionable looks are suggestive of their ambivalent position in the promotion of Western capitalist models of fashion production and consumption: 'She wearing tight white jean and lacy blouse with underwear see through it like film star and more jewellery than a bride. She call it "Bombay Look"' (ibid., p. 267). This is apparently in contradiction with Lovely's intention to create a charity to alleviate child labour. In truth, her intentions are merely masquerading her desire to assimilate to the West, taking on anti-sweatshop campaigns that, arguably, reinstate colonial ideologies of redemption (Brookes, 2007, p. 23). The problem with campaigns of the kind hinted by Lovely, while failing to understand the women and children's actual needs and circumstances, is that they relegate them to a position of 'victims' in need of outside help, rather than encouraging the development of self-agency: 'This process of salvation in solidarity's name is, then, a reenactment of earlier (colonial) salvations' (ibid., p. 24).

In this respect, Nazneen's re-appropriation of the sweatshop turns this into a positive – and utopian, perhaps – space at the end of her journey towards self-agency. While starting her career as a seamstress for work contracted out via Karim, with Razia's encouragement and entrepreneurial enthusiasm Nazneen succeeds in inverting the exploitative process of the garment industry. The creation of their own clothing factory is set upon layers of history of migrant labour in the textile industry in Whitechapel, from the seventeenth-century Huguenot silk-weavers to the Jewish tailors of the late nineteenth century. Discussing the Huguenots' history in the East End, Tarquin Hall remembers a famous inscription: '"Umbra Sumus", "We are Shadows" – it's proven a fitting motto, not just for the French but for all the immigrants who have settled here' (Hall, 2005, p. 44). In Ali's *Brick Lane*, the women's commercial venture signifies a distinctive movement away from the shadowy peripheries of the migrant's experience to the centre of power, from the sweatshop work performed in the segregated space of the domestic household, to the public space of a workshop, suggesting that London, with all its racial tensions, can also be the setting and catalyst of positive change. Looking back at Hasina's parallel story, however, the narrative appears to pose different questions: while it draws attention to the issue of exploitative labour within the late twentieth- and early twenty-first centuries garment production, it also seems to create a dichotomy between the positive fulfilment of the migrant's desire and the constraints suffered by the colonized subject in a developing country; this leads, in turn to the ideological suggestion that integration – or even assimilation – is the only way forward.

To sum up, however, I would like to suggest that in addressing the notion of the segregated body, *Brick Lane* articulates an interrogation of the complex dynamics of identity negotiation linked with the Muslim dress. Resisting any reductive and homogenizing views of the migrant predicament, as well as stereotyped views of 'the passivity of "Asian" women' (Kabeer, 2000, p. 220), the sartorial subtext of Ali's *Brick Lane* exposes instead a range of critical responses and questions a monolithic reading of the *hijab* in particular. In doing so, the novel subverts the margin/centre hierarchy of colonial and patriarchal discourse, by allowing its female characters to regain – as seen in the images of the veiled women in the works of Iranian artists Ghadirian and Anvari – a central position. As with its treatment of the *hijab*, the novel's portrayal of the garment industry draws attention to the critical overlapping of desegregation and contestation in the sweatshop/factory space. In doing so, it also highlights the ambivalent discourse of anti-sweatshop campaigns, while exposing the structures of oppression that still oppose fashion consumption in the West to garment production in the East at the beginning of the twenty-first century.

6
Overlapping space and the negotiation of cultural identity
Children's literature from the South Asian diaspora

Shehrazade Emmambokus

> 'We are. We are here.' And we are not willing to be excluded from any part of our heritage; which heritage includes both a Bradford-born Indian kid's right to be treated as a full member of British society, and also the right of any member of this post-diaspora community to draw on its roots.
>
> (Rushdie, 1991, p. 15)

Salman Rushdie, in this resonant quotation, engages with the political concerns of diaspora: the right for individuals to lay claim to both their 'home' and 'homeland' cultures.[1] The emphasis Rushdie places on the word 'heritage' signals *why* diasporic individuals should be able to lay claim to these places. But what about the *how* of such assertions? How is one able to lay claim to different cultures? How are these affiliations created? And, how are individuals able to resolve differences in cultural nuances? These questions probe the workings of cultural identity formation and negotiation, concerning which existing theories offer only partial solutions. My research into children's literature from the South Asian diaspora draws attention to this gap, but more specifically to the fact that currently there is no definitive cultural identity model which focuses solely on how post-migrant generations, including foreign-born migrant children (hereafter referred to as the 'second generation'), negotiate their cultural identities. By addressing this gap, this chapter attempts to answer questions about *how* these diasporic individuals claim cultural identities, and a model theorizing this engagement emerges which is best identified as *Overlapping Space*. Drawing on both sociological and literary discussions of cultural identity, the Overlapping Space model demonstrates the ways in which second generation identities are reliant upon practices of enculturation. Using these discussions, the Overlapping Space model ultimately illustrates how cultural identity choices for second generation migrants are negotiated.

Overlapping space: a new model for cultural identity

Cultural identities are constantly shifting and changing, and the Overlapping Space model addresses how these changes are possible. Within the site of Overlapping Space, individuals negotiate their diasporic cultural identities by *selecting and inviting* the elements that they have learned to duplicate from the parent cultures. Rather than developing a fixed hybrid identity which claims, 'I am "X" amount of "A" and "Y" amount of "B"' and so forth, Overlapping Space is a site within which the amount that is hybridized varies and is never constant. The individual is able to negotiate and renegotiate the cultural elements they want to use to create their cultural identity.

To illustrate this idea, it is useful to consider the work of Alejandro Portes and Rubén Rumbaut (2001). Portes and Rumbaut undertook two investigations, one in 1992 and another in 1995/6, to learn how diasporic children living in the USA define their ethnic identities. The two sets of tests were conducted on the same children and they discovered that there was a shift in the way that these children classified themselves ethnically. Portes and Rumbaut assert that although 44 per cent of the participants gave the same responses in the follow-up survey, the remaining 56 per cent 'reported a change in their ethnic self-definitions' (ibid., p. 156). As this investigation demonstrates, cultural identity is a mutable category, and cultural affiliations can adapt over time.

Borrowing from Homi Bhabha, Avtar Brah, and Stuart Hall, the Overlapping Space model respectively fuses ideas of Third Space, diaspora space and translation. It differs, however, from earlier models of diasporic identities as it takes account of the influences that enculturation has on individuals and, in turn, on the ways in which individuals negotiate their cultural identity as they navigate between cultures. As such, although elements of the Overlapping Space model can be applied to the experiences of the migrant generation, because of enculturation, its main focus is the second generation.

The term 'enculturation' should not be confused with 'acculturation'. Whereas *ac*culturation is the adoption of another group's cultural traits or social patterns, *en*culturation is, on a basic level, the learning of one's *own cultural group's characteristics*. Discussing enculturation, Ralph Linton states:

> No matter what the method by which the individual receives the elements of culture characteristic of his society, he is sure to internalise most of them. This process is called *enculturation*. Even the most deliberately unconventional person is unable to escape his culture to any significant degree.
>
> (1961, p. 39)

Even though an individual may be 'unconventional', they will still be subject to some of the cultural influences that they have been exposed to. Enculturation, therefore, infuses the individual with certain cultural discourses which inform that person's cultural identity.

With regards to children and adolescents, *all* children undergo processes of enculturation. A child's cultural identity, therefore, is influenced and informed by the internalization of certain cultural traits helping them to develop cultural affiliations. Many second generation migrant children develop affiliations with both their 'home' and 'homeland' cultures, depending on how they are raised and the extent of their exposure to these cultures. Through the process of enculturation, they learn to internalize both the cultural elements of their 'home' and 'homeland' environments which, in turn, grants them memberships of these cultures. Furthermore, because second generation migrant children undergo this process of enculturation with two or more, often different, cultural frameworks, the Overlapping Space model addresses *how* these individuals negotiate their cultural identities.

The word 'overlapping' recognizes the layering associated with identities which are enculturated with two (or more) cultural environments; essentially the different traits from the different cultures which construct an individual's identity overlap with one another within an internal space or site. As there is this overlapping of different cultural elements and influences, this model recognizes the possibility for contradictions; that is, it recognizes and accepts that the individual may maintain ideas which seem contradictory *because* of this enculturation process with two (or more) different cultural spheres.

This model modifies in significant ways existing theoretical approaches to cultural identity. In particular, the influential works of Hall, Brah, and Bhabha must be re-negotiated in terms of the second generation encounter. Bhabha, discussing hybridity in *The Location of Culture,* identifies a hybridized product that is 'neither the one, nor the other' (1994, p. 25), but 'something else besides' (ibid., p. 28), something that is 'in between' (ibid., p. 29). Bhabha's concept of hybridity is often applied to the diasporic individual and the construction of hybrid cultural identities. However, when asked if his ideas of Third Space represent a type of identity, Bhabha says: 'No, not so much identity as identification' (in Rutherford, 1991, p. 211). His model, therefore, does not represent identity and when we explore his ideas about hybridity, we can see why.

Bhabha claims that for him, the 'importance of hybridity is not to be able to trace two original moments from which the third emerges, rather hybridity to me is the "third space" which enables other positions to emerge' (in Rutherford, 1991, p. 211). This rationale suggests that the 'originals' or the 'parents' of the product are no longer necessarily relevant. But, as Rushdie foregrounds in the epigraph of this chapter, people's 'roots' are considered significant; the 'parent' original cultures which people are born into are important. Using myself as an example, I am *not* happy to say that I am *neither* British *nor* South Asian. As a result of enculturation, I consider myself to be part both. Within the British context I class myself as a British-Asian. I agree that I am new, in the sense that I am a second generation member of the South Asian diaspora. I see myself, however, as a product of these cultures; I *simultaneously* identify and feel as though I belong to both.

My biographical example not only declares my own interest in the project developed here, it also stands as illustration of how many second generation migrants identify with their parent cultures, to whatever degree, because they have been enculturated with one culture *and* the other. Second generation diasporic identities often embody certain cultural traits associated with their parent cultures; they, therefore, are made of the *one and the other*.[2]

Consequently, although Bhabha argues that in that moment of enunciation the 'originals' are transformed, in terms of identity construction, any model of cultural identity needs to recognize the desire for 'faithful' reproduction. During enculturation, second generation children modify and reinvent certain 'original' cultural components, making them unique. However, in order to foster a sense of cultural identification they simultaneously attempt to faithfully recreate elements from one parent culture *and* the other. As such, second generation children are able to identify with their 'home' and 'homeland' cultures, affirming that they are both the one and the other and not, as Bhabha suggests, 'neither the one nor the other' (1994, p. 25).

An alternative to Bhabha's Third Space is offered by Brah, who uses the concept of 'diaspora space' to model the experience of hybridity. What is useful about Brah's diaspora space is its invocation of 'multiple subject positions' (Brah, 1996, p. 208), *multiple layers* of cultural hybridity and multiple forms of cultural influence. However, Brah, in focusing upon the ways in which subordinated groups hybridize independently of the dominant culture, undervalues the extent to which, in the construction of a hybrid cultural identity, the individual, as Linton suggests, will have some exposure to the dominant culture(s). By contrast, the Overlapping Space model acknowledges that individuals can be influenced by many cultures – both 'dominant' and 'subordinate' cultures – at the same time.

Finally, it is useful to consider how Overlapping Space offers a partial departure from cultural studies, as represented by Hall's concerns. Hall's focus on the diasporic individual addresses the multiple layers of cultural influence that contribute to the construction of hybrid identities. Hall suggests that diasporic individuals who come into contact with different cultures are 'irrevocably translated' (1996, p. 310). However, though acknowledging that cultural purity may be lost, he recognizes that translated individuals are, as the Overlapping Space model suggests, the one and the other:

> Third generation young Black men and women know they come from the Caribbean, know that they are Black, know that they are British. They want to speak from all three identities. They are not prepared to give up any one of them.
>
> (1991b, p. 59)

Hall seems to idealize the stability of the translated diasporic identity; an identity that does not deny any of its 'roots' and is confident with projecting elements from all these 'roots'. However, though an individual may feel confident about who they are, when placed in certain environments they might not want to, or feel able to, project their identities as 'hybrid'. In addition, because of certain perceived cultural contradictions, they might have to temporarily suspend/withhold a different part of their cultural identity in order to project another. For example, when discussing the role that identification has in the construction of identity, Fuss states that:

> Identification thus makes identity possible, but also places it at constant risk: multiple identifications within the same subject can

compete with each other, producing further conflicts to be managed; identifications that once appeared permanent or unassailable can be quickly dislodged by the newest object attachment; and identifications that have been 'repudiated and even overcompensated' can reestablish themselves once again much later. The history of the subject is therefore one of perpetual psychical conflict and of continual change under pressure. It is a profoundly turbulent history of contradictory impulses and structural incoherencies.

(1995, p. 49)

Identities for *all* individuals are therefore being constantly re-evaluated. Fuss's ideas about identifying with competing external stimulants illustrate that the diasporic child may be taught to embody contradictory identifications, highlighting the potential difficulties which arise when trying to assert an identity which speaks from several cultural standpoints. The hybridity that Hall champions, therefore, might not be practical in certain situations. Nonetheless, the Overlapping Space model illustrates how individuals are able to negotiate differences in cultural nuances which allow them to reconcile certain cultural disparities.

Situational ethnicity: an example of overlapping space

To illustrate precisely the workings of Overlapping Space as an interpretive framework against existing models, one can look at how the concept functions in a specific conceptual instance. When discussing second generation migrants, phrases which now seem to border on theoretical cliché such as 'culture clash', 'caught between two cultures' and 'identity crisis' are often used to describe these individuals' experiences. Such terms suggest inaccurately that second generation migrants are somehow both culturally and emotionally lost and that they are lacking a sense of psychological stability and normality. Rather, the internal sites of Overlapping Space illustrate how second generation migrants are able to employ a technique called 'situational ethnicity' which allows the diasporic individual to navigate in and around different cultural frameworks.

Situational ethnicity is an extension of 'situational identity'. The implementation of situational *identity* is normal and is a day-to-day (even minute-to-minute) activity which *everyone* engages in because *everyone* has multiple identities.[3] For example, people speak, act or behave differently when they are in the workplace compared to when they are out with their friends or with their families. Situational *ethnicity*, however, factors in the cultural contexts and situations that the individual is in (or is going to be in) so that people adapt their personas to suit the cultural norms of that environment.

In order to employ situational ethnicity, second generation migrant youths use their internal sites of Overlapping Space. The enculturation process with both their 'home' and 'homeland' cultural spheres allows for the absorption and incorporation of cultural traits and codes into their identities. So existence within an Overlapping Space allows them to assert which specific cultural elements are projected in a particular moment. From within the site of Overlapping Space the individual can forge a particular cultural identity by selecting from the array of cultural elements they have absorbed.

Situational ethnic identities therefore illustrate the departure from conventional models of 'fully' hybrid identities. As Sunaina Maira suggests: 'Hybridity, though fashionable in theory and also literally in "ethnic chic," is not always easy to live, for families and communities demand loyalty to cultural ideals that may be difficult to balance for second-generation youth' (1999, p. 44).

Although the *idea* of culturally hybrid identities is theoretically valorized, the implementation of these hybrid identities within certain cultural frameworks is rejected because these identities may embody or assert qualities and traits in conflict with that culture's values. So migrant youths negotiate and appropriate their identities to suit the cultural environment that they are in. Employing this technique might suggest that individuals who implement situational ethnicity are placed under added strain: that is, diasporic individuals experience added difficulties and pressures as they always have to display a heightened awareness of their cultural position(s) when they move in and between different cultural frameworks, supporting 'identity crisis' theories. However, those who only implement situational identities and not situational ethnicities *also* have to display an awareness of their projected identities and personas within different situations and contexts. In this context, the employment of situational ethnicity, like situational identity, is also a normal activity people become accustomed to either consciously or unconsciously. Research into second generation South Asian youth experience, such as Maira's (1996) earlier research, and also the work of Kathleen Hall (1995), supports these ideas.

In a more recent study, Yasmin Sekhon and Isabelle Szmigin make similar observations about second generation Punjabi youth in Britain: 'All the respondents were happy and familiar with the notion of spanning the divide between their Punjabi heritage and the everyday facts of living in Britain. Situational ethnicity was an everyday occurrence for them' (2005, p. 9).

Interestingly, for Sekhon and Szmigin, situational ethnicity theory needs to be extended to include '*emotional* situational ethnicity', including:

> the emotional responses to being a second generation immigrant: the mindsets, the thought processes, and the expected reactions by others from this group. This is a process that is not as linear and structured as in the indigenous population, but one that must take account of continually changing situations and one that needs to balance host and home country expectations.
>
> (ibid., p. 5)

Employing situational ethnicity is not a conscious choice abstracted from emotion; people do not simply assert one of their cultural identities within a specific cultural environment because the situation demands it. Rather, their emotions and how they feel in terms of their ethnicity *in that environment* can also help to govern their projected identities. So, when an individual is within a 'South Asian' environment, they may indicate a 'felt ethnicity' as more Asian. However, that same person, in another context or situation, for example, in a 'British' environment, may *feel* more British (ibid. p. 5). Such individuals learn to successfully negotiate and navigate between and within their cultures by employing situational ethnicity methods. Their ease in moving from one environment to the next indicates that, if anything, they are certainly not 'caught' between two cultures at all, but, as Andrew Lindridge *et al.* argue, are in fact 'cultural navigators' (2004, p. 232).

Literary examples of overlapping space

In adolescent fiction of the South Asian diaspora, we see the Overlapping Space model in a way which complements its sociological foundation. Focusing on the characters Aisha from Marina Budhos's *Ask Me No Questions* (2006) and Dimple from Tanuja Desai Hidier's *Born Confused* (2002), we can better understand how young diasporic South Asians negotiate and assert their hybrid Overlapping Space identities and how they ultimately affirm that they are the one and the other.

Ask Me No Questions (2006), a novel inspired by the events of 11 September 2001, explores media vilification of South Asian and Islamic images following the terrorist attacks and the effect this focus had on South Asian, Muslim and Arab youths' cultural identities. The following quotation is taken from towards the end of the novel when Aisha, the protagonist's sister, who is of Bangladeshi Islamic background, gives her valedictorian address at her high school's graduation ceremony:

> Aisha's stepping onto the stage, and as she lifts the bottom of her gown, I can see the high heels Ma let her buy. They had a real fight about it too, in the Parade shoe store, but finally Ma relented and there they are: bright, shiny red satin heels with skinny straps ...
>
> 'My name is Aisha Hossain. And I am an illegal alien ... My family came here eight years ago on a tourist visa and stayed ... In those days they didn't enforce the laws. We were the people you didn't always see ...'
>
> She swallows some water, 'And then one day two planes came and smashed into two towers. A war started. Overnight, we, the invisible people, became visible. We became dangerous. We became terrorists, people with bombs in our luggage, poison in our homes ...'
>
> She pauses. 'All I ask of you is to see me for who I am. Aisha. I spell my name not with a *y* or an *e*, but with an *i*. See me. I live with you. I live near you. I go to your school; I eat in your cafeteria; I take the same classes. Now I am your valedictorian. I want what you want. I want a future.'
>
> (Budhos, 2006, pp. 150–2)

Aisha's shoes link her to popular American culture. Britney Spears, Aisha's pop idol, who in her 'Oops! ... I Did It Again' music video famously sports an all-in-one red catsuit with red heels, affirms this. Red heels, however, are perhaps made more famous by Dorothy in the movie *The Wizard of Oz* (1939). Through this secondary reference the novel foregrounds explicitly themes shared between the two texts – of leaving home, new journeys, exile and becoming an alien in a new land. For Rushdie, *The Wizard of Oz* speaks directly to migrants and exiles:

> So Oz finally *became* home; the imagined world became the actual world, as it does for us all, because the truth is that once we have left our childhood places and started to make up our lives, armed only with what we are, we understand that the real secret of the ruby slippers is not that 'there's no place like home', but rather that there is no longer such a place *as* home: except, of course, for the home we make, or the homes that are made for us, in OZ: which is anywhere and everywhere, except the place from which we began.
>
> (Rushdie, 1992, p. 57)

Metaphorically, the Land of Oz is for the exile their new home. Even though at the end of the film Dorothy returns to Kansas by clicking the heels of her ruby slippers together, Rushdie observes that in the novels that follow *The Wizard of Oz*, she eventually returns to Oz to become a princess which reaffirms the idea that the Land of Oz is Dorothy's, and therefore the exile's, new home. In *Ask Me No Questions*, the reference points to a connection between Oz and New York: Dorothy acquires her ruby slippers in the Land of Oz and Aisha buys her red shoes in New York. Consequently, Aisha's shoes symbolically assert that New York is *her* new home. Aisha is not only aligned with popular American culture but has been enculturated with American culture as well.

As Aisha is addressing a large American audience, the statement: 'I want what you want', indicates a shared ideological perspective. However, Aisha also establishes her affiliations with her 'homeland' culture as well. In her speech Aisha repeats the phrase 'we became': 'we ... became visible', 'we became dangerous', 'we became terrorists'. Her tone asserts that this 'becoming' is not meant in the literal sense: people did not suddenly become actual terrorists, but, as this novel focuses on the media's use of negative South Asian/Arab/Islamic imagery post-9/11, people like Aisha became victims of stereotype: they, as Edward Said (1997) argues in his criticisms of the media, were 'othered' and were forced to represent ideologies which were deemed un-American, uncivilized and unenlightened. In her address, Aisha demonstrates how people like her developed more pronounced feelings of what W. E. B. Du Bois (1989, p. 5) and Frantz Fanon ([1952] 1986, p. 110) call 'double-consciousness' and 'third-person consciousness' respectively: people became increasingly more aware of the cultural and religious stereotypes that their bodies supposedly represented. The subtly ironic way that Aisha describes this 'becoming', therefore, actually affirms Aisha's disassociation with these dangerous and terrorist images which, in turn, illustrates that a terrorist identity is not part of the repertoire of Bangladeshi or Islamic identities that Aisha has been taught to embody.

The 'we' identity that Aisha projects is independent of these negative images confirming that the 'homeland' culture that she has been taught is not affiliated with extremism. Aisha, therefore, serves to undo some of the myths created about South Asian, Arab and Islamic individuals. When Aisha demands that her audience 'see' *her*, she is asking them to see her as an American who represents Bangladeshi and Islamic culture and to ignore the negative images perpetuated in the news media. She is able to represent her 'homeland' culture *because* she embodies certain traits that she been taught: because of enculturation, the identity that she projects reflects parts of her 'homeland' culture.

The very specific kind of hybrid identity that Aisha projects is one that she has negotiated via her internal site of Overlapping Space, not via the kind of 'third space' or 'diaspora space' offered by Bhabha and Brah respectively. The argument that Aisha has with her mother about the shoes may indicate some of the tensions which arise when trying to affirm one's hybrid identity; nonetheless, this disagreement symbolizes the cultural identity choices Aisha makes for herself. For Aisha, it becomes important for her to employ situational ethnicity to foreground her American identity. Her valedictorian address is given within an American cultural context, and by emphasizing her 'Americanness', Aisha enables her audience to identify with her. However, this American identity does not replace her Bangladeshi or Islamic identity. Rather these three identities overlap with one another. Consequently Aisha demonstrates that the employment of situational ethnicity does not necessarily ensure the abandonment or negation of other cultural identities. In fact, though Aisha emphasizes her American identity, she, like many other multi-encultured individuals, demonstrates that she is the one *and* the other: she is American, Bangladeshi *and* Muslim. The cultural identity that Aisha projects has been influenced by all her cultural upbringings which ultimately her internal site of Overlapping Space has helped her to negotiate.

Like Aisha, Dimple, from Desai Hidier's *Born Confused* (2002), experiences similar challenges when trying to assert her hybrid Overlapping Space identity. Dimple is a keen photographer; she calls her camera 'Chica Tikka' (a tikka, like a bindi, is the red powder Indian women place on their forehead to denote the spot of the spiritual third eye) and has her own dark room at home to develop her photographs. Although Dimple's parents let her cultivate this interest, they think that it is just a 'phase' (Desai Hidier, 2002, p. 124) and her mother eventually associates Dimple's photography with American delinquent behavior (ibid., p. 74). Ironically, however, though Dimple's photography represents a part of her American identity, she was, in fact, inspired to take up this hobby by her Indian grandfather so that they could communicate via pictures (ibid., p. 15). Her camera's name also carries Indian associations since Chica Tikka is her 'third eye'. The name that Dimple gives her camera therefore symbolically asserts her associations with the spirituality of her 'homeland' culture.

Dimple's hobby is both an 'American' *and* an 'Indian' activity. Consequently, Dimple's photography can be seen as a symbol for her hybridized cultural identity: her photography is part of her, she uses it to express herself, she considers the process of development as an intimate and private activity, and it is associated with both her American and Indian cultures. Like Aisha, the disagreements that Dimple has with her mother about her photography highlight some of the tensions that may arise when trying to assert one's hybrid identity. However, these debates simultaneously symbolize the cultural decisions that Dimple chooses to make for herself. Chica Tikka therefore brings both of Dimple's cultures together: it symbolically fuses the one *and the other* and it consequently becomes representative of the overlapping spaces of Dimple's identity.

Through Chica Tikka, Dimple is able to employ situational ethnicity. Though her camera has obvious Indian associations Dimple, at the start of the novel, is more American than Indian. However, Dimple learns to incorporate an Indian identity alongside her American one when her cousin takes her to a local Bhangra nightclub. At this club, Dimple initially feels out of place. However, Dimple's alienation is resolved when she starts to take photos:

> I looked my camera in the eye. I could see down there a tiny convex me. I watched the tiny me in the lens staring back with piercing regard ... The tiny me bobbled her head to the music, which was beginning to climb like a live animal up the legs of the barstool and into my own, massaging away the knots and lifting me on a wing out of my sadness.
>
> (ibid., p. 200)

Taking photos allows Dimple to feel connected with her surroundings and we see her adopt a more Indian persona. Instead of the usual 'one, two, three' countdown, Dimple counts: 'One ... two ... *teen!*' (ibid., p. 205) replacing 'three' with the Indian word for three. Through Chica Tikka, Dimple adopts a more Indian persona, however, this persona is not superficially assumed but is born out of the environment she is in and signals emotional situational ethnicity: Dimple feels more Indian and becomes more Indian because she is within an 'Indian' context. As Chica Tikka is symbolic of Dimple's hybrid Overlapping Space identity, Dimple's cultural reframing is clearly facilitated via her internal site of Overlapping Space.

Though the selected examples foreground each of the characters' hybridity, neither Dimple nor Aisha demonstrate a 'fixed' hybrid identity. As stated, Dimple, at the start of the novel, emphasizes her

'Americanness' and chooses to mute her 'Indianness'. In contrast, when faced with prejudice, Aisha demonstrates reactive ethnicity techniques: following the events of 9/11 and the subsequent news reports, Aisha rejects 'Americanness' as she pulls away from the popular mainstream community at school. These negotiations (and subsequent re-negotiations) in cultural self-identities are facilitated via each character's internal sites of Overlapping Space. These characters, therefore, demonstrate the functionality of the Overlapping Space model and highlight that their shifts in their cultural self-identities are possible precisely because they have been enculturated with one culture and the other.

Overlapping Space: addressing contemporary demand

Children's literature from the South Asian diaspora, exemplified here by *Ask Me No Questions* and *Born Confused*, reflects the cultural experiences documented by sociological investigators such as Maira, Sekhon and Szmigin, and Lindridge *et al.* These texts give both casual and critical readers a developed insight into contemporary South Asian diasporic communities and, more specifically, into the cultural identity workings of its younger members. Consequently, these novels ask for a definitive cultural model which focuses solely on how post-migrant generations, including foreign-born migrant children, negotiate their cultural identities. Addressing this demand, existing models of identity such as Bhabha's Third Space seem inappropriate; what I have referred to here as the Overlapping Space model, in contrast, reveals how young people from the South Asian diaspora today are negotiating and renegotiating their hybrid cultural identities.

These books highlight that young diasporic South Asians are, because of enculturation, the one *and* the other and have developed cultural affiliations with multiple cultural positions. Though hybrid, these characters, however, are not fixed in their cultural positionings but can negotiate and renegotiate their cultural identities to facilitate the employment of situational ethnicity and emotional situational ethnicity. They are 'cultural navigators' and can subsequently amend and resolve their identifications with contrasting, and sometimes opposing, sets of cultural ideas and beliefs. These young people – the fiction reveals – are not neither the one nor the other; they are actually both the one *and* the other. Consequently these texts call for a new model of cultural identity which not only reflects the experiences of the characters found within these novels but the individuals who inform contemporary cultural identity studies – a demand that the Overlapping Space model ultimately tries to address.

Notes

1. Here, 'home' refers to the country in which the individual lives, and 'homeland' to where they, or their family, are 'from'.
2. As opposed to Bhabha's ideas of 'neither the one nor the other' (1994, p. 25).
3. For an analysis of 'situational identity' see Harris (1995).

7
Owning the city
Screening postcolonial Bombay in Milan Luthria's *Taxi 9 2 11*: *Nau Do Gyarah*

Caroline Herbert

This chapter examines representations of postcolonial Bombay in Milan Luthria's recent Hindi film, *Taxi 9 2 11: Nau Do Gyarah* (2006, hereafter *Taxi*), exploring its engagement with the city's social and spatial crises at the turn of the millennium. Bollywood has long projected Bombay as a Janus-faced space of desire and disappointment, emancipation and exploitation. In its opening sequence, *Taxi* offers a conventionally ambivalent representation of the city, celebrating its postcolonial modernity while gesturing towards uneven experiences of its capitalist economies. Over what might be described as a 'standard' montage sequence (Prasad, 2004, p. 68), which splices together iconic images of the city that have themselves been cited endlessly in Hindi cinema – imperial architecture, panoramas of skyscraper-studded skylines, crowded streets, overflowing trains, advertising billboards, throbbing nightclubs – song lyrics evoke Bombay's projection as 'swapaner nagari – a city of dreams' (Gangar, 1995, p. 210). Describing Bombay as 'A golden nest with no place to rest', *Taxi*'s opening track, 'Boombai Nagariya' ('Boombai, city of dreams'), traces the simultaneous possibilities and problems of Bombay's reputation as 'the quintessentially modern city of India, the country's commercial display window' (Mazumdar, 2007, p. 113). Locating urban experience as caught between the attractions of prosperity and the realities of poverty, the song's lyrical ambivalence is interrupted by a more equivocal statement of urban exclusion. As the camera pans down from billboards advertising Orange mobile phones to settle on a sleeping streetdweller – a less optimistic figure for modern itinerancy – a voice-over interjects: 'Even the footpath has no space here.' The only body upon which the camera dwells for any length of time during the opening credits, the figure reminds the viewer of those marginalized from projections of Bombay as a 'golden nest' and of the material reality of surviving in a city with 'no place to rest'.

As Ranjani Mazumdar's recent work on Bombay cinema demonstrates, '[t]he existence of two worlds [of prosperity and poverty] is not new to either Bombay or other cities in India' and 'has become the dominant visual trope to describe life in the city' (2007, p. 112). 'What *is* different about the contemporary situation,' Mazumdar continues, 'is the flush of consumption, in which global mobility and visual signage have introduced an expansive world of networks and connections, creating new desires and aspirations' that attempt to remap the spatial and imaginative landscapes of the city (ibid., p. 112, my emphasis). Mazumdar analyzes 1990s Bombay film through oppositions between 'the city of debris' – the street or footpath – and 'the city of spectacle' – real and cinematic spaces of conspicuous public consumption and privatized skyscraper living. Recent filmic depictions of Bombay, Mazumdar claims, attempt to 'mobilis[e] the fantasy of a lifestyle unblemished by the chaos and poverty that exists all around' (ibid., p. 110) by representing middle- and upper-class urbanites retreating into the glossy 'panoramic interior' of the skyscraper to occupy radically depoliticized subjectivities (ibid., p. 115). Here, Mazumdar offers a valuable reading of Bombay's spatial crisis in the 1990s in the context of globalization and economic liberalization. In what follows, I seek to extend our readings of cinematic engagements with Bombay's 'crisis of space' by examining how recent Hindi film weaves together conflict over space in the city and conflict over its secular futures. Although conventional, *Taxi*'s juxtaposition of radically different economic experiences, I suggest, reveals the complex overlaps and contradictions between discourses of ethnic and economic exclusivity within the city, between Hindu nationalism and consumer capitalism. My reading is interwoven with a concern for the film's self-conscious engagement with Bombay as a highly mediated space; attending to the traffic between the real and imagined city, I consider *Taxi*'s mobilization of competing cinematic representations of Bombay to reflect and critique contemporary conflicts over the city's identity, folding together utopian, filmic narratives of social mobility with Hindu nationalistic desires for territorial and cultural exclusivity.

My reading situates *Taxi* as part of a broader body of fictional, filmic, historical and sociological work engaging with Bombay's intersecting social and spatial crises. Bombay's transformation from paradigmatic icon of India's postcolonial modernity, to a central symbol of its crisis is, by now, a well-rehearsed narrative (see, for example, Patel and Thorner 1995; Appadurai 2000a; Hansen 2001a; Patel and Masselos 2003;

Varma 2004; McFarlane 2008). While scholars have cited the 1992–93 riots and bombings that followed the destruction of the Babri Masjid in Ayodhya as a key turning point in the city's reputation as a model of Nehruvian secular civility, what Arjun Appadurai terms Bombay's 'decosmopolitanisation' and Rashmi Varma its 'provincialization' can be traced to the 1960s, and the formation of the local Shiv Sena Party (Appadurai, 2000a, p. 627; Varma, 2004, p. 66). Combining its regional and linguistic chauvinism with the broader projects of Hindu nationalism, the Shiv Sena made significant political gains in the 1980s and 1990s, positioning Bombay at the centre of a nation rescripted as a sacred, Hindu space, a project culminating in – and symbolized by – the city's official name change to Mumbai in 1995.

Scholars have been careful to situate the rise of a localized version of Hindu nationalism in relation to the city's changing economies. While contemporary Hindu nationalism 'became politically conspicuous in the context of economic liberalization and in relation to it' (Rajagopal, 2001, pp. 2–3), Bombay's steady ethnicization has been linked to struggles for access to the city's economies in the wake of liberalization. The shift from an industrial manufacturing to a service economy, and the radical inequalities in access to housing and resources that have often accompanied such changes, intersect with and contribute to the rise of violently exclusionary understandings of urban identity, as communities marginalized from narratives of Bombay's globalized modernity compete for material and cultural space in the city. Appadurai explains:

> As struggles over the space of housing, vending, and sleeping gradually intensified, so did the sense of Bombay as a site for traffic across ethnic boundaries become reduced. The explosive violence of 1992–93 translated the problem of scarce space into the imaginary of cleansed space, a space without Muslim bodies.
>
> (2000a, p. 644)

At the turn of the millennium, then, nationalist geographies and capitalist economies coincide in their attempts to remap Bombay as Mumbai, an 'ethnically cleansed ... gateway to the world' (ibid., p. 645).

Such remapping is evident in *Taxi*'s opening credits and scenes. After a sweeping shot of the city's skyline, the camera pans down to a suited man hailing a taxi. In the background of this establishing shot – repeated three times – scaffolding hints at the building of luxury real estate. Alongside visual gestures throughout to construction sites, and a repeated positioning of the camera at low angles to capture the city's new vertical heights, this shot reminds us that, at the beginning of the twenty-first century, Bombay is a city in the midst of extensive social and spatial (re)construction, in the aftermath of communal violence and deindustrialization. If a new Mumbai is being built in the background to *Taxi*, its central narrative prompts us to ask for whose benefit this city emerges; what inequalities are produced, compounded, and occluded by the rising skyscrapers of the city's post-Ayodhya modernity?

   Taxi negotiates the complex overlaps and contradictions between narratives of the city's ethnic and economic exclusivity through issues of space, place, and property. The film follows the fraught relationship between a hard-up taxi driver and a wealthy Mumbaikar who, after a chance encounter, become increasingly dependent upon each other in their attempts to maintain a space of belonging in the city. Raghav Shastri – 'A. K. A. Raghu' (Nana Patekar) – is a frustrated taxi driver in financial crisis. Unable to sustain employment due to a fiery temper, Raghu is in arrears on domestic bills, the taxi rental, and his son's school fees. The action begins when Raghu picks up Jai Mittal (John Abraham), son of a recently deceased industrialist, Shyam Mittal. Although more prosperous than Raghu, Jai similarly faces imminent financial ruin. Dispossessed by his father's will, which bequeaths the Mittal estate and business assets to an old family friend, Arjun Bajaj (Shivaji Satham), Jai needs Raghu to take him across Bombay, first to a bank vault containing an earlier, more favourable – but fraudulent – document and then to the High Court to present his case. Encouraged to speed by Jai, Raghu crashes the taxi. As Jai disappears into the gathering crowd, Raghu is arrested, later escaping custody to spend much of the film on the run from the nation-state (police) and predatory capitalism (Jai). Discovering that the key to the vault fell into the taxi during the collision, Jai is forced to pursue an uncooperative Raghu to regain the key, access to the vault and, in turn, his inheritance.

   Revolving around a disputed inheritance, *Taxi* uses anxieties over property – as financial capital, material shelter, and space of imaginative belonging – to raise issues of economic and cultural entitlement. As Jai and Raghu vie for possession of the key to the vault and the will it contains, these props accrue significance as points of access to, and authority over, Bombay's material and imaginative cartographies. Written by Shyam Mittal, the will documents a specific understanding of the city, more in line with 'classical Bombay' than contemporary Mumbai. Thomas Blom Hansen explains that from the mid-nineteenth century to the 1960s, 'classical Bombay' was a space in which a multicultural industrial elite fostered a cosmopolitan, secular city, a 'hub of organized capitalism, working-class culture, trade unions, and modern institutions' (2001a, p. 39). Visual references to colonial architecture associate the Mittal business – founded on motorcycle manufacture – with an older city of secular civility, and *Taxi* emphasizes Shyam as 'a charitable man' who paired corporate success with civic obligation. Awards, certificates, and a photograph of Shyam with then Prime Minister Indira Gandhi adorn a memorial in the imperial Mittal Group headquarters, apparently associating him with a commercially oriented, but socially committed, bourgeois nationalism.

The photograph, however, cautions against an unequivocal idealization of the Shyam era, gesturing towards civic unrest, authoritarian rule, and a period of decline in Bombay's (and India's) inclusive outlook. Taking the death of 'classical Bombay' as its starting point, *Taxi* traces the legacy of the retreat of Bombay's iconic secular, industrial modernity in the 1970s and 1980s. Already associated with a fading and failing ideal, Shyam's death prompts an inheritance battle that re-stages the contemporary conflict over the city. In the triangulated dispute – between Raghu and Jai, Jai and Arjun – an ideological as well as an economic inheritance is at stake that has ramifications for Bombay's secular futures, as different visions compete for what Hansen might term the 'political "property rights" to the city' (2001a, p. 69).

As heir apparent, Jai has squandered his father's legacy. Enjoying the proceeds of Shyam's business, Jai is less concerned with its social commitment, preferring to consume Bombay's pleasures rather than engage with its realities. His disinheritance forces him to negotiate with a city excluded by his consuming desires, and to recognize the precariousness of his own comfortable existence. In the taxi, he tells Raghu that, 'If I don't get to court on time, I'll be hanging around begging at this traffic light'.[1] If one concern of the film is to reveal the slim margins between prosperity and destitution, another is to expose how Jai's pursuit of private capital impacts upon the city around him, marginalizing – even as it depends upon – less privileged subjectivities.

Taxi's engagement with competing claims to the city is made explicit in the initial taxi journey, which, unsurprisingly given the film's title, establishes its central dynamics. Bringing two modes of urban subjectivity into close proximity, the scene in the taxi re-enacts the contested terrain across which it travels. Introducing taxi-driver and passenger, a voice-over announces that each 'says that this is his Mumbai', explaining that 'If [Raghu] had his way, he'd take people like Jai and drop them off outside Mumbai'; Jai, meanwhile, 'wishes that people like Raghu were prevented from entering the city'. Verbal and visual markers indicate what kind of city each envisions. Raghu's claims implicitly intersect with the nativist agenda of the Shiv Sena. A saffron wrist-thread, polyester shirt and cheap watch code him as a working-class Hindu, while his earlier insistence that his son emulate the Bombay-born Maharashtrian cricketer Sachin Tendulkar, rather than the North Indian – and Muslim – fielder, Mohammad Kaif, hints at a regionalist, Hindu chauvinism. His occupation similarly privileges the local, his cab driver badge acting as a 'civic insignia of occupancy' (Appadurai, 2002, p. 36) that seems to officially endorse his identity as a Mumbaikar.

Taxi exploits the local 'star text' of Nana Patekar. Patekar's work has been associated with often violent articulations of frustrated masculinity and, for some, the actor has become 'the closest one gets to a film icon of the ideal [Shiv Sena] sainik, the assertive, no-nonsense man from a modest background' (Hansen, 2001a, p. 214). Rachel Dwyer suggests that the 'populist or mobilizing roles' played by Patekar – a 'known Shiv Sena supporter' – indicate the connections between Bombay's film industry and its Hindu nationalist voices (2000, p. 111), a point I will return to in my conclusion. In the post-crash confrontation, Patekar offers just such a populist performance of aggressive nativist masculinity. Wearing cotton shirts and expensive jeans, the driver and passenger of the over-sized luxury car into which the taxi crashes clearly belong to Jai's class of Bombayite, and they similarly construct Raghu's identity as interruptive to Mumbai's modernity. In the taxi, chatting on his mobile phone, Jai tells his girlfriend Rupali that Raghu 'belongs in the twentieth century. Bullock-carts are going faster. Milkmen on bicycles will pass us by soon.' Jai locates Raghu as an obstacle to progress, a signifier of a pre-industrial nation, anachronistic to the time and space of India's urban modernity. The wealthy driver reproduces Jai's attitude, similarly eliding his own part in producing the city's violent congestion: 'Why do all of you come to Mumbai?' he naively asks. Raghu's response at once asserts the legitimacy of his presence and appropriates his perceived outsideness as justification for it. Thrusting his badge forward, Raghu articulates the anger of a disenfranchised Maharashtrian underclass who are encouraged to view themselves as the true inheritors of the city, but who continue to be marginalized from its economic prosperity. Declaring that 'We have come to Bombay to straighten out the likes of you,' Raghu performs an urban subjectivity in line with the Sena's promotion of a violently assertive local masculinity in opposition to the 'excesses of modernity' embodied by a westernized economic elite (Hansen, 2001a, p. 51).

While Raghu's badge highlights his sense of belonging as constructed through an anxiously exclusionary association of cultural authenticity with place, Jai's is located in economic privilege, symbolized by the key that hangs around his neck. Dressed in a tailored white suit and sporting an expensive Rolex watch, Jai wears the garb of Bombay's economic elite. More used to travelling in private, air-conditioned cars, Jai makes little attempt to hide his disdain for the less exclusive taxi, repeatedly checking his suit for stains and smells, anxious to prevent Raghu's identity from infecting his own. While Jai distances himself from Raghu, he is nevertheless willing to exploit what he assumes are Raghu's ideological perspectives. Encouraging Raghu to speed, he ironically urges the driver to follow the example of his 'Maharashtrian hero, Shivaji' who 'rode like the wind with just one horse ... Put [the car] in gear and say "Jai Maharashtra" ("Long Live Maharashtra").' Jai's strategic use of regional and religious chauvinisms reveals a significant overlap between discourses of an ethnically cleansed and an economically exclusive city. Although Raghu is more closely identified with a nativist agenda, Jai shares something of the Hindu Right's vision of a modern, global city. Hansen explains that while the Shiv Sena evinces a populist 'rhetoric, profile, and constituency' (2001a, p. 210), its approaches to Bombay's economies and infrastructure are more complex, frequently 'marked by a distinct upper-middle-class view' (ibid., p. 207). Housing schemes in the 1990s in particular seemed to 'serv[e] the interests of entrepreneurs and builders', appearing 'more concerned with the physical dimensions of the city than with the lives of the poor' (ibid., p. 210). It was clear, Hansen suggests, that the Shiv Sena and BJP wished to remove 'all signs of the poor and the plebeian from Bombay ... all who were seen as encroaching on the comfort and physical security of the middle class' (ibid., p. 211). Although apparently sceptical of the Sena's vernacular populism, Jai's desire to maintain a pristine suit bears a worrying resemblance to the Sena's desire to address what its leader Bal Thackeray termed 'the major problem of dirt' – that is, house-poor and Muslim denizens (cited in Hansen, 2001a, p. 208).

While voice-over, costume and flashbacks emphasize the differences between Jai and Raghu, Jai's strategic mobilization of nativist symbols reveals a complex overlap between their understandings of urban space, which draw on a similar desire for a culturally and spatially exclusive city. Commentators have noted the interactions between the Hindutva agenda and liberalization in 1990s India (see, for example, Hansen, 2001b). According to Arvind Rajagopal, the 'rhetoric of market reform and that of an insurgent cultural politics went public together', an 'opportunistic alliance' forming between 'aspiring middle classes and business elites' and a party keen to gain mainstream electoral success

(Rajagopal, 2001, p. 3). '[F]ashioning political participation on consumer choice rather than ideological commitment per se' (ibid., p. 18), the BJP appealed to an expanding middle class by promoting itself as the party of liberalization and globalization, most notably during the 2004 'India Shining' electoral campaign which worked to associate the BJP government with India's touted global economic success through 'images of upwardly mobile consumers' and 'middle-class aspirations' (Wyatt, 2005, p. 470). Although the campaign was unsuccessful – precisely because of the glaring inequalities in India's 'shining' economy – Andrew Wyatt rightly argues that '[w]e need to [continue to] take the narratives and aspirations communicated by the India Shining campaign very seriously' (ibid., p. 478), not least because, as Pankaj Mishra observes, India's middle and upper classes were revealed as 'likely to support the Hindu nationalists, even the extremists among them, as long as they continued to liberalize the Indian economy and help create a consumer revolution' (Mishra, 2006, p. 109).

Jai's lifestyle reveals the co-implication of discourses of economic liberalization and Hindu nationalism. His penthouse suite is a gallery of conspicuous consumption; crowded by commodities bearing little relation to local production, the space recalls the aesthetics of the 'panoramic interior' prevalent in the 1990s family film, produced after globalization and liberalization. Such high-rise, high-spec interiors create, Mazumdar claims, a 'virtual city' into which middle and upper classes withdraw from the overcrowding, poverty and violence of the city below (2007, p. 110), creating and occupying a 'privatized and depoliticized subjectivity' (ibid., p. 115). *Taxi* reveals Jai's preference for a privatized 'virtual city' as politically problematic, connecting conspicuous consumption with the politics of Hindu nationalism. Ordering an expensive ring for Rupali over the telephone, Jai glances at a newspaper article announcing the 'Mittal Court Case Today'. Although the accompanying photographs are of Jai and Arjun, on freezing the frame it becomes clear that the text itself concerns a contested inheritance of a broader, national significance, and is a version of an article by Mohua Chatterjee, originally published in *The Times of India* in 2005 under the headline 'LK to step down in December' (Chatterjee, 2005, np). This piece concerns L. K. Advani's resignation as leader of the BJP, following what has become known as the 'Jinnah episode'.[2] Departing from long-standing Hindu nationalist demonizations of Pakistan's first Prime Minister, Advani controversially praised Jinnah as a secular statesman, in a move widely viewed as an opportunistic attempt to project himself as a moderate, secular leader. Chatterjee notes that Advani's resignation triggered 'a succession battle'

(2005, np), as the militant RSS wing of the Hindutva movement com-
peted for authority over the saffron agenda with the BJP, which had, by
the 1990s, gained political hegemony and electoral legitimacy.

By juxtaposing the fictional and historical inheritance disputes in this
way, *Taxi* endows the Mittal case with significance beyond the personal,
situating it within the broader crisis of secularism, as well as gesturing
back to earlier instances of communal conflict. But the article also potentially reframes the conflict between Jai and Raghu as one involving different articulations of Hindutva, one appealing to India's economic elite
even as it relies upon – and mobilizes – other, more violent expressions of
national identity. Although *Taxi* critiques both Raghu and Jai as invested
in violently exclusionary narratives of urban identity, it seems particularly critical of Jai's failure to engage with the politics of the present. The
camera holds the article in frame long enough for the attentive viewer
to note the discrepancy between headline and content, something Jai
clearly fails to do. Jai's willingness to overlook national and local politics,
in favour of hedonistic consumption, implicates him within what Mishra
terms a 'politics of evasion and amnesia' (Mishra, 2006, p. 109) that is
complicit in – if not proactively supportive of – the machinations of the
Hindu Right.

As the inclusion of the newspaper indicates, *Taxi* foregrounds the traffic
between the material and mediated spaces of the city, revealing the role
of visual cultures in producing urban desires and disrupting their exclusionary impulses. According to Sara Dickey, '[c]onsumption of cinema,
and consumption within cinema, ... provide access to the luxuries of
public culture through the spectacular and utopian fantasies', offering 'a
momentary experience of luxury and ease' while 'suggesting that wealth
and the comforts it buys are within reach' (1995, pp.132, 147). *Taxi* is
explicitly packaged as drawing together two cinematic traditions – the
social realist and the glossy spectacle – with two 'local' stars performing,
and appealing to, different constituencies: Patekar's 'local', Marathi appeal
to the 'quintessential Mumbai crowds' of working-class Maharashtrians,
contrasting with Abraham's rising currency as a cosmopolitan model-
turned-actor from a multicultural background.[3] Form reflects these differences. Patekar's performance of an almost archetypal angry working-class
man is situated within realist traditions: *mise-en-scène*, muted lighting,
depth of characterization and performance style, and unsteady, hand-
held camerawork lend a documentary feel that implies a privileging of
Raghu's experiences and the city spaces he occupies as reflective of those
of the majority of Bombayites: that is, as more 'authentic', or 'real'. Jai,
meanwhile, is positioned within a glossy cinematic mode and urban

milieu that celebrate luxurious, easy living. Juxtaposing these contrasting cinematic and material spaces to highlight their simultaneously disruptive and mutually constitutive existence, *Taxi* folds together utopian, filmic narratives of social mobility with nationalistic desires for territorial exclusivity, suggesting that frustrations over uneven access to Bombay's wealth – frequently projected within film – are translated into violent parochial politics on the ground.

Domestic spaces reveal how modes of being at home in the city are informed and interrupted by mediated ideals of modernity, and Raghu's home contextualizes his anger within the failures of the real city to live up to its projected promises. Raghu's family occupies a small flat in a crowded *chawl*. Inside, a cramped space functions as living room and bedroom, with Raghu and Sunita's makeshift bed – a thin mattress on the floor – cordoned off from their son's by a curtain. Although the flat offers precious private accommodation, the ad hoc bedroom gestures towards issues of housing poverty within the city; Raghu and Sunita are rendered temporary floor-dwellers, a pile of suitcases in the room lending a further air of itinerancy. In Bombay, even private spaces of home are haunted by the proximity of public homelessness.

A television hints at the importance of visual culture in mediating Bombay's reputation as a site of social mobility, and as the Shastris discuss their financial difficulties, cinema's implication in the frustrations of urban desire is emphasized. Settling into bed, Raghu flicks through a magazine, lingering on a feature about Aishwarya Rai, one of India's leading film actresses, a former Miss World, and 'face' of the international cosmetics corporation, L'Oréal. If the image of idealized, consumable beauty prompts Raghu to cajole Sunita into intimacy, the kitchenware occupying the shelf above the bed indicates that more mundane realities will intervene. Economics disrupt erotic desire here and, while Raghu promises to address their financial crisis 'tomorrow', Sunita remains too preoccupied with their problems in the present, whispering that the 'imaginary tomorrow will never come when everything will suddenly be fine'.

The heavily gendered presentation of the tensions between erotic pleasure and economic need here certainly deserves further attention – not least because it is a dynamic repeated throughout *Taxi* – and I return to the problematic gender dynamics of the film in my conclusion. I want to remain focused here, however, on the traffic between the projected and the experienced city that underlines the couple's dialogue and which is reiterated in the closing tableau of this scene. As Sunita curls around Raghu, a high-angle shot brings back into frame the magazine, open on the image of Rai. Arjun Appadurai and Carol Breckenridge point out that magazines and films offer 'Indians of a variety of classes' information on 'where and how they can gain access to knowledge of the emergent lifestyles of modernity' (Appadurai and Breckenridge, 1995, p. 8). Here, however, glossy images of social mobility grate against the experience of surviving the city, putting a strain on everyday life. Raghu's attempt to access, or at least escape into, an 'imaginary tomorrow', where debt does not disrupt desire, entails an economically damaging performance of middle-class identity, in which he pretends to Sunita he is an insurance broker. Perceiving, along with Jai, that his real occupation is incommensurate with narratives of urban modernity, Raghu performs a role he cannot afford.

If Rai's photograph implicates cinema within the frustrations of urban desire, it is also a transitional image in *Taxi*'s negotiation of the city and its cinematic representation, as we move from Raghu's to Jai's space. In both form and content, Raghu's narrative suffers an excess of 'reality'; Jai, by contrast, enjoys an excess of pleasure, occupying that emergent lifestyle of unbounded consumption – the 'imaginary tomorrow' – to which the Shastris aspire. I have already noted how Jai's penthouse suite elides ground-level economies in favour of sky-scraper living. An introductory song sequence reiterates his occupation of an affluent urban subjectivity familiar to recent 'Bollywood' films, such as those featuring Rai. Crucially, what Christopher Pinney terms the 'pleasurable affirmation' of 'shared desire' (2001, p. 1) offered by song is revealed as reliant upon a subordination of the material. In 'Maine Suna Hai' ('Love Affects Such'), as rain-soaked bodies dance between billowing flames, it becomes apparent that erotic enjoyment is enabled by an economic prosperity that allows the transcendence of everyday, ground level realities. 'Suspended in the air / We walk on the clouds', Rupali sings; 'Joys transcend the limits of the skies,' Jai responds, implying an interplay between carefree skyscraper living and sexual pleasure. The lyrics claim that 'Love affects such' transcendence of the city, but *Taxi* suggests that cash plays its part too. Celebrating the possibilities of cinematic escapism, *Taxi* nevertheless positions Jai's consumption of a luxury 'imaginary tomorrow' today as predicated upon a precarious marginalization of economic reality. *Taxi* complicates the pleasure promoted, Bollywood style, in 'Maine Suna Hai' by insisting that Jai's erotic desires are interrupted by economics and Rupali, like Sunita, defers sexual pleasure until 'tomorrow' when Jai's finances are settled. While films 'feed hopes that a spectacularly easier life is attainable' (Dickey, 1995, p. 147), *Taxi* reveals the pleasurable 'imaginary tomorrow' as precisely that: a persistently deferred, danger-ously unsustainable fantasy.

As Mazumdar notes, '[t]he movement of the eye and the desire to look out [onto the city] can never ensure the perfectly sanitized and ordered vision that many of the city's middle- and upper-class residents desire' (2007, p. 115). Similarly, *Taxi* problematizes Jai's disregard for the impact of his consumer habits on the city through a dynamic of performance and spectatorship that moves in two related directions: by forcing Jai to 'look out' at and engage with Bombay's ground-level realities; by allow-ing Raghu to move beyond his position as aspiring viewer and enter into the (material and cinematic) spaces of social mobility occupied by Jai. Raghu is consistently figured as a spectator, an outsider looking in on Jai's hyper-visible prosperity. In the taxi, Raghu watches Jai via the rear-view mirror, ambivalently observing a lifestyle he simultaneously desires and suspects, at once resistant to and unable to access the prosperous modernity for which he labours. Later, having escaped custody, Raghu returns home to find Jai 'narrating [his] life' to Sunita, silently watching through an internal window as Jai reveals his occupation as a taxi-driver, in a scene that suggests the potentially destructive impact of predatory capitalism on domestic space. If Raghu watches silently here, his frustra-tions at his spectatorial position are clear in a preceding scene in which he watches media coverage of the Mittal case through the window of a store selling television sets and other electronics. As Raghu extinguishes his cigarette on the glass, over the eye of a televised image of Jai, his later violence is framed as an attempt to penetrate the 'screen' of the global city and render his experiences visible to its elite.

Possession of the vault key offers Raghu temporary access to the spaces of Jai's prosperous modernity – the bank and the skyscraper in particular – and to narratives of social mobility. Wearing the shirt and tie of his insurance broker costume, Raghu ascends Jai's high-rise, gazing out over Bombay, allowing its streets to fade from view. Here, Raghu occupies a narrative of upward mobility, settling into the luxury apartment, perus-ing the will, before travelling to pay his son's school fees and present himself as a financially secure citizen. Jai's appearance at the school with police in tow again disrupts this performance of a middle-class identity. Criminalized even in his attempts to become respectable, Raghu is re-arrested, implying that narratives of social mobility are not, in fact, as easily accessible as cinematic – or nationalist – representations imply.

While Jai initially fails to look beyond his privatized world, the loss of the key forces him to enter spaces he has previously ignored – taxi, street, custody cell, *chawl* – and *Taxi* borrows conventional modes of cinematic representation – notably the melodrama and the action genre – to bring into view the impacts of Jai's capitalist pursuits on his local environment. The melodramatic scene of father–son separation that follows Raghu's re-arrest, for example, repositions Jai as witness to the social impact of his actions, all the while reminding him of the loss of his own father, of a social inheritance thus far eclipsed by his focus on his economic disinheritance. In the last of three car chases, meanwhile, Jai watches Raghu struggle to remove his taxi from a railway track as a train – so often a cinematic symbol of progress and modernity (see, for example, Gopalan, 2002, pp. 85–90) – approaches, finally destroying the vehicle. Against a backdrop of towering scaffolding, which again reminds us of Bombay's reconstruction, the scene combines filmic spectacle with the material impact of the city's global aspirations and, as Jai looks on, the taxi is transformed from cinematic prop to economic object, the very means of Raghu's survival in the city. In each scene, the everyday struggle of urban existence is rendered visible through generic filmic spectacle, rather than occluded by it, with cinematography, point-of-view shots and performance placing spectator sympathy firmly with the struggling working-class hero, rather than the economic elite.

It is not until Bombay's violence enters his domestic space that Jai finally recognizes his implication in the everyday realities of the city. After failing to recover the will, Jai returns home, to find that Raghu has destroyed the document and pinned scraps of it to the wall surrounding a large portrait of Jai. Arguably, this image is more John Abraham than Jai Mittal, the sweat-drenched body congruent with publicity shots of the model/actor in public circulation. Placing the ripped up will around this highly mediated image, Raghu reveals the traffic between the material exclusions of Bombay's modernity and the projections of its prosperity in film. Moreover, by destroying the will – the symbolic deeds to the secular city – Raghu re-enacts the public violence of contemporary Bombay within Jai's private space, implicating his careless capitalism in recent communal conflicts. Here, the escapist spaces of the skyscraper (and the filmic narratives of privileged modernity with which they are associated) are disrupted by the street below, as Raghu simultaneously rejects, and insists on being seen by, a city – real and cinematic – that fails to acknowledge his labour.

Taxi has already reminded us that the will is a counterfeit document that does not reliably bear witness to the Mittal legacy of socialist secular nationalism. Moreover, Raghu later reveals that he has destroyed a photocopy of the will – a fake version of an already counterfeit city of capitalist excess. In *Taxi*'s movement towards reconciliation, Jai must similarly reject this counterfeit Bombay and recover a more inclusive city. Thus, he repeats Raghu's gesture, destroying the will and returning it to Arjun Bajaj. 'Today I'm missing my father a lot,' he says, continuing: 'I couldn't be like him in his lifetime, but now I want to follow in his footsteps.' Jai has already begun this journey, paying Raghu's bail, before reuniting the driver with his family, in a move that recuperates Shyam's social philanthropy and the potentially positive contribution of capitalism to urban reconciliation. Here, destroying the will signals renewal rather than violence, or renewal after violence, of Bombay's earlier promise of reciprocally responsible citizenship and socially committed capitalism.

Nevertheless, even as *Taxi* evokes an inclusive future, its resolution includes the terms of its own critique, following patterns of social affirmation familiar to Bombay cinema which tends to 'push vital differences to the margins of the frame' (Virdi, 2003, p. 14; see also Prasad, 1998, pp. 217–37). The newspaper earlier alerted us to the ongoing erasure of non-Hindu and minoritized subjectivities from the city space, and *Taxi*'s conclusion potentially reiterates such exclusion. In his reading of *Sangam* (1964), M. Madhava Prasad notes that the 'bond of dosti [friendship]' offers 'a prototype of the compact among men that institutes the social contract' (Prasad, 2004, p. 83). In *Taxi*, social contract is similarly presented as homosocial, with an emphasis on father–son reunion that marginalizes the productive contributions of female citizens to imagining Bombay's futures. Sunita's professional potential as a nurse, for example, recedes from view in favour of family reunification. Reconciliation and urban renewal are firmly situated as transactions between Hindu men. Similarly, despite *Taxi*'s insistence on reincorporating material 'reality' into the imagined city, the conclusion seems to leave economic disparities unquestioned. Jai retains privileged access to the profits of capitalist modernity, and although Raghu's family reunion is crucial – as is his rejection of a utopian narrative of social mobility occupied by access to Jai's space – we are left wondering what has materially changed; the bills, after all, remain pending. In its promotion of a utopian reconciliation in resistance to the city's post-Ayodhya spatial and social cartographies, *Taxi* sublimates its earlier politics, marginalizing its critique of nativist and capitalist narratives of Bombay in favour of a resolution that potentially reiterates, rather than unsettles, the status quo. As such, *Taxi* problematically leaves unquestioned the exclusionary Hindu nationalist voices dominating the city's public agenda at the turn of the millennium, the very voices it earlier positioned as bringing the city to its contemporary crisis.[4]

Notes

1. Translations of the screenplay are those provided as subtitles to the film.
2. See also Mohua Chatterjee and Owais Tohid (2005).
3. See the promotional leaflet accompanying the DVD version of *Taxi 9 2 11* and Luthria's director's commentary.
4. This chapter is part of a research project generously supported by a Canadian Commonwealth Postdoctoral Research Fellowship, funded by the Department of Foreign Affairs and International Trade, Canada, and a Postdoctoral Fellowship funded by Figura: Centre de Recherche sur le Texte et l'Imaginaire, based at Concordia University, Montreal. I would like to thank Jill Didur, Michael Parrish Lee, and Bart Simon for their valuable input into different versions of this chapter, and Ananya Jahanara Kabir for pointers on language/translation.

8

Postcolonial purgatory
The space of migrancy in *Dirty Pretty Things*

James Graham

Stephen Frears's (2002) film *Dirty Pretty Things* is a compelling thriller-romance much lauded for the way it reveals the invisible underworld of twenty-first-century Britain's unregulated immigrant workforce (Hovet, 2006). The film weaves a poignant love story between two such migrants, the Nigerian Okwe and Turkish Senay, into a much darker plot surrounding the illegal trade in body organs. Both have fled their home countries in search of new identities, only to become trapped in a hellish existence in London. With only a limited awareness of the dangers she will face, Senay volunteers to be a kidney donor in order to gain a passport to leave the country. Against his convictions, Okwe, a trained doctor, agrees to do the operation in order to protect her. By entering the illegal trade Senay unwittingly exposes herself to a sexual attack. Throughout the film bodies and body parts are traded for official identities in a similarly violent and exploitative way. This insidious economy makes both love and any definitive sense of home or community for the migrants seem impossible.

Rather than celebrating the liberatory possibilities and spaces of migrancy in an era of unprecedented global flows of capital, commodities and people, Frears's film unflinchingly depicts the abject lives of *sans papiers*: migrants denied the right to stay or work in, but also *to leave*, the host country. The film is thus animated by a central irony. The dramatic power of *Dirty Pretty Things* derives not so much from its bearing witness to the plight of those attempting to gain permanent residency and citizenship in Britain, but from those who struggle *to escape from it*. Not only does this irony usefully challenge the all too familiar picture of benefit-grabbing immigrants conjured by Britain's right-wing press and politicians by focusing on the way the 'bare life' of global migrants is produced and experienced in terms of the non-places of the global city

(Sharma, 2009, p. 140) – it also allows us to develop a critique of the way migrancy, and specifically spaces of migrancy, have come to be viewed in postcolonial theory.

The film's central moral dilemma seems to be this: do the protagonists have the necessary combination of individual integrity and love for one another to gain some kind of absolution – to finally find a home, wherever that might be? Or do the political, economic and social conditions of their migrancy damn them to stay, alone and exploited, in an inhospitable city? London, depicted as a truly *unequal* global city in the film (see Hamnett, 2003), is also quite deliberately represented as a penitential and, more specifically, purgatorial space for these new migrants. It is the overlooked significance of this last point that this chapter is concerned with. The key to understanding the purgatory leitmotif is Okwe's friend Guo Yi, underworldly mortician and reader of Greek myth – a symbolic gatekeeper who mediates Okwe and Senay's passage between worlds. This chapter examines the purgatory leitmotif and places it in the context of current debates about the theorization of migrancy – a critical task I believe to be necessary and important. Necessary, because allusions to different cultural ideas of purgatory, penitence and absolution in the film are manifest, but have yet to be adequately theorized in criticism of the film. And important, in that the use of the leitmotif in this film marks a significant moment in British cultural production. The thematic and aesthetic concerns of *Dirty Pretty Things* represent a movement from the post-imperial to the global in a manner that challenges the dominant paradigm of migrancy in British cultural and postcolonial studies

In the film's critical reception to date, three dominant and interrelated themes emerge. The hotel where the main characters work and the migrant body, which it hosts, are both explored as metaphors for a qualitatively new migrant experience. How this experience is presented to the viewer in the *mise-en-scène* then provides a subversive perspective on a third theme: London as it has been popularly promoted at home and abroad in at the beginning of the twenty-first century. The first of these themes, the hotel, is taken to reveal Britain's exploitative treatment of global as opposed to post-imperial immigrants; that is, of forced rather than voluntary migrants: refugees and others seeking asylum since the collapse of communism and the changing world-order in the early 1990s (Gibson, 2003, 2006; Elsaesser, 2006; Foster, 2006). The metropolis, for a long time the destination for migrating citizens of the commonwealth, is increasingly experienced as a space of transience rather than settlement. Recognition and citizenship become conditional on economic and political expediency rather than legal rights.

In this reading, *Dirty Pretty Things* reveals how Britain has become a hotel rather than a home on the global stage.

The second area of attention concerns the levels of meaning the migrant body assumes in relation to the sovereign nation-space: to its literal dismemberment and symbolic 'metaphorization' (Zylinska, 2004, p. 534) as conditions of acceptance and assimilation in the host nation. In order to gain legal identities, prospective immigrants are compelled to sacrifice their bodily integrity through the illegal trade in organs. To keep her silence about her compromised asylum seeker status, Senay is sexually exploited by an Asian sweatshop owner in East London and Señor Juan, the organ-trade ringleader, in the hotel. As Emily Davis argues,

> [The] mission of the film's central characters becomes finding a way to navigate the underground economy of immigrant labor while minimizing the fragmentation and commodification of their own and each other's bodies for capital, whether it is through providing kidneys or sexual favors.
>
> (2006, p. 48)

But as well as damning the 'Western-driven economic globalization' that Davis's article focuses on, so too does the manifold exploitation and violation of Senay's body reveal the gross and gendered imbalance in human rights and power relations between the different kinds of global migrants seeking to make their home in Britain.

This sexualized focus on the female migrant body is a central feature of two other powerful British films of the 2000s that confront the problems facing the most vulnerable kinds of migrants, *Last Resort* (2000) and *Eastern Promises* (2007). In *Last Resort,* Tanya, a young Russian mother, arrives at a British airport without money or a work permit, waiting to be collected by her British fiancé. He never materializes and Tanya and her son are taken to a holding centre for asylum seekers on the coast. As she reaches her nadir in this 'last resort' – what, following Sarah Sharma, we might describe in terms of Agamben's concept of 'the camp' (Sharma, 2009, p. 130), perhaps the definitive example of migrant space as a modern-day purgatory – without contacts or money, and with no means of making a living, Tanya takes up the offer of work from an internet pornographer. While, unlike Senay, she is in a position to escape to a more loving relationship before she is involved in any actual sex acts, her invidious predicament is essentially the same. Also focusing on migrants from Russia, *Eastern Promises* has been reviewed as a 'transgressive' meditation on the 'body-horror' of the tattooed gang members of Vory V Zakone, the Russian mafia (Bradshaw, 2007). But arguably the most significant bodies in the film are not the criminals' (as inscrutable signs of threatening otherness), but those of a Russian girl and her baby. We learn that Tatiana came to Britain in search of work but instead found herself trafficked into prostitution. She dies having been raped and forced to take drugs by the leader of the mob, Semyon. Her death and the baby's birth are graphically portrayed and the baby, whose existence indicts Semyon and all he represents, subsequently becomes the key object of circulation from which the plot unfolds. In all these films the bodies of female migrants are unable to escape the literal and metaphorical meanings ascribed to them as a condition of their residence in Britain. This dual burden invariably corresponds to harrowing representations of sexual violence.

The third strand of interpretation links together these readings of the hotel-nation and the abject migrant body. The depiction of the central characters, exhausted and abject yet going about the quotidian business of living as best they can, has been compared and contrasted with the way London is depicted (which is to say marketed) as a global city in contemporary London-based films such as *Sliding Doors* (1997), *Notting Hill* (1999), *Love Actually* (2003), *Closer* (2004), and *Wimbledon* (2004) (Murphy, 2001, p. 296). Yet while such comparative discussions enable a timely critique of the collusion between global capital and the biopolitics of immigration in western Europe, they have less to say about the ways in which the spatialization of migrancy in this subversive vision of global London are registered in this particular film's *mise-en-scène* through a range of purgatory motifs. These motifs present the dilemma these new migrants face in a compellingly succinct way. They dramatize the everyday difficulties faced by migrants compelled to work illegally in Britain while allegorizing the material implications of their being immobilized in a purgatorial space. Before exploring these motifs and their theoretical implications in detail, however, I first want to clarify what I mean by describing Okwe and Senay as 'new' or 'global' migrants.

From post-imperial to global

> *Dirty Pretty Things* confirms that a new character has appeared in the London version of the ancient narrative of the arrival of the stranger in the city. This figure is the global migrant: the asylum seeker, the refugee, 'the illegal'.
>
> (Brunsdon, 2007, p. 117)

If it is a truism to say that London has always attracted immigrants then, as Charlotte Brunsdon suggests, from the perspective of twenty-first-century Britain, the kinds of migrants that feature in *Dirty Pretty Things* can nonetheless be understood as representing a qualitatively (and as the tabloids never tire of declaiming, also quantitatively) different kind of migrant to those who arrived in Britain following the dissolution of the formal British Empire in the post-war period. The difference is manifest in the very term used to describe this figure. As all good histories of post-war Britain now tell us, in 1948, the *SS Windrush* brought the pioneers of a whole generation of West Indian immigrants to the metropolis.[1] Since the mid-1980s, however, Britain has received from war-torn parts of Africa, poverty-stricken South Asia, post-communist Eastern Europe, and elsewhere, the forced migrations of people increasingly referred to not as immigrants but as migrants: the refugees, asylum seekers and 'illegals' to whom Brunsdon refers. Where the former are popularly viewed as having come *to stay* – as having embarked on a difficult journey, an epic struggle even, to be recognized as being British (see Fryer, 1984) – the latter are characterized by the transiency of their status. They are treated as guests, *passing through*, whether wanted or unwanted by the host nation, and are expected to reciprocate this dubious hospitality by surrendering fundamental human rights and, more often than not, their embodied labour. Where the former were faced with a struggle to *earn* their permanent place, the latter are made to *pay for* temporary residence.

Admittedly, there is nothing new about this pattern of immigration insofar as these 'new' migrants are characterized as being in flight from political and social pressures in their homelands. Britain, and especially London, has a long tradition of providing shelter to the persecuted and displaced. During the eighteenth and nineteenth centuries, Huguenot, Irish and Jewish immigrants settled in large numbers in east London. At the end of the Second World War, some 150,000 displaced Poles settled throughout Britain – and went relatively unnoticed compared to the more visible influx of West Indians in the 1950s and 1960s, and Asians fleeing from persecution and poverty in East Africa and South Asia from the 1970s. As Panikos Panayi suggests, the imperial metropolis was attractive to immigrants in the earlier period because of the jobs provided by the world's first industrialized economy, but also because 'for most of the nineteenth century Britain had no immigration laws, which meant that people could basically enter the country as they wished'(1999, p. 5). In the twentieth century, the demand side of Britain's immigrant labour economy remained; not so for the supply side. Since the 1960s, 'As Britain has implemented increasingly tight immigration controls, the flow of newcomers with dark skins has decreased drastically' (ibid., p. 1).

It is ironic, then, that what *is* new about the late twentieth-century, early twenty-first-century pattern of migration is the truly global provenance of those attempting to enter the country, on the one hand, and the increasingly dominant role they play, according to Stephen Castles and Mark J. Miller, in 'domestic and international politics and their enormous economic and social consequences' (2003, p. 2), on the other. Both features of this new pattern of migration testify to the economic and cultural logic of globalization. But it is the social as well as economic climate within the borders of contemporary Britain, exacerbated by its party-political system, that are responsible for its ever more hostile forms of hospitality. While the culture shock of post-war immigration was justified to the electorate as being economically expedient – filling gaps in the labour market in the period of national reconstruction between 1945 and 1975 – it was the legal status of the immigrants, as variously enfranchised citizens of the commonwealth, which enabled them to lay claim to Britain as their home. Not sharing or indeed denied this status, and facing increasingly hostile regimes of media representation and state regulation in the post-9/11 'War on Terror' climate, these new migrants are forced underground into the informal economy; their claims to citizenship are systematically marginalized and, increasingly, rejected.

The distinction between post-imperial and global migration is thus complex, perhaps not yet historically definitive. In terms of its cultural resonance, however, it is more clearly discernible in the medium of British cinema. Brunsdon, for instance, argues that films from the 1970s and early 1980s that depict the black experience in London, ranging from 'angry' films such as Horace Ové's *Pressure* (1976) to Stephen Frears's more playfully transgressive *My Beautiful Launderette* (1985),

> speak from a post-colonial moment in which there is, or has been, an imagination of settlement, of accommodation, of coexistence, even if obstructed at every turn. In these 1970s/early 1980s post-colonial London films, however angry they are, there is a narrative of entitlement.
>
> (2007, p. 69)

In contrast to this narrative of entitlement, where the immigrant's aim was to claim belonging, to be *recognized*, the new figure of the global migrant is 'characterized, above all, as seeking to avoid recognition.' (ibid., p. 72) This new figure 'is found simultaneously in films such as

Jasmin Dizdar's *Beautiful People* (1999), Michael Winterbottom's *In This World* (2002) and Pawel Pawilkowski's *Last Resort* (2000)' (ibid., p. 117), as well as *Dirty Pretty Things*; films that represent the experiences of migration from the perspectives of a diverse range of peoples from Africa, Asia, the Middle East and Eastern Europe. In all these films, the global migrant typically attempts to remain mobile and become invisible, to keep his or her identity fluid or hidden. These traits are exemplified in the opening scenes of *Dirty Pretty Things* in which Okwe, on returning to his mini-cab firm from a pick-up at the airport, hands on his identification card to another 'illegal' driver and has to remind him that, as 'Mohammed', he should really get rid of the cross he is wearing. It is a reminder of how precarious the tenure of these 'illegals' in this country is; but for both the characters and the viewer, it is also comical moment. Despite this neatly staged performance of the migrant's fluid identity, subsequent scenes make clear that not only do Okwe and those like him survive by their wits, in the process they necessarily establish some kind of new affective identity in the city, and indeed some kind of home for themselves – however precarious or contingent either may be (Sharma, 2009, p. 142). Yet survival carries a heavy cost.

Surviving in purgatory

Three of the film's central characters – Okwe, Senay and their Chinese companion Guo Yi – have fled their native countries in the global South and East only to find themselves trapped in a vicious circle of exploitation in this iconic global city of the West. Contrary to the dominant paradigm of migrancy circulating in postcolonial theory, however, their lives are marked by immobility rather than mobility. They want deliverance from the hell of London's underworld, as it is symbolized at various points in the film, but can only gain it by striking a terrible Faustian pact with another migrant, the hotel concierge Señor Juan. Sneaky, as Señor Juan is known, offers forged passports in exchange for donor organs: a documented identity for undocumented bodies. It is a truly modern, or rather globalized, form of metempsychosis – the transmigration of a dead person's soul into another form. But these three migrants, along with the prostitute Juliet, turn the tables on Sneaky, the 'modern Mephistopheles' (French, 2002, np). He prepares passports for Senay (as the proposed kidney donor) and Okwe (for performing the illegal operation), but after drugging him they take *his* kidney to fund their passage out of the country. The film finishes where it begins, at an airport, with Senay following her quintessential migrant dream of going to New York and Okwe finally able to return home to his daughter in Nigeria. By assuming official identities gained through sly complicity within an exploitative system, Senay and Okwe are poised to travel onwards to what Salman Rushdie, the most celebrated fabulist of the post-imperial migrant experience, might call their 'imaginary homelands' (1991, p. 9). Yet while undoubtedly subversive, the actions of Okwe, Senay *et al.* are problematic in that they imply that the migrant dream – the right to cross borders and become a citizen in a new nation-space – is only possible through complicity with the vampiric economy of illegal migrant labour. As such, their escape is ambiguous. In duping Sneaky, have they made a pact with the devil or achieved metempsychosis?

How we answer this question might vary from character to character. The migrant underworld dehumanizes individuals and renders them invisible. The film's triumph is to reveal the humanity of these lost souls and the richness of their lives and friendships through their different ways of resisting both the systems and agents of their disempowerment and exploitation. The characters are also – quite deliberately, I think we are safe to assume – distributed across distinct positions in the spectrum of British migrancy circa. 2002 (specifically, the positions codified in the 2002 Nationality, Immigration and Asylum Act). Granted temporary asylum but denied the right to seek employment, Senay works illegally in the hotel and later the sweatshop, and illegally sub-lets her couch to Okwe. Guo Yi, a 'certified refugee' who has been granted conditional residency, steals medical supplies for, and offers shelter to, his friend Okwe. The most 'illegal' of all the characters, Okwe is the moral core of the film. Quite appropriately for a film that constantly draws attention to the integrity of the migrant body – especially the unregulated circulation of migrant bodies and organs – Okwe quite literally is its heart and soul. Together, these characters create a micro-community of resistance, a confederacy of the underclass. Individually, however, resistance takes much more ambiguous forms, what Emily Davis describes as 'calculated self-commodifications by characters with limited options in the global economic order' (2004, p. 37). In following her migrant dream, Senay suffers sexual exploitation at the hands of Sneaky and an East End sweatshop owner; trying to protect her, Okwe has to compromise his moral integrity and agree to work for Sneaky; Guo Yi risks his 'certified' legal status to help them both. In all these examples the invidious position that these new migrants find themselves in is made brutally clear. The spaces of migrancy in *Dirty Pretty Things* are a potentially soul-destroying purgatory.

The purgatory leitmotif works at three levels in this film, or through three distinct codes: the literal, the economic and the cultural. At the literal level, the film testifies to the attempts made by global migrants to survive in the informal economy and unflinchingly conveys the bleak reality of exploitation, immobilization and criminalization that this entails. This is invariably tragic given the circumstances of the characters' residence in the city: Senay has escaped from her family and wants to reach the promised land of America; Guo Yi, a political exile from China, is searching for religious enlightenment; Okwe desires only to be able to return home to his daughter with a new identity, to somehow be purified of a sin he never committed. And yet their individual narratives, their life-journeys, have all stalled. They are all immobilized, trapped in London with neither the official documents nor the means to allow them to travel to where they truly desire to be.

The position of the global migrant in this purgatorial space also allegorizes the postcolonial world's position in a global market economy. While for several decades the IMF and the World Bank have embraced the developing countries of former empires with open arms, compelling them to open up their markets to investment, these nations of the global South are denied reciprocal rights because of the protectionist measures the Western economies are afforded. They are embraced at arm's length, pending the purification of a Western-style democracy and the complete liberalization of their fragile economies. Like the souls of the dead in the Greek myths that Guo Yi frequently alludes to, they are marooned on the banks of the river bordering Tartarus (the postcolonial, developing world) and Elysium (the developed world – the West). To cross and enter Elysium they must be able to pay their way. In the meantime, of course, they suffer as if damned: economically underdeveloped, their resources siphoned off by the rich countries in the West while it dumps its surplus commodities on their unprotected markets.

At a cultural level, and binding the first two codes together, is the migrant underworld: a richly symbolic place in the *western* cultural imagination. From Guo Yi's reading of Robert Graves's *The Greek Myths* (1974), it translates as the mythic underworld of Hades. Quite appropriately he works as a porter in the hospital mortuary, preparing the dead for their passage between worlds. In dialogue toward the end of the film, Guo Yi equates the hotel doorman Ivan with Charon, ferryman of the underworld: 'Pylades was the boatman who ferried the souls to the land of the dead. If you didn't put a coin under the tongue of your dead relative, Pylades wouldn't take them to Hades, no matter how good you had been in your life.'[2]

Earlier in the film we come across Guo Yi preparing a dead Chinese man – another anonymous global migrant – for cremation. Before that he hands Okwe a copy of *The Greek Myths* he finds on another body. 'It's blown my world wide open', he says. 'You should try it. Medicine for your soul.' But it later becomes clear that he too is in need of absolution, that he too is immobilized in a kind of embodied purgatory. When we next see him he is disposing of medical waste – including body parts – in an incinerator, giving us a brief glimpse of the hellfire that potentially awaits all the migrant donors. He is himself a Charon-like figure, standing on the border of salvation and damnation, awaiting his own transportation to another world. As Okwe persists in his mission to expose Sneaky's organ-trafficking, Guo Yi confides, 'If I had the courage, I'd sell my kidney. Just to get out of here. Just to save my brain.' But, like Okwe, Guo Yi cannot risk deportation: he cannot risk the dangers of return, even with a new identity, no matter how unhappy he is in exile in London.

It is Senay, the character most vulnerable to exploitation in this multivalent underworld, who finally reveals to the others the purgatorial truth of their predicament: 'You put me in the house of the dead, Okwe. You are all dead', she says. Yet it is Sneaky who reveals to Senay the impossibility of leaving this purgatory, of gaining the transcendence she desires in her migrant's dream, without submitting to the evils of the exploitative system that face them all. 'This is hell', Sneaky says to Senay, before raping her, 'I'm helping you to get away.' But if the London underworld is indeed hell, and the spaces of migrant dwelling are a kind of purgatory, then the film's mediation on the variegated experience of migrancy is very much expressed through a western paradigm of metempsychosis, or the transmigration of souls. So what do I mean when I describe this as being *postcolonial*?

Migrancy and 'diaspora discourse' in postcolonial theory

As Andrew Smith notes in his critical discussion of the subject, '"Migrancy" is now ubiquitous as a theoretical term' in postcolonial studies. He adds, however, that it 'specifically refers to migration *not* as an act, but as a *condition* of human life' (2004, p. 257). In much academic discourse, the migrant appears as the archetypal figure of the globalization era. The caveat is that it is predominantly their novel perspective on the world rather than their specific experience of migration that is focused on. All too often, Smith argues, the particular reasons for migration, the brute facts of poverty and persecution, as well as, of course, aspiration, are not taken into account. Perhaps the best example of this problem is found in Homi Bhabha's (1994) celebrated reading of Salman Rushdie's *The Satanic Verses*.

In an essay which offers a postcolonial corrective to Fredric Jameson's (1991) influential Marxist reading of postmodern space and modernity, Bhabha explores migration as a condition of cultural translation by which 'newness enters the world', and pays particular attention to Rushdie's playful representation of migrant metempsychosis:

> Translated, by Sufyan, for the existential guidance of postcolonial migrants, the problem consists in whether the crossing of cultural frontiers permits freedom from the essence of the self (Lucretius), or whether, like wax, migration only changes the surface of the soul, preserving identity under its protean forms (Ovid) ... This liminality of the migrant experience is no less a transitional phenomenon than a translational one; there is no resolution to it because the two conditions are ambivalently enjoined in the 'survival' of migrant life.
>
> (Bhabha, 1994, p. 224)

Bhabha's reading of the essentially interruptive – or rather, irruptive – qualities of the migrant's ambivalent identity is fantastically suggestive. Moreover, Bhabha is concerned not merely to illustrate the phenomenon at a theoretical level. He goes on to situate his reading of the novel in the political discourses that attended the novel's publication, discussing, for instance, how

> women's groups such as Women Against Fundamentalism and Southall Black Sisters ... have been concerned less with the politics of textuality and international terrorism, and more with demonstrating that the secular, global issue lies uncannily at home, in Britain ... Feminists have not fetishized the infamous naming of the prostitutes after Mohamed's wives: rather they have drawn attention to the politicized violence in the brothel and the bedroom, raising demands for the establishment of refuges for minority women in coerced marriages.
>
> (ibid., p. 229)

However, where these groups are interested in *The Satanic Verses* in so far as it enables them to publicize some of the brute facts of what Bhabha calls 'the "survival" of migrant life' (ibid., p. 217), Bhabha is more concerned with the abstract value contained in the ambivalent 'location' of this condition. The key to the popularity of this theory among other scholars of migration and its representation lies in the positive spin they are thus able to give to the 'condition' of migrancy – as being inherently resistant to the dominant cultures of the host nation – irrespective of what this might mean for those actually attempting to 'survive'.

Consequently, where Bhabha's work has influenced debates over migration (postcolonial studies) and immigration (British cultural studies), there is a conflict between critics who focus on the translational and disruptive tropes of travel and mobility (nomadism, cosmopolitanism, becoming), and those who call our attention to the material experiences of belonging and immobility (refugeeism, settling, being). According to James Procter, the former tendency has come to constitute a 'diaspora discourse' in these fields, which in turn has

> contributed to a wider sense of subjectivity as decentred, uprooted, dispersed, mobile. Significant here is the extent to which diaspora has become an increasingly *figurative* concept associated as much with a series of travelling metaphors and tropes as with any particular, referential community or geography.
>
> (2003, pp. 13–14)

In the film, the main characters certainly exhibit elements of this protean condition. But not to the extent that such a condition is abstracted from their – often quite different – quotidian and affective experiences of migrancy-as-survival. Rather than focusing solely on the fluidity of their identities, Frears uses a range of techniques to foreground the different ways in which migrants move through, but are also immobilized within, London. Though he writes about literary representations of post-imperial immigrants, Procter's work nonetheless speaks to the representation of the 'new' global migrant in the film in this respect. As he puts it, 'dwelling constitutes a kind of para-site, *within* travel' (ibid., p. 14). In the underworld of *Dirty Pretty Things*, this equates to spaces of migrancy that assume purgatorial character. While such spaces are not without hope, and indeed the main characters do eventually pass on to other worlds, the premise of resistance that underlies Bhabha's theory is severely hollowed by the uncompromising depiction of survival as a vicious circle of criminalization and exploitation.

However, just as with Bhabha's positive take on migrancy as metempsychosis, it is important to note that the kind of immobilization that Procter describes in his concept of dwelling is similarly construed as an essential and positive aspect of migrant experience. And as much as the characters are shown to be trapped in a purgatorial space, such a sense of dwelling emerges in the film as a dialectic between practical adaptation to the host environment and the sustaining and empowering role played by cultural memory. In one particularly touching scene in Senay's flat, for example, Okwe improvises a Nigerian dish for them both. She is grateful for the meal though playfully admonishes Okwe for washing glasses while she runs a bath: the water runs cold. 'Everything here is connected to everything else', she quips, innocently capturing the dialectical nature of the world they make for themselves. In contrast to the conditional forms of hospitality on offer at the hotel where they both work and, by extension, the British nation or even 'Fortress Europe' (see Gibson, 2006; Elsaesser, 2006), the simple gift of the meal turns the transitory space of the council flat, however briefly, into a shared space: a home.

This moment of hope soon gives way to tragedy, however, when the immigration police raid the flat. In Okwe's and Senay's situation, mutual hospitality can never be completely unconditional. Senay loses the flat and her legal asylum seeker status because of her hospitality to Okwe. As a result, she spirals further into the illegal underworld, working in the sweatshop and falling prey in turn to the boss and to Sneaky. As Kevin Foster somewhat bleakly puts it, in such situations '[t]rust begets betrayal, reliance invites abuse, vulnerability brings exploitation.' (2006, p. 690) Yet despite this, the dialectic of dwelling – the positive sense of survival – persists. After losing her job at the hotel and fearing that Okwe has abandoned her, Senay searches for consolation and escapism – for some kind of immediate, worldly transcendence – when she dances to Turkish music, clinging on to her migrant dream (kept alive by a postcard from her cousin in New York which Okwe gives her during the meal). It is Guo Yi who provides them with a refuge from the immigration authorities, first by offering them the mortuary and then by referring them to his relatives in Chinatown.

These vignettes all give a certain presence to what Procter calls a diasporic 'referential community or geography' (2003, p. 14), but without making direct representations of them. The allusive presence of these forms of cultural memory adds to the affective *thickness* of the spaces they inhabit. It conveys a sense of how the different characters continue in their attempt to *make* a home in an unremittingly hostile world. It dramatizes how they do so within the immediacy of the everyday, rather than abstracted as a universalized condition, or as a transcendent perspective on that condition. This latter perspective is dangerous. It threatens to ape the very forces that dehumanize the global migrants and limit our appreciation of how these characters mediate their immediate experiences of home and homelessness, on the one hand, with their longings for belonging or escape, on the other. These dangers are explored in Josefa Loshitzky's article on cinematic 'journeys of hope into fortress Europe'. Loshitzky argues that *Dirty Pretty Things* is one of a growing number of European films that 'push the mise-en-scène to the geographical and symbolic margins of famous cities and turn them from globally recycled iconic images of fantasy and glamour into non-places' (2006, pp. 746–7). The photography and location selections of *Dirty Pretty Things* certainly present a quite different London to what one may encounter in more mainstream media representations of the global city. Though he makes no direct reference, Loshitzky undoubtedly has in mind here what the anthropologist Marc Augé describes as the 'non-places' of 'supermodernity' (1995, p. 78).

On the one hand Augé's concept seems to capture perfectly the global migrant's immobilization in the purgatorial space of global modernity – or supermodernity as Augé terms it:

> The hypothesis being advanced here is that supermodernity produces non-places. Meaning spaces which are not themselves anthropological places and which, unlike Baudelairean modernity, do not integrate the earlier places ... [these constitute] a world where people are born in the clinic and die in hospital, where transit points and temporary abodes are proliferating under luxurious or inhuman conditions (hotel chains and squats, holiday clubs and refugee camps, shanty-towns threatened with demolition or doomed to festering longevity).
> (ibid., p. 78)

In Augé's Baudelairean understanding of modernity (time as tableau rather than narrative), identities are integrated with, indeed through, the presence of the past in spatial forms. Modernity is a site of *cohabitation*. In supermodernity, by contrast, identities *coexist* only insofar as they are 'equivalent and unconnected' (ibid., p. 111). And so in their quest to find a place in Western society, the global migrants enter under the promise of freedom through anonymity, but then struggle to establish their place within it, to cohabit. The result is to be detained in a socio-cultural purgatory. They are 'in' Britain but not 'of' British society. In contrast to Bhabha's emphasis on the productive spatio-temporal irruption of postcolonial migration, of newness entering the world, Augé describes this form of experience as being an interruption that has no transformative affect:

> When individuals come together, they engender and organize places. But the space of supermodernity is inhabited by this contradiction: it

deals only with individuals (customers, passengers, users, listeners), but they are identified (name, occupation, place of birth, address) only on entering or leaving … It is in the manner of immense parentheses that non-places daily receive increasing numbers of individuals.

(ibid., p. 111)

These observations should caution us from assigning an exclusive connection between the figure of the global migrant and the non-places of supermodernity. For what Augé really has in mind in this essay is not the plight of Western society's abject peoples – migrants and others who inhabit the underclass of the informal service economy – but a malaise at the heart of western society itself.[3]

In the film, the relationship between individuals and the spaces they move between, live, and work in, is arguably more significant than Loshitzky implies through his brief allusion to Augé. The film dramatizes immobility but also reveals transformative possibilities *within* the 'geographical and symbolic margins' (Loshitzky, 2006, p. 747) of the city. To return to Procter, it expresses the paradox of dwelling as a 'para-site within travel' (Procter, 2003, p. 14). And to set the record straight by Augé:

We should add that the same things apply to the non-place as to the place. It never exists in pure form; places reconstitute themselves in it; relations are restored and resumed in it; the 'millennial ruses' of 'the invention of the everyday' and 'arts of doing', so subtly analyzed by Michel de Certeau, can clear a path there and deploy their strategies.

(Augé, 1995, pp. 78–9)

In the scene in the flat described above, for example, the camera follows its subjects Okwe and Senay closely and eventually simultaneously. What James Monaco would call the 'closed' (2000, p. 185) form of the frame composition discloses the intimacy of their co-habitation, their dwelling together. By contrast, when Okwe travels to the home of the Somali man who has been infected by Sneaky's transplant operation, the scene begins with a long-shot of the Millennium Dome (the 'O2 Arena' since 2007) from inside a flat, high up in a tower block. The Greenwich peninsular is only in shot for a second, however, before the camera pans and tracks back into the flat, into the cramped and confined quarters of the Somali family and Okwe's discovery of another 'African story'. From the briefest of glimpses of one of London's newest 'globally recycled iconic images' (Loshitzky, 2006, p. 747) – the 'open' (Monaco, 2000, p. 185) form of a panoramic shot which gestures to the vast expanse of London, city of plenitude and possibility – we cut to a claustrophobic closed shot juxtaposing Okwe, a travelled, educated and English-speaking 'illegal', with a refugee family barely able to communicate but prepared to suffer indignity and exploitation in order to stay in the foreign city.

All the elements that Loshitzky sees as representative of London's 'non-places' actually encourage the viewer to reflect on the different kinds of migrant experience invoked in the different perspectives offered by the 'closed' and 'open' shots. Seen from the Somalis' flat, the Millennium Dome identifies London's iconic global status. But by shifting the gaze from panorama to the flat's interior, it contrasts this with the illegal immigrant's marginal presence, trapped within the city, struggling to communicate and struggling to create a sense of place or community. In another example, the busy market outside Senay's flat in Dalston, where Okwe buys his khat (the stimulant that allows him to work as a taxi driver by day and a hotel concierge by night), gestures to the overlapping formal and informal economies that the characters are similarly caught between. The location of the Baltic Hotel in Whitehall, opposite the Ministry of Defence (see Hovet, 2006), suggests a close relationship between the immigrant workforce and the world of European politics. Okwe's taxi journeys from the airport (Augé's quintessential non-place), along the city's congested arterial routes and under the railway bridge, ending in the cramped mini-cab office, signal the inward impulse of migrants, to be absorbed and immobilized within the national body-politic while simultaneously being excluded from it.[4]

Like Bhabha's notion of postcolonial migrancy, the purgatorial underworld of London's migrant labourers constitutes a 'thirdspace', but not simply of hybridized, largely benign global modernity as Bhabha might suggest, but of a global modernity where the postcolonial world's liberation continues to be suppressed by what David Harvey describes as the 'new imperialism' of Western neo-liberal and, more recently, neo-conservative ideology (2003, pp. 183–212). And whereas the ideologues argue that the *right kind* of migrants desire a Western metempsychosis – for their souls to leave behind their long-suffering migrant bodies, to be granted new, official identities in Western society – the particular representations of immobility, dwelling and transformation in *Dirty Pretty Things* show something different. The film dramatizes a very tragic kind of resistance to this ideology. It shows how migrants live different lives and aspire to different things; it shows how some migrants turn some non-places into places of hope, yet others into a living hell. It shows how Britain and especially London can be transformed into home, but it also shows how some migrants become trapped there, and that, conditions being different, they would rather escape than be granted permanent residency in this postcolonial, global purgatory.

Notes

1. But as Andrea Levy's novel *Small Island* (2006) eloquently reminds us, the date of June 22 1948 is a much mythicized moment of arrival and should not necessarily be taken as the 'beginning' of a substantial black presence in Britain: many West Indian men served in the armed forces in Britain prior to and during the Second World War and either stayed on or used the experience and contacts they gained as a means of returning in subsequent decades.
2. Though he refers to Charon, incorrectly, as Pylades, the friend and accomplice of Orestes, who avenged his father's (Agamemnon) death by killing his murdering mother, Clytemnestra. See Graves (1974, pp. 56–84).
3. This irony is developed at some length in the film. As Foster notes, 'Okwe's readiness to love selflessly without expectation of gain or reward, to sustain the forms and practices of a civilized society, is an isolated and almost heroic gesture, a reminder of all that this community seems to have lost' (2006, p. 690).
4. In this respect, Okwe is abject in relation to the national *body-politic* in the sense expressed by Julia Kristeva (1982). As a politically and culturally rejected, yet economically necessary, migrant he is not so much the body-politic's 'constitutive outside', as Zylinska (2004, p. 523) puts it in her article, as what Anne McClintock, in describing the socio-historical phenomenon of abjection in imperial and neo-imperial culture, refers to as the body-politic's 'inner constitutive boundary' (1995, p. 71).

9
Third space, abstract space and coloniality
National and subaltern cartography in Ecuador

Sarah A. Radcliffe

Introduction: indigenous peoples' map-making

Indigenous peoples in Ecuador have seized map-making as a critical tool in their struggles for postcolonial justice. The topic addressed by this chapter is the politics of producing maps, a process and a symbolic and meaningful practice that speaks to postcolonial power differentials in South America. Specifically, the chapter examines how the production of maps of nation-state territory occurs when indigenous organizations (representing diverse cultural-linguistic groups claiming descent from pre-Colombian populations) engage in a politics of struggle against dominant, European-oriented norms of statehood, identity and knowledge.[1] Although established geographical and cartographic institutions often dismiss these maps – and the practices that give rise to them – they can be viewed as evidence of struggles by indigenous subalterns for voice and recognition. In this context, how do indigenous national maps articulate and further these struggles? What means do indigenous organizations have at their disposal to challenge the exclusions of postcolonial nationhood? And in what ways can alternate forms of belonging and purpose be expressed cartographically?

In theoretical terms, this chapter aims to bring into conversation the concept of 'third space' together with the materialities of indigenous mapping production in Ecuador. The production and practices of map-making can be understood as an arena within which subaltern subjects shift the languages and knowledges resulting in 'heterogeneous histories of contending peoples, antagonistic authorities and tense locations of cultural difference' (Bhabha, 1994, p. 148); in other words, they enunciate claims in/produce a third space. Although for many

129

decades in Ecuador, Indians were represented as minority, isolated and anachronistic cultural groups, the emergence of indigenous political activism has combined contradictorily with liberal measures of cultural recognition to lead to new cartographies. Indigenous map-making occurs in contexts of multiculturalism and postcolonial independence, so why do indigenous cartographers and confederations view it as a critical practice? To answer this question requires an examination of the tensions between state-led multiculturalism, and indigenous struggles for decolonization and interculturalism. Such tensions can be initially understood in terms of the fraught distinction identified by Homi Bhabha between cultural *diversity* and cultural *difference*.

Rather than describe in detail how indigenous organizations produce maps (see Radcliffe, 2009, 2010a), this chapter explores the theoretical frameworks through which these maps might be described and analyzed. I examine Bhabha's third space from a critical geographical perspective, questioning its power as a spatial metaphor and asking questions about how it meshes with other understandings of space, disruption and resistance. To do so, I establish how cartography engages continuously and directly with state claims to sovereign power over territory (following the geographer Matt Sparke's discussion of Bhabha and nationalism (Sparke, 2005)), and to introduce postcolonial critic Walter Mignolo's concept of 'colonial difference' (Mignolo, 2000). The chapter works to analyze the material and metaphorical consequences of Bhabha's concept of third space from the perspective of indigenous populations that critique current citizen regimes and the politics of representation. Both indigenous maps and cultural production are linked by their formation within the context of postcolonial nation-states. Bhabha conceives of national cultural productions as comprising two interlinked and simultaneous processes, namely the authorization processes of official nationhood ('the pedagogical') and continuous repetition of elements of these significations ('the performative'). As part of state-led processes of multicultural re-articulation and re-signification, maps represent one dimension of shifting and highly value-laden cultural products (Harley, 2001). As a result, 'neither can cultural homogeneity, [n]or the nation's horizontal space be authoritatively represented within the familiar territory of the public sphere' (Bhabha, 1994, p. 154).

Since independence in 1830, Ecuador, like many Latin American states, has placed mapping and geographical information at the centre of numerous projects to know, create inventories of, and control territories as well as to shore up geopolitical claims near international borders (Deler, 1981). Through the nineteenth century, Ecuador's territorial integrity and consolidation as an independent republic relied upon geographical imaginations of its spatial extent and content, as well as on the deployment of geographical expertise in statecraft (Radcliffe, 2001). As a component of nation-states' cultural productions, maps reflect society's endorsed meanings *and* suppress meanings (Harley, 2001). From the nineteenth century, geography – encompassing map-making and the collection of spatially referenced data – was often a tool of specialist military cartographic and geographical teams (Craib, 2004; Radcliffe, 2009). National atlases were a means to display the state's abstract space as self-evident, sovereign and discrete, where the nation-state within international borders exists as a decorporealized, modern, singular and self-evident space (Smith and Katz, 1993; Sparke, 2005), and thereby 'institutes a forgetfulness of antecedent spatial configurations' (Rabasa, 1993, p. 192). Citizens have been introduced to enduring patriotic geographical imaginations often centred on the national territory and geopolitical-territorial grievances (Anderson, 1991); in Bhabha's terms, maps are a tool in nationalist pedagogy. Indigenous and popular cultures have been represented cartographically as fading folklore about-to-disappear. Over recent decades, however, transformations in cartography have been driven by the country's early and powerful indigenous movement, processes of re-democratization, formal recognition of the country's pluricultural and multiethnic composition, and legislative and institutional efforts to establish multiculturalism.[2] Consequently, national maps have shifted in content and meaning (Radcliffe, 2009). It is in this context that indigenous peoples in Ecuador produce maps and, by doing so, enter metaphorically and materially into what Bhabha terms 'third space'.

Why choose third space as the starting point for an analysis of postcolonial space? In one sense, the concept of third space has become less prominent in geographical postcolonial theorizing and debate than ideas around ambivalence and hybridity. Yet it offers a crucial concept for understanding postcolonial space for a number of interwoven reasons. First, third space speaks to the politics of change, to the ways in which the highly differentiated landscape of postcolonial conditions might be challenged and transformed, not so much by mimic men as by critics (and in this sense the concept is perhaps unlike Bhabha's other tools for postcolonial criticism). In analyzing the indigenous maps as a critique, as an exemplary enunciation in a third space, the chapter explores the ways in which – and the extent to which – maps produced by subaltern subjects can be viewed as a form of resistance, in the process of moving towards a new politics of recognition. A second reason for analyzing the term is that the concept of third space has intellectual purchase in part due to its powerful spatial metaphor that speaks of something beyond the colonizer–colonized binary (Loomba, 1993). As spatial metaphors have been widely deployed in social theory – including postcolonial criticism – so too geographers have been engaged in deconstructing these metaphors, and simultaneously clarifying how space can be analyzed and represented in ways that have epistemological and political coherence (Pratt, G., 1992; Smith and Katz, 1993). In other words, spatial metaphors offer an opportunity to reconsider what third space might mean analytically and politically within broader *spatial* theory (Soja, 1996; Routledge, 2009), as well as critically examining the force of spatial metaphors for theorizing the *social*. By analyzing the concept of third space in relation to national maps produced by indigenous organizations, the chapter works towards an account of indigenous cartographies that encompasses their materiality and symbolic and metaphoric force.

Representation, enunciation and the subaltern: Bhabha's third space

Bhabha's account highlights the emergence of third space precisely through ambivalence, and the construction of hybrid identities and positionalities that challenge the binary distinctions of colonizer/ colonized, West/rest (Bhabha, 1990c, 1994; cf. Routledge, 2009; Walsh, 2009; Radcliffe, 2010b). Indigenous cartographic productions are inherently ambivalent as they utilize the form, convention and content of state maps just as they use their maps as tools in struggles for profound political transformations. Indigenous maps take a number of forms, including maps of 'global titles', which provide cartographic support for claims to large territories by one ethnic group, individual land tenure maps to ensure security of rural livelihood and – the focus of this chapter – increasing numbers of maps of the Ecuadorian national territory. In the latter, the national territory is frequently represented as populated by a number of indigenous nationalities and peoples. Indigenous nationalities and peoples were recognized in the 1998 and 2008 Constitutions. Yet, given the suppression in official maps of the present-day indigenous presence in the national territory, these indigenous cartographies serve as an insurrectionary intervention in nationalism's visual cultures. In these terms, Bhabha's third space is welcome, asking the question of whether these maps comprise an arena where progressive after-colonial enunciations can take place.

Ecuador's indigenous movements have produced a series of national maps as posters. An early example is that of the re-drawn and re-signified map produced by the major national indigenous confederation, the Confederation of Indigenous Nationalities of Ecuador (CONAIE) (see Radcliffe, 2010a). The map became a component of the confederation's political project, a campaign tool for a spatial politics to demonstrate ethnic groups' widespread distribution across the nation-state's territory. As a meaning-laden product, it demonstrated 'who we are, where we are in civil society', in the words of one indigenous leader involved in its production.[3] CONAIE adapted an existing national map – one originally drawn in 1982 by the Ministry of Education, Culture and Sport – to show the distribution of diverse indigenous peoples, adding an indigenous language title, 'Ecuador Llactapac Aillucuna' ('the location of Ecuador's indigenous peoples' in the major indigenous language of Kichwa), and the CONAIE symbol and the flag representing pre-Columbian populations. In other words, this map is a quintessentially hybrid cultural product that re-fashions the pedagogic tools of nationhood to make a performative intervention, overturning the prevailing invisibility of indigenous populations in the nation's cartography. Picturing indigenous groups as territorially and numerically significant, the map demonstrates that claims for land rights, development assistance and distinctive socio-cultural identity are legitimate and proportionate to indigenous groups' spatial distribution. In the words of one Indian leader (whose history was entwined with this map), the CONAIE map was not about cartographic accuracy as much as it was about a renaming, a re-spatializing, and a de-Othering of indigenous presence in Ecuador: 'technically it isn't real, but politically it is good' (author's interview, 2007).

In conceptualizing cultural difference, Bhabha draws upon postcolonial scholars (especially Franz Fanon) as well as psychoanalysis, post-structuralism and post-Althusserian Marxism.[4] In an interview dealing with third space, Bhabha discussed the importance of an analytical distinction between cultural diversity, on the one hand, and cultural difference, on the other. Bhabha suggests that 'cultural diversity' is associated with a liberal tradition of viewing the diversity of cultures as a 'good and positive thing', appreciated by the civilized western connoisseur. Cultural diversity refers, in his account, to the politics of multiculturalism where a plurality of cultural meanings are contained within the framework of equivalence, each element of diversity being equivalent to any other and, in consequence, no challenge to the dominant culture. As Bhabha goes on to say, this mode of cultural diversity is recognized only through dominant society's terms and can coexist with – and indeed often masks – racism (1990c, pp. 207–8). In contrast, Bhabha delineates a concept of cultural *difference* which rests – metaphorically – 'in that position of liminality, in that productive space of the construction of culture as difference, in the spirit of alterity or otherness', that departs from a recognition of the frequent '*incommensurability* of cultural difference' (ibid., p. 209, original emphasis). Cultural difference can then be associated with an array of meaning-producing subjects, whose terms of reference are not set merely in relation to a (western, liberal, multicultural) norm.

As a consequence, third space represents not the offer of voice from a dominant interlocutor, but the unprecedented, contested and improvised beginnings of a different cultural production.[5] Third space thus 'displaces the histories that constitute it, and sets up new structures of authority, new political initiatives, which are inadequately understood through received wisdom' (ibid., pp. 210, 211). Indigenous confederation maps and the *Ethnos: Ethnographic Atlas of Ecuador* (Moya, 1998) displace histories of Europeanization, and respond to the new structures of authority employing indigenous professionals and leaders (Figure 9.1). The new structures of authority here emerged with the creation of the Indigenous Development Council (CODENPE in its Spanish acronym), establishing indigenous social movements within the state, endowing them with resources and political leverage, and the broadening of the bilingual intercultural education programme (Andolina *et al.*, 2009). Moya's *Ethnos* atlas was produced under the auspices of the bilingual education system (itself an early – albeit under-funded and politically weak – stronghold of indigenous professional presence in the nation-state). Departing radically from previous national atlases, the *Ethnos* atlas provides schematic maps and ethnographic detail on each indigenous nationality and population across (and beyond) the Ecuadorian territory. Heavily reliant on formal ethnographic studies (overwhelmingly produced by non-indigenous authors), the *Ethnos* atlas nevertheless conveys a vivid sense in which the abstract national territory contains within it cultural difference. For Bhabha, third space is about identification in a psychoanalytical sense, 'a process of identifying with and through another object, an object of otherness, at which point the agency of identification – the subject – is itself always ambivalent, because of the intervention of that otherness' (1990c, p. 211). The Ecuadorian ethnic atlas speaks precisely to the difficulty of identifying un-reflexively as 'Ecuadorian' given the intervention of Otherness via the *Ethnos* atlas. In this context, cultural difference rests significantly not at the level of 'contents' but on interpellative practices, 'because all cultures are symbol-forming and subject-constituting' (ibid., p. 210).

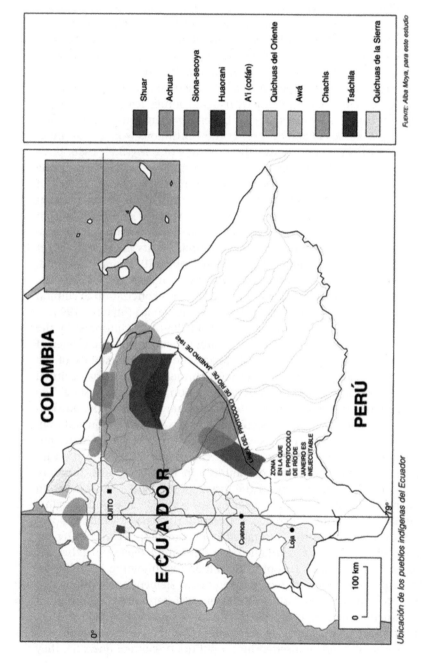

Ubicación de los pueblos indígenas del Ecuador

Figure 9.1 Ubicación de los pueblos indígenas del Ecuadori
Source: Moya (1998).

In indigenous cartographic production, what matters is not so much the taken-for-granted national territory but the possibility of imagining a form of socio-spatial belonging that interpellates Indians as co-constitutive of nationhood. In the continuous work of culture, these symbols are produced not out of an original but from 'a self-alienating limit' that enables other positions to emerge (ibid., p. 210). This form of cultural production, originating with an encounter across cultural *difference,* represents the third space. In his engagement with Fanon's *Black Skin, White Masks,* Bhabha expresses the continuous work of culture as 'the state of emergency ... also always a state of *emergence*' (1986, p. xi, original emphasis). In Ecuador, the 'emergency' – the injustices of the postcolonial condition as perceived by indigenous organizations – of dispossession and neo-liberal economies permitted the materialization of a neo-liberal multicultural state that inaugurated programmes such as bilingual education, health and social development. The *Ethnos* atlas appears, in this moment, indeterminate in its effect although it did shore up the material accoutrements of multicultural statehood. Ambivalence arises precisely around the indeterminability of outcomes, around whether emergence is dominated by the exoticization of cultural diversity, or the re-signification of cultural difference (Bhabha, 1994).

In the third space, the negotiation of subalternity is informed by the production of what Bhabha terms a supplement to the pedagogies of the nation. For Bhabha, the ambivalence and indeterminability of the third space can be further understood through the fact that cultural interjections supplement the pedagogic action of the nation-state. The supplement – the performative interjection that constitutes the possibility of a third space – is highly significant, as it is not merely 'an addition' to the cultural diversity expressed within a tolerant liberal state, but an interruption. Such an interruption causes alienation from the easy banalities of the 'imagined community'. In Bhabha's words, the 'supplement is ... a meditation on the disposition of space and time from which the narrative of the nation must *begin*' (1994, p. 155, original emphasis). This supplement acts to interrupt the seriality of the national narrative, which has the cultural effect of 'not simply confronting the pedagogical ... with a contradictory or negating referent'; rather, he argues, 'it interrogates its object by initially withholding its objective' (ibid., p. 155). Indigenous cartographies supplement the cultural sign of postcolonial statehood adding 'a sense of belatedness to the original structure, interrupt[ing] the seriality of its narrative' (ibid., p. 155). Although indigenous maps were produced in the context of multiculturalism (and thereby inserted into a politics of cultural *diversity*), they acted as a supplement to nationalist narratives by insinuating notions of ethnocultural presence and territorial heterogeneity (see ibid., p. 155).[6] Indigenous maps declare a subaltern presence, denaturalizing national myths of Europeanization, and introduce a politics that exceeds state-led multiculturalism and thereby denaturalizes it. In contrast to the apparent ease of cultural translation in multicultural 'cultural diversity', doubling or non-plurality is founded upon cultural difference, a politics that expresses the 'discourses of emergent cultural identities' (ibid., p. 154).

In summary, third space offers a theoretical frame that can be applied to the analysis of indigenous cartographies, bringing into focus how the objectives of indigenous cartographers (and their organizations) exceed the terms of neo-liberal multiculturalism. National maps produced by indigenous cartographers and their organizations in Ecuador can be understood as supplements to the nation-state's claims to sovereignty and territoriality. The metaphor of third space highlights how postcolonial national narratives have to shift to radically different ways of enunciating, recognizing and acting on diverse groups' claims. Questions remain, however. Is this interruptive capacity sufficient? And how does presence on a map translate into material rights on the ground? It is to these questions that the next section turns.

Third space, abstract space and coloniality

Geographer Matt Sparke starts his constructive critique of Bhabha's understanding of nation and difference by opening up a distinction between spatial metaphor (Bhabha's 'location' of the nation) and the *production* of space and its framing. According to Sparke, spatial metaphors such as space, location and territory are used in theory as 'metaphorized sites of performativity; [space, location, and territory which] become the three spaces and, indeed, his idealised "Third Space" of displacement and difference, the space of hybridity' (2005, p. 13). In his words, 'the more ... space is used to metaphorise other things such as politics and identity – [e.g.] mapping multiculturalism ... – the less ... are the geographical contexts of politics and identity adequately explored' (ibid., p. xxvii). Widely used in recent social theory, spatial metaphors underpin analyses interested in differentiating diverse social actors and perspectives, although they are rarely linked systematically with geographical theory (Pratt, G., 1992; Smith and Katz, 1993, p. 78). Metaphors work by associating the familiar with the unfamiliar, but by that move risk obscuring other unfamiliar ways of viewing the world. Alternative conceptions of space as socially produced and irredeemably contested offer alternative insights into multi-ethnic cartographies. Postcolonial critic Mignolo likewise argues that Bhabha's account is 'decentred', operating at the metaphorical margins of colonial power, thereby echoing Sparke's critique of Bhabha's third space for being automatically disruptive, and its lack of a more substantial account of the *locatedness* and *specific nature* of colonial authority. By this move, Mignolo cuts across Bhabha's concepts of third space and hybridity in a number of significant ways. While he acknowledges his intellectual debt to the concept of third space, Mignolo instrumentalizes a stronger stress on the critical insights of those at the margins. In this way, Bhabha's concept of third space is reformulated in the light of geographical theory, and more geographical-historical accounts of (post)colonialism.

In the words of geographer Paul Routledge, third space 'attempts to map the silences of the dominant geopolitical positions and undo these by invoking multiple scales of enquiry and knowledge production' (2009, p. 754). In this endeavour, and building on theories of space, Sparke insightfully picks up on the fact that Bhabha 'offers no account of the historical production of abstract space' (ibid., p. 13), an aspect that he remedies with an analysis of statehood's investment in abstract space. Cartesian logics and conventions reinforce the association of statehood with sovereignty and assumptions of a *tabula rasa* for states and their maps. Yet, contradictorily, the nation's constant shoring up of abstract space relies upon the continuous materialization and representation of the nation, as a particular territory defined by geopolitics that presents itself as natural and enduring. Yet in practice, national maps are tools in, and reflections of, a struggle and contestation over abstract space, as exemplified by indigenous demands for collective territories.[7] In this sense, indigenous maps work to 'articulate claims to territory in the way the [authorities] understand ... effectively cartographing their lands as First Nations within the abstract state space of Cartesian cartography' (Sparke, 2005, p. 17). Rather than space being automatically disruptive (*pace* Bhabha's third space), 'the ongoing regulative production of space' (Sparke, 2005, p. xix) can function to co-opt cultural diversity.[8]

In Ecuador, indigenous critiques of national territoriality and cartography are based on an understanding that the nation-state's territoriality is partial and power-saturated. The map produced by the CODENPE Indigenous Development Council (Figure 9.2) exemplifies the core conventions of Mercator-ized and national mapping in ways that the authorities understand. As a key multicultural agency, CODENPE is caught between representing indigenous constituencies and acting within the state, resulting in ambivalent cartographies that are open

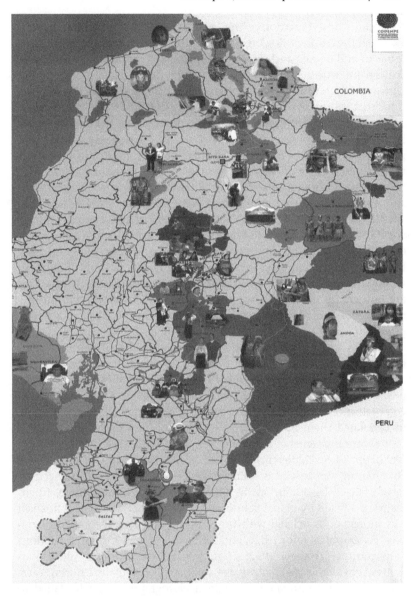

Figure 9.2 Mapa de las Nacionalidades y Pueblos del Ecuador
Note: Nacionalidades refer to ethno-cultural-linguistic populations (e.g. Shuar; Awa). Pueblos refer to culturally distinct sub-groups within nationalities (e.g. Salasaka pueblo in Kichwa nacionalidad).

Produced by the Department of Intercultural Communication of CODENPE, under the coordination of Ana Lucía Tasiguano. Design: Wayra Coro. Sources: Members of the Council of Nationalities CODENPE, SIDENPE, and INEC. Photos: Department of Communication of CODENPE, and Ayañawi Films. 2008. Reproduced with permission.

to various interpretations. The performativity exemplified by the CODENPE map is, following Sparke, ultimately contained within the terms of and denied authority by the pedagogy of the state that 'finally policed [it] within the spatial abstractions of the state' (ibid., p. 28). However in discussions about the map and how to produce it (conversations that cannot appear in the map itself), CODENPE cartographers are engaged in questioning how the state 'knows' about indigenous populations. It is initiating practices that build up more finely-grained geographical data on the location and size of ethnic groups. In this sense, there is much going on 'behind the map' in ways that are not hampered by the state's assumptions of national territory as a 'space [that] stands still, fixed, unproduced' (Smith and Katz, 1993, p. 78). These politics exceed the terms of reference of state-led multiculturalism, resting upon capillaries of Other means to relate geography and identity. Moreover it doubles the temporal interjection of subaltern resistance, representing their past/present on maps as a means to articulate notions of different *futures* articulated in contradistinction to state multiculturalism. 'Maps are not the territory, but also ... the process of inventing and putting the Americas on the map was not an episode in the past but an open process towards the future' (Mignolo, 1992a, p. 61).

Whereas Bhabha stresses the incommensurability of cultural difference, Mignolo argues that the *colonial* difference is more significant, as this sets the terms for designations of cultural difference, and the power to recognize such difference (or not) (2000, p. 338).[9] Relations of colonialism established colonial power over 'unnamed' territories, and incorporated them into a system of meaning that makes them visible only under the terms of colonial inscription (Said, [1978] 1995; Rabasa, 1993, pp. 93–5; Godlewska and Smith, 1994b). Given that European colonialism was based on a Euclidean geometry, colonial cartography territorialized its dominions as spaces that 'were already there, [their] reality predicted by global coordinates' (Craib, 2004, p. 6). Colonialism was moreover associated with the suppression of indigenous cartography, geographical knowledge, and forms of representing social relations with territory (Harley, 1992; Mignolo, 1992b). Although indigenous guides provided expert knowledge to Spanish colonialists during early exploration and settlement, European cartography generally failed to acknowledge indigenous contributions and institutionalized instead Cartesian abstract space (Mignolo, 1992b). Postcolonial critic Mignolo's account suggests that the very possibility of producing abstract space of the (colonial) nation-state rests upon the colonial difference, namely the colonization of the world and the differentiation between places that could *achieve* abstraction (the Occident in his terms), by means of dominating and removing authoritative knowledge from colonized spaces. The erasure of indigenous topographic, cosmological and geographical knowledges through conquest and subsequent national programmes to create and settle 'empty lands' has been extensively documented (e.g. Harley, 1992; Scott, 2009). In this sense, 'Eurocentrism permeates the world by means of a semantics of space that reduces the meaning of cartographical representations to the signs Europeans appropriate and project on the surface of the Earth' (Rabasa, 1993, p. 249). Moreover, conquest was often premised upon the concept of empty lands (*terra nullius*). A dominant understanding of abstract space – the notion that the territory within international borders exists as a singular, self-evident space – arose out of the conquest and colonization of indigenous-held territories, a co-production whose specific – and often violent – history has only recently been written by geographers and others. Extending Fanon's point, we can say that colonization wrote its own legitimizing history on *maps* as well as in the history books.[10] The 'universalism' of cartography – and the kinds of statehood it instantiated and represented – can be viewed analytically as the product of particular histories of *claims* to universalism and the entanglements of postcolonial modernity (Castro Gómez, 1999). Although Ecuador became independent from Spain in 1830, the production of national maps and geographical knowledges has been strongly shaped by French imperial interests that naturalized racial hierarchies, marginalized indigenous knowledges, and created forms of statehood that designated Indians as non-modern (Mignolo, 2005, pp. 58–9; Coronil, 2006; Radcliffe, 2009).[11]

In the postcolonial construction of abstract space, the dispossession of indigenous populations remains an unacknowledged underpinning to state cartography. The present-day reality for many indigenous and black populations is to be dispersed across a series of overlapping, fragmented and often insecurely titled lands, in material geographies that dis-empower and restrict their access to resources. Under Ecuadorean law, the state claims the subsoil and hence its claims over natural resources can – and do – cut across and disrupt indigenous territories (even if the latter have been granted collective rights under global titles). Moreover, the nation-state awards concessions to mining and petroleum to companies, resulting in the despoiling of indigenous territories and their precarious livelihoods. In other words, the very abstractness of postcolonial state maps denies the representation of colonial dispossession and the possibility of Other territorialities and social configurations. The conventions of cartography – that make invisible the state's foundation at modernity's/coloniality's inception – systematically erase the ways that national maps rest upon the material fact of colonial conquest as well as on colonial claims to 'universality'.

The claim of universality is countered by analytical and political recognition that in particular colonial spaces – namely what Mignolo terms 'deep settler societies' – the 'coloniality of power endured with particular brutality' (e.g. Algeria, Bolivia, Kenya) (2000, pp. 96–9), giving rise to a qualitatively different postcolonial politics and identity, characterized by more extensive and enduring patterns of epistemic and embodied violence against the colonized. In this regard, Fanon locates himself in a global horizon shaped overall by coloniality, but speaks from within a 'deep settler society' (ibid.). In deep settler societies, such as the Andean republics, internal colonies were formed in which the demarcation between settler and colonized was etched through material and epistemic violence, materialized and reproduced via the uneven spatial arrangement of populations and resources. Yet within these internal colonies, subalterns engage politically and intellectually with the postcolonial nation-state from a perspective of colonial difference, a difference that encompasses and exceeds cultural difference. In this sense, it is not surprising to find that the most disruptive and least 'nationalized' cartographic production arises in Ecuador's Amazon region, arising from long histories of colonializing metaphorical and material marginalization. AmazonGISnet is the name taken by a diverse group of 30 indigenous cartography technicians and leaders located in the Ecuadorian Amazon, where starting in the early twenty-first century they began to use geographical information systems to strengthen their political goals of autonomy, socio-cultural identity and self-management. AmazonGISnet uses Google Earth images overlain with self-generated spatial data to produce maps of indigenous designated zones (zones not found on Ecuadorian national maps), and nationalities' global titles. Such cultural productions supplement national maps but can only be understood fully in the context of coloniality, and a politics of decolonization. AmazonGISnet maps ignore national boundaries (to map ethnic populations that straddle the Ecuador–Peru border), and use maps as a strategic tool in the 'defence of national territory' and 'to show our space on a world map' (AmazonGISnet, 2008, 2010).

In this positionality *vis-à-vis* Latin American postcolonial nationhood, subaltern reason articulates what Mignolo terms 'border thinking' which metaphorizes identity and politics.[12] Border thinking arises directly from the geographies of colonial intervention, hidden and overt forms of violence, and the distinction between local histories and global forms of knowledge production, as it is 'attached to particular places ... resulting from and produced by local modern/colonial histories' (Mignolo, 2000, p. 326). As subaltern perspectives are necessarily critical, decolonization for the subalterns trapped in internal colonies is thereby articulated through a double consciousness, a new '*mestiza* consciousness' (Anzaldúa, 1987), which aims to 'undo the subalternization of knowledge' from the perspective of subalterns themselves. As coloniality works to subalternize knowledge as well as subject material bodies, indigenous cartography articulates its alternatives *by means of* a critique of Ecuadorian postcolonial nationalism, drawing on indigenous knowledges and ontologies, as in the example of AmazonGISnet. Moreover, through the framework of colonial difference, we can delineate how indigenous subalterns instantiate *pedagogic* (not merely resistance) projects.[13] AmazonGISnet's project to create an *Atlas of Ecuador's Amazon Nationalities* to document regional life, and to designate cartographically the autonomous systems of indigenous governance, economy, health and education, exemplifies this (AmazonGISnet, 2010). Cartographic productions by indigenous populations become part of a wider project to decolonize knowledge and substitute postcolonial national pedagogies with alternative pedagogies (Radcliffe, 2010b).

Back to third space? Concluding thoughts

As with all spatial metaphors, third space offers a richness of associations and meanings that conveys the profound complexity of cultural production in postcolonial societies, specifically by acknowledging the ways in which subaltern, racialized Others have to transform the vocabularies, meanings and dynamics of cultural production. However, Bhabha's third space rests upon a common post-foundational theoretical position, namely, the assumption that space is in itself inherently disruptive. Bhabha's formulation draws an equivalence between a spatial move (however metaphorically that is done), and a counter-hegemonic move (Sparke, 2005). If spatial moves and counter-hegemonic moves are kept distinct analytically, third space can be understood as conditioned by the metaphorical and *material* production of space itself. Furthermore, the production of abstract space is the product of coloniality. The authority of nation-states rests not only on the production of abstract space, but reiterates the authority of *colonial* ways of seeing. Indigenous cartographers find themselves bound up in coloniality, having to produce maps whose conventions and authority rest upon the erasure of indigenous geographical knowledges and the realization of colonial (and postcolonial) rule. As a result, indigenous activists struggle to represent cartographically the dimensions of their political agendas that refer to colonial dispossession and its present-day impacts, and represent pictorially their politics of intercultural respect. Internal colonies remain doubly invisible, un-representable either in the languages of republic postcolonial nationalism or in its cartographies.

In 2008, Ecuadorians ratified a new constitution that draws extensively on indigenous movement arguments for a politics of 'interculturalism', a form of participation and knowledge-sharing that treats indigenous subjects as equal interlocutors in political life. Yet the extent to which the 2008 Constitution shifts the basis for realization of subaltern rights remains to be seen. At the time of writing, Ecuador's indigenous movements are mobilizing against a government that disregards indigenous proposals and delegitimizes their cultural productions, and accuses their leaders of sabotage and terrorism. If postcolonial criticism constantly prompts us to make connections between current patterns of racial hierarchy and material dispossession, it also provides tools by which to question colonialism and its aftermaths. Indigenous peoples have seized map-making as a critical tool in struggles to enunciate cultural difference; the challenge is to found a decolonization project on understandings of space and spatial metaphors that support a progressive articulation of space, power and colonial difference.

Notes

1. According to disputed 2001 census figures, Ecuador's pluriethnic society comprises mestizos ('mixed' descent, 77.7 per cent), 'whites' (10.8 per cent), self-identified indigenous (6.1 per cent), and Afro-Ecuadoreans (5.0 per cent). However, the census under-estimated indigenous populations, due to officials' prejudice; surveys suggest Indians (the terms indigenous and Indians are used interchangeably in this chapter) comprise around one-fifth of the population. Ecuador in this respect is distinct from Bolivia, where over half the population is self-identified indigenous, and where President Evo Morales was elected in 2005, proclaimed as the first indigenous president.
2. Pluricultural refers to the existence of multiple cultural and linguistic groups. Multiculturalism refers to official programmes to recognize the existence of 'minority' groups and to award some rights on the basis of cultural difference.
3. Author's interview with Kurikamak Yupanki, lawyer, Fundación Tinku, Quito, July 2007.
4. Althusser introduced varied spatial metaphors into Marxist social theory (Smith and Katz, 1993, pp. 71–2).

5. In this way, culture becomes 'based not on the exoticism of multicultural- ism ... but on the inscription and articulation of culture's *hybridity*' (Bhabha, 1994, p. 38, original emphasis; cf. Young, 1995).

6. The supplementary is a 'space of doubling – *not plurality* – where the image is presence and proxy, where the sign supplements and empties nature'; it is here where 'discourses of emergent cultural identities' can appear 'within a non- pluralistic politics of difference' (Bhabha, 1994, p. 154, original emphasis).

7. Abstract space is commonly represented and discussed as if it were appreci- able and accessible to an all-seeing viewer, positioned above and beyond abstract space. The disembodied view brings into play the impression of a view from nowhere, an un-located observing self who can transcend an embodied and located self (Rose, 1993). In other words, one must ask ques- tions about the maps' readership, its configuration in terms of (il)literacy, and diverse interpretations across cultural difference.

8. In other words, the relationships between space, nationhood and disrup- tion show 'how space can be operationalized *pedagogically* in attempts to convene and thereby potentially co-opt plural traditions and histories into the abstraction of the single territorial collectivity we call the state' (Sparke, 2005, p. 13, added emphasis).

9. By contrast, Sparke acknowledges legacies of colonialism but suggests that the postcolonial nation-state can expansively incorporate that colonial dif- ference (Sparke, 2006, p. 40).

10. In other words, 'the very understanding of space as a stage has a history' (Craib, 2004, p. 5), a history of colonialism.

11. At a global scale, moreover, this re-emplacement into the history and geopolitics of third space reasserts the importance of variability in colonial experiences across the world (Loomba, 1994; McClintock, 1994).

12. Of course, Mignolo's concept of 'border thinking' relies on a spatial meta- phor and as such, it is as liable as any spatial metaphor to contain limita- tions. However, this metaphor is based on a firm understanding of abstract space (and its history) as well as of the uneven power relations of postcolo- nial Latin American nations, as outlined above.

13. In Bhabha's words, 'the pedagogic founds its narrative authority in a tradi- tion of the people, ... as a moment of becoming designated by *itself*, encap- sulated in a succession of historical moments that represents an eternity produced by self-generation' (Bhabha, 1994, p. 147, original emphasis; cf. Sparke, 2005). However, Latin American postcolonial elites viewed indig- enous subalterns as the paradigmatic 'non-pedagogic' subject, making them subject to violent state-led pedagogies, including hygiene campaigns and efforts to 'civilize' them.

10

Security, territory, and colonial populations

Town and empire in Foucault's 1978 lecture course

Stephen Legg

This chapter explores Foucault's ([1978b] 2007) *Security, Territory, Population* lecture series, which situates the extremely influential *Governmentality* (Foucault, [1978a] 2001) lecture in the context of the 12 other lectures delivered that year (Foucault, 2000, pp. 67–71). It will also draw comparisons with *The Birth of Biopolitics* (Foucault, [1979b] 2008) lectures delivered the following year, which extend the methodological and empirical matter of the former work. These lectures contain explicit considerations of empire, which have been notoriously absent in Foucault's other work (see Legg, 2007a). But they should also be of interest to postcolonial scholars who are keen to follow Young's (2001, p. 386) injunction that postcolonial theorists consider discourses beyond the textual, so as to explore their materiality, heterogeneity and power. The lectures provide an invaluable resource to those concerned with colonial and postcolonial government, in the broad sense of the conduct of conduct.

But the lectures also have much to add to considerations of Foucault's spatial sensibility. These have, so far, included examinations of disciplinary spaces (Driver, 1985; Elden, 2001) reserved for the poor (Driver, 1993), the sexually threatening (Ogborn, 1993; Howell, 2000a; Legg, 2009a), the unhealthy (Philo, 2000) and the 'insane' (Philo, 2004). There have also been studies of heterotopic (Hetherington, 1997), heteronormative (Hubbard, 2000) and entangled (Sharp *et al.*, 2000) spaces of power. Governmentality, as a concept, has been used to consider the ways in which territory is conceived (Braun, 2000; Hannah, 2000) and how spatial and environmental logics have causal effects (Huxley, 2007). Recent work on the spatiality of Foucault's thought have reflected further upon the concept of governmentality (Rose-Redwood, 2006; Elden, 2007b; Huxley, 2008), of calculation (Crampton and Elden, 2006), of the census (Brown and Knopp, 2006), and of sub-disciplinary engagements with Foucault's texts (Crampton and Elden, 2007).

While Elden's (2007a) overview of the lectures correctly points out that they lack an explicit focus on territory, they do display a new level of spatial awareness of the imperial and the urban. The latter goes beyond the lecture which explicitly refers to urban examples of different modes of power (Foucault, [1978b] 2007, Chapter 1; see also Foucault, 2007). Rather, the town is persistently referred to as the site in which, and because of which, modern governmentalities emerged. There is also the suggestion that 'Europe' emerges in distinct relation to its conception of, and relations with, the rest of the world. Taken together, these two scales of spatial insight present exciting new avenues of postcolonial research.

This chapter explores these spatialities, but will be unable to portray the true richness of the lectures, or to highlight the other contributions that these works will make to understanding Foucault's thought more broadly. In brief, these contributions must include a refutation of Foucault's discursive or social determinism. Besides the lecture on counter-conduct, there is also an ongoing attentiveness to the reversibility and contestational nature of power, and to its permeability and accessibility to struggles or attacks (Foucault, [1978b] 2007, p. 119; see also Foucault, [1982] 2001b; Ransom, 1997). There is also a much more detailed explanation of how sovereign, disciplinary, and governmental power were mutually imbricated and how they continued to function in harmony or discord through modern governmentalities. Finally, those who criticize Foucault's microphysics as neglectful of larger scales (see Moss, 1998) will find considerations of the national and international in this work, as discussed at the end of this chapter. Finally, these lectures should help rebalance postcolonial scholarship, much of which grew out of 'commonwealth literature' studies which foregrounded textual or semiological analyses over the material experience of colonial rule, and colonial cities, on the ground.

Security, territory, population

The principles of governmentality have been extensively commented upon and critiqued (Burchell *et al.*, 1991; Barry *et al.*, 1996; Rose, 1999; Dean, 1999; Hannah, 2000; Joyce, 2003; Huxley, 2008). The *Governmentality* lecture itself dwelt on the shift from a sixteenth-century Machiavellian literature that advised the Prince, to the emergent arts of governing the disposition of humans and materials. The concept of governing gradually evolved, during and after the eighteenth century, from an art of dispositions, which sought to benefit the sovereign, into the science of processes, namely those of economy, demography, and society, which sought to benefit the population. The influence of the sovereign remained, as did the intra- and extra-institutional influence of disciplinary power, but all within the framework of the new science of government, tactically deployed as governmental rationalities ('governmentalities').

In the following lecture (8 February 1978), Foucault put to the audience a series of questions: why study the state and population with such an obscure notion as that of governmentality? 'Why attack the strong and the dense with the feeble, diffuse, and lacunary?' He answered that his aim was to effect a triple displacement, as had occurred when studying discipline outside of disciplinary institutions (Foucault, 1977a, pp. 209–28). This entailed an emphasis on, first of all, broader technologies of power, a functional inversion of strategies and tactics on to the outside world, and, finally, studying the creation of objects of knowledge, rather than the study of pre-existing forms. Governmentality, as a concept, attempts to shift attention outside of the state, situating bureaucracies, the reason of state, and its material manifestations as the result of wider governmental rationalities. The state was the result, not the originator, of apparatuses of security, or, as Foucault would claim the following year: 'The state is nothing else but the effect, the profile, the mobile shape of a perpetual statification (*étatisation*) or statifications' (Foucault, [1979b] 2008, p. 77).

As a proponent of genealogy, rather than linear history, Foucault darts between dates and causal links throughout the lecture series. The first three lectures, covered last here, address the apparatuses of security which were the product of the new governmentalities that were summarized in the famous fourth lecture. However, the following nine lectures chart the inspirations for these governmentalities, starting in the ancient world. Here Foucault explored the Christian-Hebrew pastoral tradition involving the 'government of souls' in which prime concern was given to subsistence and devotion to each individual, rather than an anonymous whole (as further explored in Foucault's 1980 lectures: see Landry, 2009). This pastoralism was posed as a prelude to sixteenth-century governmentalities because of the relation it established between salvation, law and truth, but also because of the constitution of a specific subject: 'of a subject whose merits are analytically identified, who is subjected in continuous networks of obedience, and who is subjectified (*sujectivé*) through the compulsory extraction of truth' (Foucault, [1978b] 2007, p. 185).

While this pastoralism marked an alternative art of government that would re-emerge in later strands of individualized government, Foucault

([1978b] 2007, Chapter 9) suggested that between 1580 and 1660, across Europe, sovereigns sought to augment their power not through the individualization of the pastorate but through the new arts of government which gave birth to state reason. Such reason essentially concerned the state's ability to preserve its integrity. This might involve the decision to suspend laws in exceptional cases so as to allow the wielding of violence in defence of state interests (see Agamben, 2005), or collecting statistical information on the reality of the state (for the nineteenth century, see Porter, 1986). Such actions were necessary to strengthen emergent state administrations. Yet Foucault stressed that, at the end of the seventeenth century, the happiness of the state was still prioritized over the happiness of the population. The latter, a key feature of governmentality, would only emerge through the influence of policing technology, but this itself was intertwined with what Foucault termed the diplomatic-military technological assemblage, the second model on which the new governmentality would draw.

State reason introduced more explicit discussions of internal politics, and posited the state as the arbiter of governmental reason and the interpretation of reality. Yet this reason sought not only to preserve the state, but also to expand it. This was connected to the geographical realization that states coexisted in 'spaces of competition' (Foucault, [1978b], 2007, Chapter 11). Replacing the Christian eschatological temporality and the spatial unity of the Holy Roman Empire came the open time (that is, secular, non-millenarian, non-apocalyptic) and multiple spatiality of a post-Reformation Europe emerging from the crisis of pastoral power. Rivalries were replaced with geopolitical strategies and competitions that tested the *force* of a state, its dynamic capacity to exert influence both internally and externally.

Military-diplomatic techniques were developed in the mid-seventeenth century to limit the mobility of states while facilitating their growth. The objective was a balance of Europe, seeking to orchestrate the host of plural and different, yet not imperially hierarchized, states, what Schmitt ([1950] 2003) termed the formation of a world *nomos* via the international law of the *Jus Publicum Europaeum* (see Legg, 2011). An equality of power between the strongest states, and the potential combination of smaller states, aimed for a peace that allowed increasing force alongside stability. The instruments of this peace would be political wars, a diplomatic society of nations, and internal infrastructures that formed the military apparatus (*dispositif*). This consisted of a professionalized soldiery as part of a permanent armed structure, a means of tactically reflecting on military matters and war, and back-up facilities of strongholds and transport. With this military apparatus Foucault turned to a discussion of the actual means by which this prelude to governmentality manifested itself in spatial relations of policing.

Diplomatic militarism and policing were linked in the seventeenth and eighteenth centuries, Foucault ([1978b] 2007, Chapter 12) argued, by their devotion to increasing state force. 'To police' referred neither to the previous loose definition of a public authority or body, or to the later definition of a crime-fighting force. Rather, the object of policing was the good use of the state's forces, and as such can be linked to the balance of Europe in three senses. 'Morphologically', both sought to balance the growth of different forces with the maintenance of state order. In terms of 'conditioning', the equilibrium of Europe relied upon the equilibrium of forces developed by states internally. Finally, the 'instrumental' statistics that were needed to make comparisons between states were made not just necessary but also possible by the police, which provided the state with knowledge of itself and its rivals.

Foucault identified five integrative tasks for the police, bridging the cameralist (internal) and mercantilist (external) force requirements of the state. The first concerned the number of people in a territory: counting their numbers and ensuring that there are as many as possible, as well as their development in relation to resources or territory. The second task concerned providing these people with the necessities of life, and the third with ensuring that the people were put to work.

The last two tasks welded the police to the maintenance and creation of the infrastructures that would facilitate a healthy and productive economy, society, and population. The circulation of goods would be provided for by two types of infrastructure: first, by 'material networks' such as roads, rivers and canals that constituted the 'space of circulation'. But there also needed to be, second, an infrastructure of regulations, constraints or facilities to allow circulation. The last task of the police was to safeguard health: not just to protect from epidemics, but to promote health itself. This necessitated not just a new infrastructure ('a whole new politics of amenities') but also a new approach to towns and cities ('new urban space') (also see Foucault, 2001, p. 99).

In the following lecture (Foucault, [1978b], 2007, Chapter 13), Foucault expanded on the relationship between the town and the police. The widely accepted objects of police action in the nineteenth century were unified by being 'urban objects', whether because they only existed in towns (markets, squares, commerce) or because they were especially significant in towns (vagrants, health, subsistence). As such, the police contributed to the 'urbanization of territory' through facilitating communication between towns and organizing territory-like towns. While the market town was central to this urbanization, this was not government in the name of individual happiness or profit. The early arts of government still served to benefit and secure the state first and foremost: 'In other words, police is the direct governmentality of the sovereign qua sovereign' (ibid., p. 339). Foucault also briefly commented that the spread of the police should be seen as the context of the general disciplinarization of society from the end of the sixteenth to the eighteenth centuries (Foucault, 1977a), which he described as: 'a general regulation of individuals and the territory of the realm in the form of a police based on an essentially urban model. Making the town into a sort of quasi-convent and the realm into a sort of quasi-town is the kind of great disciplinary dream behind police' (Foucault, [1978b] 2007, p. 341).

This contextualization serves as a reminder of the place of this work in Foucault's larger and ongoing project. It situates this last precursor of liberal governmentality in the wider emergence of biopower, between the two poles of discipline and government, in relation to sovereign power. Stuart Elden (2008) has shown that throughout the 1970s Foucault was collaborating in research projects that demonstrate his commitment to the urban sphere as a material and political space. These projects included one entitled 'the equipment of power' with Gilles Deleuze, Félix Guattari, and François Fourquet which focused on urban infrastructure, analyzing the town as machine and metaphor, through its roads, plans and organization of territory. Further works examined hospitals and the 'politics of habitat' (1800–1850). The latter explored the effects of cholera on urban life, public health, housing, and the notion of habitat. The town thus emerges as a distinct and persistent feature of Foucault's work, in addition to his more broadly commented upon interests in space (Foucault, [1982a] 2001) or geography (Foucault, [1976] 1980).

In the light of this work, the *Security, Territory, Population* lectures seem to be tracing the genealogies of the modern urban form back to the early modern market town and the arts of government associated with mercantilism, discipline and regulation. Police and the diplomatic-military technological assemblage marked the final preludes to modern apparatuses of security. These apparatuses would not just seek to extract, tax, or organize, nor would they seek to observe, survey and individualize. These *dispositifs* would revel in the circulation of the unknown, but an unknown that was statistically monitored; they would grant freedom to their subjects, but would also distribute the burdens of liberty; they would relinquish control over the minutiae of territory, yet seek to guarantee at every scale the state's territorial security. Securing individual freedom was the hallmark of European liberal *government*, which Foucault discussed, in the first instance, as the government of cities and towns.

Apparatuses of security: the problem of the town

The first three lectures of Foucault's 1978 course addressed the general features of security apparatuses, which were identified in the summary *Governmentality* lecture as the essential mechanisms of the triangle of sovereignty–discipline–government which targeted the population. These apparatuses do not operate through distinguishing and punishing, in the sovereign model, nor do they survey, diagnose, and correct, as with discipline (Foucault, [1978b] 2007, Chapter 1). Rather, security deals with probable events and weighs up an appropriate response in relation to optimal functioning. These three models cannot be completely distinguished, but do have separate techniques, such as the cell in disciplinary institutions, or statistics in security. More generalized than these specific techniques are security technologies, which may use the techniques of discipline or the sovereign juridical model, but use them to address the population, not a group of individuals. Three features of security apparatuses were addressed during the lectures, namely: space (the town); the uncertain (grain and dearth); and normalization (vaccination and smallpox).

Foucault ([1978b] 2007, p. 11) immediately began his discussion of the spaces of security through dismissing a temptingly simple generalization, namely that 'sovereignty is exercised within the borders of a territory, discipline is exercised on the bodies of individuals, and security is exercised over a whole population'. The dismissal was based on the phenomena of the multiplicity. This mass of people denied any notion of a sovereign actually ruling over an unpopulated territory, as it might appear in juridical discourses. Similarly, whilst focusing on individuals, discipline did this in the context of a multiplicity that needed managing, organizing and protecting. As such, all three modes of power and social organization concern multiplicities, yet they each had different approaches to space.

Foucault again returns to the town, in the seventeenth and early eighteenth century, just as the policing arts of government were developing. The town was problematic in its specificity: in terms of law and administration, physical containment, and its socio-economic heterogeneity. It had to be integrated into emerging administrative states, it needed its growing population to be catered for, and it needed to trade with the countryside: 'Broadly speaking, the question was that of the

Table 10.1   Apparatuses of the City

	Period	Power	Space	Features
Le Maître's *La Métropolitée* (plan)	1682	Sovereign	Capitalized	Segments, domination ornamentation
Richelieu	Late 1600s	Discipline	Structured	Hierarchy, enclosure
Nantes	Late 1700s	Security	Circulation	Hygiene, trade, surveillance

spatial, juridical, administrative, and economic opening up of the town, and this was what was at issue in the eighteenth century. Resituating the town in a space of circulation' (ibid., p. 13). This marked the emergence of apparatuses of security, the distinctiveness of which was stressed in the lecture by picking three paradigmatic cities for studying the spatial relations of sovereign, disciplinary and security apparatuses (these cities are not discussed in depth as the lecture has been reprinted as Foucault (2007); see also Rabinow, 1982, and Elden, 2007a). The main features can be summarized as shown in Table 10.1.

Speaking of this new city of security, Foucault ([1978b] 2007, p. 18) commented that '[i]n other words, it was a matter of organizing circulation, eliminating its dangerous elements, making a division between good and bad circulation, and maximizing the good circulation by diminishing the bad.' The aim was that of development, and the means of achieving this sketched out a radically new conception of space and time. First, space was not empty, which would allow the unhampered construction of multiplicities; it was materially constituted by flows of water, air, food and people. Second, authoritarian space would not be constructed; rather the positive elements of its organization would just be maximized. Third, the poly-functionality of the city was acknowledged: filled with simultaneous spaces of health, trade, riot, and sociability. Finally, security in the town was shown to work on an unknown future, but one that could be predicted through the calculation of a series of events and their probabilistic recurrence. The space of this recurrence is the *milieu*, the environment which supports actions of one body on another. The milieu is both natural (rivers or hills) and artificial (individuals or houses) and is a space of positive and negative feedbacks:

> The milieu is a certain number of effects that are mass effects bearing on all who live in it. It is an element within which a circular link is

produced between effects and causes, since what it is an effect on one side will become a cause on the other.

(ibid., p. 21)

This necessarily affects the nature of intervention, as infrastructures now have to target not a legal subject or a performing individual, but a population:

> I mean a multiplicity of individuals who are and fundamentally and essentially only exist profoundly, essentially, biologically bound to the materiality within which they live. What one tried to reach through this milieu, is precisely the conjunction of a series of events produced by these individuals, populations, and groups, and quasi natural events which occur around them.
>
> (ibid., p. 21)

Yet what the new lectures furnish governmentality theory with is a description of socio-spatial relationships that retain the power of panoptic subjectivization but are more open, less subject to surveillance, and less amenable to the sovereign's manipulation. Security moves from an art of governmental objects to a science of governmental processes through its orchestration of population geography (Legg, 2005). The following two apparatuses of security (dearth–grain and epidemic–contagion) detail these orchestrations of space and subjects, and are unified by their puzzling over the problem of the town:

> The town as market is also the town as place of revolt; the town as a centre of diseases is the town as the site of miasmas and death. Anyway, it really is the problem of the town that is, I think, at the heart of these different examples of mechanisms of security.
>
> (Foucault, [1978b] 2007, pp. 63–4)

Foucault (ibid., Chapter 5) stressed not only that sovereign, disciplinary, and security techniques continued to inform each other, but that it was the territorial sovereign who was the architect of disciplinary space and the regulator of milieus. In relation to this, the second security apparatus Foucault studied addressed dearth, a scarcity of food that led to positive feedbacks which worsened the scarcity. This was a problem for the sovereign not just in terms of public health, but also of public order, through the riots that dearth produced. The response of the police model was to prevent shortage through monetary controls, banning hoardings of grain, and permanent supervision. These mercantilist anti-dearth policies were unsuccessful, as peasants were impoverished by artificially low grain prices and thus could not sow as much grain, increasing the likelihood of future dearth.

The security response was embodied in the physiocratic doctrines of the mid-eighteenth century that laid the foundations of political-economic thought and attacked the regulatory assemblages of the police. A belief in free circulation was argued for by appealing to the reality of the grain, to its conditions of growth and fluctuations in supply. Thus, price rises would be accepted, for they would direct money to the peasantry, who would invest in the land and reduce prices through increased supply, while also decreasing the chance of further dearth.

Thus, in accordance with the spaces of the city, but applied to rural land, the space of security is centrifugal and integrative, not centripetal as with the enclosure and partitioning of discipline. While discipline and the police sought to regulate everything, security lets things happen. While discipline forbids and permits, security observes what takes place and instils an infrastructure that can work with this reality and encourages its components to work together. While law prohibits and discipline prescribes, security regulates a geography that it accepts and moulds itself around. This grants a freedom to pre-existing socio-spatial relations, but it also grants freedom to its subjects as the founding act in the great game of liberalism that has found its fullest flourishing in what we know now as neo-liberalism (Foucault, [1979b] 2008; see also Barry *et al.*, 1996). This freedom was *produced*, and was thus historically and geographically specific. This was woefully apparent to colonial populations who were placed under programmes of 'civilization' that constantly deferred the benefits of European liberty. Yet, beyond the political-philosophical denial of 'liberty', other apparatuses of security took shape in colonial cities, governing movement so as to create an orderly, profitable and clean city.

The final security apparatus concerned the successful smallpox vaccination that linked statistical knowledge to other mechanisms of security (Foucault, [1978b] 2007, Chapter 3). Cases of the disease were plotted through time and space, not in association with people or miasmas. Calculations were made of the risk of catching the disease which could be used to plot zones of risk. Yet the aim would not be to eradicate disease, but to restore its recurrence to normal levels. The norm here is a distribution of death, not a healthy subject.

Epidemiological zones of risk naturally centred on urban forms, around which the technology of securities had appeared by the mid-eighteenth century (ibid., p. 64). They allowed the population to be considered as an object of political government in a new manner. The mercantilist and cameralist (police) arts of government of the sixteenth century *had* considered population, but only as the dynamic of state force that had to be increased: the labour behind the harvest; the manpower behind manufacturing; the competition behind low prices. The population thus needed regulation and discipline. The physiocrats of the eighteenth century envisaged the population not just as a mass of sovereign subjects, but as a set of natural processes. These processes varied with material surroundings and thus not only *would* they not obey sovereign orders, they *could* not.

Yet this nature was not impenetrable to infrastructural regulation. It could be transformed by calculations and regulations of factors which affected the population, such as currency, exports and imports. The sovereign thus had to deploy reflected procedures of government within nature. The population was certainly not immune from violence, as Foucault's (1979b) later brief remarks on genocide and Dean's (2002) comments on the dark side of biopolitics suggest. Indeed, it is only with the emergence of the mechanisms of security–population–government that the field of politics, as we know it, emerged (Foucault, [1978b] 2007, p. 76).

This field marked a new governmentality, which Foucault (ibid., Chapter 13) returned to summarize in his last lecture. This emerged against the police state not on the jurist objection of infringement of rights by the sovereign, but through the physiocratic critique of the mercantilist and cameralist art of government. In the case of grain and dearth, physiocrats argued for high grain prices in the belief that the 'just price' would be created by the natural processes of free trade, just as population would arrive at the optimum rate in relation to its territory. This was against the police regulation that sought low prices in fear of continually rising cost and the largest population to decrease labour wages.

This new approach to security introduced the fundamental lines of modern and contemporary governmentality. While it still operated within the bounds of state reason, seeking a European balance and internal order, it modified this reason in five key ways. First, it acknowledged the naturalness of processes that were external to the state, such as society, economy and population (on the scalar logic informing this emerging concept of domains, see Legg, 2009b). Second, these processes could be accessed by scientific knowledge, such as sociology, political-economy and demography. Third, the latter scientific discipline sought knowledge of the population as a reality that was affected by wages and work levels, but which also possessed its own laws – the fourth innovation – that could not be targeted by the regulation of individuals. Rather, it could be influenced by intervention that targeted the population, via social medicine or public hygiene, for instance. These constituted the mechanisms of security, the fifth modification, that would ensure that natural processes of population regulation worked, or that clumsy intervention did not make them veer off course:

> The fundamental objective of governmentality will be mechanisms of security, or, let's say, it will be state intervention with the essential function of ensuring the security of the natural phenomena of economic processes or processes intrinsic to population.
>
> (Foucault, [1978b] 2007, p. 349)

While such mechanisms did not act directly on the individual, the withdrawal from natural processes inevitably meant a liberal reduction in subject regulation. This was one of the elements of the new governmentality, besides society, economy, population, and security. The state did not withdraw in the face of these new realities, but reorganized the nature of government as intervention, not regulation. This was achieved through economy, population management, respect for liberties, and apparatuses of police (reduced to a negative function in relation to crime), diplomacy and the military. This does not suggest a benevolent state, or one that was not resisted. Foucault stressed the importance of modern counter-conducts that would use these new elements, posing society against state, error against economic truth, collective against private interests, the living reality of the population against its processes, danger against security, and liberty against rules and regulations: that is, civil society, the population, or the nation against the state.

These reflections on the town, and the modern urban form more generally, could be of great interest to postcolonial scholars. There is a re-emerging emphasis on colonial urbanism, for instance, which has replaced an earlier centrality on cities as places of economic exploitation with an emphasis on power relations and government (Çelik, 1997; Hazareesingh, 2007; Kidambi, 2007), often in explicitly Foucauldian terms (Yeoh, 1996; Legg, 2007b; Glover, 2008). But the lectures also have much to say about Empire and imperialism, if not colonialism, directly.

Europe and Empire

Postcolonial scholarship has long insisted upon the constitutive role of Europe's colonial outside: from Said's ([1978] 1995; 1993) discipline-founding assertion of the importance of the colonial Other to the

European Self; to the new imperial history's emphasis on blurring the core–periphery boundary (Hall, 2000; 2002; Wilson, 2004); to the contested discussion of imperial sexuality (Hyam, 1990; Stoler, 1995; Howell, 2000b; Levine, 2004). Yet within this scholarship has been a recurrent objection to the *lack* of a colonial vision in Foucault's previously published work (Legg, 2007a). His discussion of Europe is contiguous with the discovery of the Americas and the beginning of the Spanish and Portuguese ages of empire in the New World, to be followed by the French and English led colonization of the Old. The changes in Europe that the new biopower had to adapt to could be said to result not just from the breakdown of feudal order, but also from the financial, material, geopolitical, and imaginary intrusion into, and exploitation of, the colonial outside.

On the basis of Foucault's published work, a somewhat weak claim has been made that the smattering of references to colonialism denote a consideration of its importance (see Foucault, 1961, p. iv; 1972, p. 210; [1975–6] 2003, p. 103; 1977a, pp. 29, 314; [1979b] 2008, Chapter 6; 1980, pp. 17, 77; 2006, Chapter 4). A stronger claim has been made by Ann Laura Stoler (1997) that the *Society Must be Defended* lectures (Foucault, [1975–6] 2003), along with the *History of Sexuality* vol. I (Foucault, 1979a), suggest the formative role of race and imperial circuits of power-knowledge for the European bourgeoisie. It is in the spirit of both of these claims that I would like to provide a brief postcolonial reading of *Security, Territory, Population*. This will rest on two claims: that the lectures are saturated with the idea of *Europe* as post-imperial space; and that embedded in Europe's negotiation of this status was a geopolitical sensibility founded upon colonial space.

Post-imperial Europe

> In other words, the two great forms of universality, Empire and Church, which, in the case of the Empire at least, had for a number of years, for decades and maybe centuries, no doubt become a sort of empty envelope, an empty shell, but which still retained their power of focalization, attraction, and intelligibility, these two great forms of universality had lost their vocation and meaning, at least at the level of this universality. This is the reality on which the principle that we exist within a politically open and multiple state space is articulated.
>
> (Foucault, [1978b] 2007, p. 291)

Foucault's ([1975–6] 2003) *Society Must be Defended* lectures pose the birth of discipline and biopolitics as a result of post-*feudal* demographic and industrial change. The *Security, Territory, Population* lectures, in contrast, situate the emergent arts of government as an explicitly post-*imperial* phenomenon. The Holy Roman Empire and the unchallenged authority of the Catholic Church had been 'the two great poles of historical-religious sovereignty that dominated the West and promised salvation, unity, and the fulfilment of time' (Foucault, [1978b] 2007, p. 229). As such:

> The time of the Middle Ages was still one that, at a certain moment, had to become unified as the universal time of an Empire in which all differences would be effaced, and this universal Empire will herald and be the theatre of Christ's return. The Empire, the last Empire, the universal Empire, whether of the Caesars or of the Church, was something that haunted the medieval perspective, and to that extent there was no indefinite government.
>
> (ibid., p. 260)

Although successfully married under the banners of temporal and spiritual universalism, the Church and secular Empire had remained distinct as mystical pastor and imperial sovereign (ibid., p. 155). The denouement of this union came with the end of the post-Reformation hundred years of political and religious struggle (c.1555–1648) which had seen 'German' states fight to free themselves from the 'yoke of imperial pre-eminence' (and which Schmitt ([1950] 2003, p .57), described as the collapse of the *Respublica Christiana*, precipitating the formation of a new European world-*nomos*). These revolts of conduct can thus plausibly be posited as anti-colonial, rejecting the papal authority of the Vatican, or the peripatetic authority of the Holy Roman Emperor.

It was from this collapse of imperial sovereignty that the need for a balance of power in Europe arose between self-asserting and purposive bodies in 'multiple state space' (Foucault, [1978b] 2007, p. 290). Peace could be conceived without the over-arching unification of a temporal or spiritual imperialism; indeed, the arts of government consciously sought to avoid the rise and fall of another empire (ibid., p. 289; [1979b] 2008, p. 6). The succeeding order was embodied in the 1648 Treaty of Westphalia which established each sovereign as emperor in their own domain in an order of different but not hierarchical states (see Elden, 2005, for a discussion of the actual complexities of the Treaty of Westphalia). Imperial unity thus gave way to the society of nations.

Therefore, all of the processes hereby described in this chapter can be considered to be responding to the reverberations of a collapsing imperial compact between Church and Empire. This Empire had exerted its influence through the aesthetic, ideology, and domination associated with 'imperialism' (Said, 1993, p. 8). It was also an Empire forged through conquest and violent suppression over a thousand years before, and as such can also be considered very much a colonial edifice (see Jones and Phillips, 2005, on pre-modern empires). Yet Foucault also outlined a much more direct role for colonialism in the forging of post-imperial Europe.

Post-imperial colonialism

> We are now dealing with absolute units, as it were, with no subordination or dependence between them ... in a space of increased, extended, and intensified economic exchange. They seek to assert themselves in a space of commercial competition and domination, in a space of monetary circulation, colonial conquest, and control of the seas.
>
> (Foucault, [1978b] 2007, p. 291)

State reason's emphasis on expansion in a space of competition can be seen as a post-imperial reality. The 'balance of Europe' did little to satiate this expansionist desire, but colonialism did. The very problem of the conduct of conduct was said to arise between two movements: one to devise spiritual guidance in the wake of the Reformation, the other, 'the process that, dismantling feudal structures, organizes and sets up the great territorial, administrative, and colonial states' (ibid., pp. 88–89). Spain was the earliest exemplar, aggregating itself a 'more or less worldwide quasi-monopolistic colonial and maritime empire' (ibid., p. 292), but finding itself vulnerable to more spectacular and rapid collapses than the Holy Roman Empire before it. There are also passing references to other colonial contexts in the lectures: to the experimentation with statistics in Ireland due to its military occupation by England, and a brief mention of the Quakers in America. There is even an acknowledgement of the formative framing nature of colonialism. Referring to the calculation of forces:

> You can see that this development that takes place entirely on the basis of a historical reality and identifiable historical processes – the discovery of America, the constitution of colonial empires, the

disappearance of the Empire, and the withdrawal, the fading away of the universal functions of the Church.

(ibid., p. 295)

From this context, Europe emerged not just with an historical determination towards colonialism, but with a hunger for economic domination, colonization or commercial utilization: the only type of relationship that Europe would have with the rest of the world. The thought that was formed at the end of the sixteenth and beginning of the seventeenth century, which crystallized in the middle of the seventeenth century with the set of treaties signed at that time, and which:

> is the historical reality that is still not behind us ... that of Europe as a geographical region of multiple states, without unity but with differences between the big and small and having a relationship of utilization, colonization, and domination with the rest of the world. That is what Europe is.

(ibid., p. 354)

Unlike the dismantling of the police model of the sixteenth to seventeenth centuries, the diplomatic-military apparatus that emerged in the post-imperial but thoroughly colonizing space of Europe was said to have hardly changed since the eighteenth century. This system weighed upon the distribution and ordering of forces in the emergent European states, even after the mercantilist and cameralist regulatory forces had been replaced by the interventionist apparatuses of security.

These ideas were expanded upon in the *Birth of Biopolitics* lectures when Foucault briefly diverted his attentions outside of Europe. Three characteristics of the liberal art of government were listed: the problem of economic truth and the truth of the market; limiting government by the question of utility; and, finally, 'international equilibriums, or Europe and the international space in liberalism' (Foucault, 2008 [1978–9], p. 51). Liberalism is posed as supplanting the mercantilist belief that the wealth of one state could only increase at the cost of another with the idea of mutual enrichment and unlimited economic progress. But, this would require permanent and continuous inputs:

> It is necessary to summon around Europe, and for Europe, an increasingly extended market and even, if it comes to it, everything in the world that can be put on the market. In other words, we are invited to a globalization of the market when it is laid down as a principle,

and an objective, that the enrichment of Europe must be brought about as a collective and unlimited enrichment, and not through the enrichment of some and impoverishment of others.

(ibid., p. 55)

Europe itself thus emerges as a player on the world market, whereas the rest of the world becomes the stake. Foucault suggests that these developments around the middle of the eighteenth century were later than colonialism but earlier than imperialism, and should thus be thought of as 'a new form of global rationality, of a new calculation on the scale of the world'(Foucault, ibid., p. 56).

Despite this clear statement that colonialism was at the very core of the constitution of Europe itself, and continued to define what Europe *was*, there is no continued analysis of the colonial experience in either of the lecture series. This marks conformity between Foucault and liberal thought through a failure to expose the dependency of the liberal dream of perpetual growth on the expropriation of the rest of the world (Cooper, 2004, p. 521; also Venn, 2009). This was viewed not only as a free space of competition, but as an empty space of acquisition and, as such, a colonized zone administered as the new, interstate, Eurocentric, spatial order of the earth (Schmitt, [1950] 2003, p. 140). In the colonies, modern governmentalities were articulated with greater degrees of violence, a slighter disciplinary archipelago and a form of government that appears more akin to the regulation of police than the distanced intervention of liberalism (Legg, 2007b, p. 25). As such, while these lectures expand on the very limited extent to which Foucault had considered imperial or colonial relations in previous work, there is still much work for postcolonial scholars to do in relating this body of work to the burgeoning field of colonial governmentality studies and, perhaps, reading these suggestions alongside Foucault's comments on urban security to imagine some innovate approaches to studying colonial urbanism. Just as the governmentality work has been adapted to a host of scales and environments beyond its original application, so a postcolonial reading of the 1978 lectures suggests myriad potentially productive applications. Among the many provocative questions raised by the lectures, I would like to conclude with the following:

- How did apparatuses of security operate in the colonial realm? What was the nature of colonial governmentality?
- To what extent did anti-colonial movements form thoroughgoing revolts of conduct? If so, do the five forms of medieval counter-conduct (ascetism, communities, mysticism, scripture, and eschatology)

have parallels in appeals to pre-colonial traditions by anti-colonial nationalist?

- How did nationalists make claims over the actual apparatus of security, rather than just over political sovereignty?
- Were the post-imperial geopolitical experiences of sixteenth-century Europe similar in any way to those of de-colonized territories in the twentieth century?
- Rather than being simply comparable to colonialism, are the origins of neo-liberalism to be found in the colonial experience?

Acknowledgements

This chapter was originally presented at the 'Political infrastructures: governing the fabric of the city' workshop held at the Open University in April 2006. It has benefited greatly from comments on an early draft by Stuart Elden and Gerry Kearns.

11
The geography of theory
Knowledge, politics and the postcolonial present

Tariq Jazeel

As a formulation, *postcolonial spaces* clearly has much critical purchase in terms of the colonial spatial presents and continuing inequalities it is positioned to make visible. But just as we can turn critical postcolonial thought towards the traces of colonialism in our geographical present, at a time when the world is being remade by globalization, there is also a need to turn critical thought towards critical intellectual praxis itself. In this chapter I depart from the premise that working effectively through the term *postcolonial spaces* necessitates due attention to the spatialities inherent in any critical theoretical language and praxis so implicated in the metropolitan and Euro-American academy.[1] My concern is to work through some of the geographies of the theory culture that drives academic knowledge production. Specifically, I aim to unpick the spatial politics of theoretical knowledges demarcated by monikers such as 'postcolonialism' in what is an increasingly corporate and unequally global academic knowledge production complex.

Uncovering the Eurocentrism of the theory cultures that pervade academic knowledge is of course not new. Subaltern Studies scholarship has sought in different ways to uncover the European squint of archives of world history and knowledge (see Guha, 1982, [1983] 1999; Chakrabarty, 2002), and in a world continually being remade by transnational flows of different varieties and paces, it remains a fact that postcolonial and other modes of critical theoretical scholarship proceed in an unevenly global landscape of academic knowledge production. What I am concerned with here are the theory cultures that drive disciplinary and interdisciplinary debates and conversations. I write from a dual positioning. First, I engage with these concerns as a disciplinary social scientist – a human geographer – whose ongoing work and thoughts around identity, difference and the politics of 'nature' in Sri Lanka have profited greatly from postcolonial theoretical interventions with the spatial (see Jazeel, 2005). Simultaneously, I write as an invited contributor to this important collection that thematizes the postcolonial spatial as theory object. In the context of this dual positioning, I am particularly interested in the spatial politics of knowledge that emerges from theory-driven constellations across a transnational academic landscape in which university space aggressively territorializes theory but in which many of us also continue to work on place. How can academic practitioners think and work humanely and responsibly through the geographies of theoretical praxes (like postcolonialism) in which we are inevitably immersed, as we simultaneously seek productive and progressive engagements with 'field' spaces? In this context, how can postcolonial scholarship itself proceed effectively in the light of an awareness of some its own iniquitous spatial presents? In pursuing such questions, it is absolutely my intention to take seriously this volume's awareness of an inherent spatiality in postcolonial theory, but I do so by signalling some thoughts about what an awareness of the geography of theory might mean for practitioners of postcolonial criticism.

To be clear, forcing the postcolonial as theoretical object is what I seek to avoid in this chapter. As I elaborate below, it is precisely the reification of 'postcolonialism' as a theoretical canon that perennially runs the risk of consolidating the contours of something as dogmatically defined as 'postcolonial theory'. But it is also worth stressing that *if* a postcolonial endeavour seeks a critical engagement with the lingering traces and inequalities of colonial encounter and anti-colonial nationalism in the present, then to that goal this chapter is firmly committed. In the context of critically engaging the spatiality of postcolonial criticism itself, then, it is my contention that degrees of theoretical ambivalence and practical introspection are required: what Edward Said (1983, pp. 1–30; 1994) refers to as an exilic disposition toward critical praxis itself, a readiness to intellectually shift one's orientation in the pursuit of a politics grounded in place. In this sense, this chapter is written as a methodological meditation on 'strategies' of critical praxis in disciplinary contexts and the theory cultures employed in them, within unevenly global landscapes of knowledge production.

In the next section of the chapter, I sketch more fully some of the contours of an unevenly global landscape of academic knowledge production that characterizes our postcolonial present. My concern here is to outline what I refer to as the 'shape of knowledge' that emerges within contemporary transnational academic space, and in doing so to suggest some of the spatial politics of the teleology of contemporary theory culture, particularly within the disciplinary social sciences and humanities. In the following two sections, I more squarely address two particular aspects of the academic knowledge production process that, I suggest, Euro-American researchers might, usefully, carefully think through in relation to theory culture as a way of honing effective modes of critical intellectual praxis in this global postcolonial moment: the politics of abstraction, and the mechanics of representation. Working through both, I suggest, affords a valuable way of attending to the cultural geographies and spatial politics of critical theoretical projects.

Sketching the present: globalization and the geographies of knowledge

Globalization has preoccupied the Euro-American academic world for at least three decades now. A phenomenon as troubling socially and politically as it can be hopeful, globalization research and commentary have become familiar terrain for social scientists, literary and cultural theorists and political scientists alike. Yet globalization does not just impinge on academic space as a phenomenon to be critically researched. It also constitutes and continually remakes the shifting transnational landscapes in which academic knowledge production takes place (see Appadurai, 2000b; Mohanty, 2003, pp. 169–89). The implications of this are acknowledged to varying degrees across university faculties and disciplines, and it is perhaps fair to say that those scholars engaged in the business of thinking through colonialism's own discursive and material footprints are some of those most familiar with the effects of globalization's uneven contemporary cartography on academic knowledge production.

As Arjun Appadurai has pointed out, the 1950s and 1960s were the high points of a somewhat expansive faith in the confident notion that theory and method were naturally modern, metropolitan and Western. This coincided with high modernization theories that instantiated teleological readings/renderings of a world in which less developed regions were thought to play catch up to the West's modernity. Marxist critiques, despite their criticality, did little to refute that sense of a world cartographically bifurcated into a theory-rich west and the rest of the world construed more or less as field: 'The rest of the world was seen in the idiom of cases, events, examples, and test sites in relation to this stable location for the production or revision of theory' (Appadurai, 2000b, p. 4). As Appadurai goes on to remark, however, this faith has gradually dissipated among critical social theorists. The reconstitution of Area Studies in a post-Cold War era (Miyoshi and Harootunian, 2002), Lyotardian suspicions of master narratives, and subalternist revisions to South Asian historiographies have been among those intellectual developments that have played their role in establishing a rather more reflective take on the exclusions effected through a Eurocentric hegemony in the global circuits of academic knowledge production, especially in terms of theory culture. The development of postcolonial perspectives have also played their own role in such revisionings, as they have constituted some of the most productively unsettling engagements with globalization thought simply as high modernization (see Gikandi, 2001).

Despite these critical intellectual developments, the infrastructures through which the knowledge we call theory is produced takes place in a world that still bears the imprints and inequities of globalization. The production of academic scholarship itself is embedded within a geography marked by the residual asymmetries of power emerging from both colonialism and neo-colonialism. In this section I want to roughly delineate some practical and conceptual effects of our own embeddedness within this global postcolonial moment; in particular, I sketch what I take to be an unevenly global geography that characterizes the present condition of transnational academic knowledge production. Doing so suggests exactly why, in this global postcolonial moment, it is necessary to turn the interventionary and critical postcolonial gaze of this volume back on itself, to introspectively interrogate university space and the cultural geographies of theory that pervade metropolitan criticism, precisely in order to work toward what the geographer Jenny Robinson has called 'a reconfigured field of the transnational production of scholarship in which entrenched power relations (of different kinds) and dominant geopolitical relations can be dispersed in the interests of new kinds of productive engagement' (2003, p. 274).

Chandra Talpade Mohanty's recent reflection on the US academy within globalization offers a useful and provocative take on the politics of twenty-first-century academic knowledge production. She refers to the university's role in the commoditization of knowledge amidst a landscape of global capitalism. Research in the US university (and I would add, the Euro-American university more generally) revolves around the business of producing knowledge, and knowledge – including theory – has thereby become a marketable commodity; intellectual property is both owned and sponsored (Mohanty, 2003, p. 173; see also Rennie-Short, 2002, pp. 23–4). It remains true that the professional criteria that determine grant funding, as well as the processes and codas that arbitrate on the 'quality' of research output are located historically, epistemologically and geographically (particularly in the social sciences) (Jazeel, 2009). Western-based academics working on texts, materialities and contexts situated variously in the Global South are invariably positioned and subjectivized by this landscape of global capitalism. Paraphrasing Stanley Aronowitz (2000), research emerges from universities that are structured as 'knowledge factories'.

As a tenured academic who has enjoyed the secure footing of the Euro-American academy, it seems a perverse and bourgeois contradiction to complain about this global knowledge economy. Profound privileges come attached to the Euro-American academy: access to grant-funding, free or cheap access to bibliographical resources, the safe space and time that academic salaries afford to think and work intellectually, and conference funding, to name just a few. All of which I continue to benefit from. Indeed, Mohanty prefaces her critique of the political economy of an increasingly corporatized US academy by reminding the reader that the academy is 'one of the few remaining spaces in a rapidly privatized world that offers some semblance of a public arena for dialogue, engagement, and visioning of democracy and justice' (2003, p. 170). These are privileges that those of us who enjoy them should not easily forget.

Despite these privileges, what I want to signal with these observations on globalization and academic knowledge production are some of the resultant geographical orientations of critical intellectual praxis and their potential effects, because this unevenly globalizing knowledge economy has both practical and conceptual effects on research and critical theoretical praxis. Foremost, it affects what knowledge is produced from within that capitalist, transactional landscape. This is not to argue against professional mechanisms like peer review or any of the other criteria, checks and balances that help shape high quality knowledge production. But it is to suggest that precisely because of the political economy of an increasingly corporatized university system, it is difficult for research (readings, analyses, theoretical interventions) to be determined solely by a utopian or exilic commitment to a politics accountable to the places about which we write. Critical praxis itself is immersed in an unevenly globalizing geography toward which the corporate university increasingly leans, and any kind of critical postcolonial engagement with the spatial must continue to take these geographies and their effects on knowledge production seriously.

As well as a slew of resulting practical concerns and questions relating to the politics of academic community formation – who gets funded, who gets access to journals and other bibliographical resources, who is able to enter the space of critical conversation itself, for example – the unequal globalization of academic knowledge production also raises a series of related, more epistemological issues concerning the *shape* of theoretical knowledge itself. Such concerns are not new. They emerge with various critiques of modernity's Eurocentrism.[2] However, I want to pick them up because it seems to me that sounding some warnings about the 'shape of theoretical knowledge' produced *about* the rest of the world from within the corporate, largely western, academy is precisely what can enable further discussion of the rather more careful and introspective processes necessarily required for simultaneously humble and effective modes of critical thought and engagement. Something like postcolonial intervention, in other words, has much to gain from engaging the geographies of critical theoretical praxis itself.

In his recent engagement with the complexities of 'global comparativism', Aamir Mufti (2005) provides a striking analysis of the hierarchical epistemological systems that have come to dominate cultural life since the colonial era. In a clarion call for *creativity* in the research process, he draws attention to the Eurocentrism that regulates 'theory' as 'a discrete set of practices' (ibid., p. 475). Mufti's goal is to encourage contrapuntal modes of reading, analysis and criticism such that the critic might step outside the embedded theoretical conventions that have coagulated in the corporate spaces of the western academy. Doing so is not a voguish invitation to write *new* theoretical paradigms. Rather, it is posed as a challenge to bring incommensurable difference (that is to say, ordinary texts written in scripts unfamiliar to western theory) into representation on terms true to the singularity of their difference. In other words, this is a call to make visible the implicit comparisons (the comparativisms), and thereby erasures, embedded in the epistemic paradigms through which 'theory culture' sees the world and makes its critical interventions.

This, of course, is no easy task. To illustrate the complexity and challenge of this kind of epistemic and critical creativity, Mufti draws on one powerful moment in the Sudanese author Tayeb Salih's novel *Season of Migration to the North* (1969; hereafter *SOMN*). The passage that concerns him is set in Sudan toward the end of the novel, in a remote village on the banks of the Nile, where the narrator – a native of the village, who has recently returned from England with a PhD in English poetry – encounters a locked room in the house of the novel's main character. For Mufti, 'it is the jarring juxtaposition of what [the narrator] ... discovers in this room, in this mud house in this village on the banks of the river Nile in the heart of Africa' (2005, p. 479) that speaks directly to the epistemological problematic that global postcolonial culture poses. For in this locked room is a perfect replica of an English study and sitting room, with books, books everywhere. Books on Astronomy through to Zoology, reference works like the *Encyclopaedia Britannica*, authors from Hardy to Woolf, philosophers from More through Wittgenstein, even The Qur'an and Bible in English. But not a single Arabic book. And as the narrator remarks, the room is at once 'A prison. A huge joke. A treasure chamber' (ibid., p. 480). Of course, what both Mufti and Salih show us is the face of that unevenly globalizing knowledge economy that structures the habitus of a knowledge production and theory culture that remain deeply Eurocentric. Knowledge of the non-West is available only through this painfully out-of-place library, in English, as Mufti writes '*in translation*, assigned its place as Oriental text-object within the architecture of the Western library' (ibid., p. 480).

This matters for a couple of reasons. First, as much of the recent work on alternative modernities has shown (Gaonkar, 2001; Chakrabarty, 2002; Johnson, 2007), the theoretical languages that drive predominantly Eurocentric modes of critical disciplinary inquiry are often not commensurable with the social and political formations in place, especially in the Global South, that academics might seek to engage. *SOMN* poses a question about whether any of those books in that library can effectively 'speak to' the pressing social and political questions that abound in that place specifically. Probably. But as I discuss below, probably only partially, because the library stands for the ghettoization of knowledge. It stands for Eurocentric theory culture's abstractions – knowledge's organization and categorization according to the patinas of European modernity. In the corporate academy, difference, such as it is, is increasingly made to respond to – and be read through – the categories brought into play by European thought. It is not insignificant in this sense that *SOMN*'s narrator has returned from England with a PhD in English poetry, for his specialization and qualification as literary 'expert' are dependent upon his own migration to, and training in, the heart of empire. *SOMN* is a reminder that critically intervening in new contexts requires equal degrees of creativity, humility and uncertainty. It requires working with the awareness that any answer, moreover any question, that the library can generate is only a repetition of existent ways of thinking (Said, 1983, pp. 111–25; Allen, 2003). Mufti's thoughts around this epistemic bind of a 'global comparativism' within which we all must work remind us that knowledge needs to work hard, and creatively so, to iteratively serve the singular, to not be afraid of the unverifiable.

Most of all, he reminds us that knowledge must set new understandings and possibilities to work. It is worth adding here that though I focus predominantly on criticism practised from and within the Western academy (or as I refer to it in this chapter, the Euro-American academy), epistemologically we (meaning scholars positioned across the Global North and South) are *all* Eurocentric in terms of the theory cultures that incarnate globalizing landscapes of academic knowledge production. The very out-of-place-ness of the library in *SOMN* suggests how

> Humanistic culture is saturated with this informal developmentalism – a 'first in the West, and then elsewhere' structure of global time … – in which cultural objects from non-western societies can be grasped only with reference to the categories of European cultural history, as pale or partial reflections.
>
> (Mufti, 2005, p. 474)

Second, Mufti's warnings about the shape of knowledge produced within this global postcolonial moment matter simply because in a world where research proliferates as one of the dominant modes of contemporary knowledge production (academic or otherwise), it is important to remember that research *is* the optic through which we typically find out about something (Appadurai, 2000b, p. 9). So, each time we are enjoined as 'theorists' or 'scholars' to contribute to particular intellectual debates, our research is invariably coaxed in a certain direction. We may, for example, have to focus on 'cosmopolitanism', 'nature', 'religion', 'space', 'materiality', 'subjectivity', or other debates that drive our disciplines. Then it is also true that as the knowledge we produce is coaxed in that direction, we produce place in a particular kind of way, through those essential conceptual categorizations. In other words, we write place through our research. Conceived this way, the world simultaneously emerges with our knowledge of it (a point to which I return in some detail below). Recognition of this inalienable connection to place demands some thought on how to proceed critically, theoretically and responsibly as a professional academic in this unequally global moment. As a way of elaborating on this, I turn now to two particular aspects of academic knowledge production: the politics of abstraction and the representational mechanics of theory culture. Thinking these through as we go about the process of knowledge production is, I suggest, a step towards engaging the cultural geographies of theory culture in the service of fashioning hopeful futures at this global postcolonial conjuncture.

Abstraction

As I have suggested so far, knowledge production in the globalizing spaces of the increasingly corporate academy is just as much the production of commodity attached to tangible rewards like promotion, tenure, salary and professional standing, as it is a process of dialogue, intellectual engagement and democratic envisioning. Epistemologically as well, global landscapes of academic knowledge production play an influential role in shaping demands regarding which debates we are enjoined to contribute to. These debates can often be quite particular to, and located in, disciplinary contexts. For example, my own research on the politics of human relationships within the environment in Sri Lanka acquires currency within my discipline – human geography – for its broader contribution to understandings of the geographies of nature, or perhaps even postcolonial natures (Jazeel, 2005). To be sure, these kinds of disciplinary demands are important intellectually as well as pedagogically. The privilege of learning and tackling (through teaching as well as research) the philosophical and political conundrums of our time from a kaleidoscopically worldly array of perspectives is not just part of what many of us academics hold most dear about our jobs, it is also something we should strive to protect for it is central to the intellectual freedom that propels the dynamism of knowledge production.

But the very teleology of these kinds of privilege and disciplinary/ theoretical demand can signal simultaneous movements away from the spaces of public accountability in which our research is mired in the first place. Increasingly, in disciplinary contexts theory makes its own kinds of space whose smooth insularity can easily abstract us from a 'field' located elsewhere, especially for those of us working somehow *in* the Global North, *on* the South.[3] The 'field', however we may construe that space, has its own politics, urgencies, necessities, to which anyone who has a relationship with it is also in some sense responsible. But to orient one's iterations toward the corpus of a discipline-bound theory culture whose own maps betray the Euro-American squint and power structures of the twenty-first-century corporate academy, does not necessarily require the very same rigour, care and discipline that engaging the politics, urgencies and necessities of the 'field' demand. Another way of putting this is that if we are located as academics within the unevenly global spaces of the corporate academy, it is worth remembering that we are also located within the spaces and communities – the 'fields' – in which we do our research. The two locations, however, are not always intellectually commensurate.

There is an unavoidable tension then between the demands of a kind of place-based knowledge production more associated with the new (and old) Area Studies (see Miyoshi and Harootunian, 2002), and the dynamism of (inter)discipline-bound theory culture that prefers a vague familiarity with a litany of case studies over in-depth, contextual knowledge and sustained engagement with any one single place.[4] This tension should not be taken to be disabling. But it does exist and requires some negotiation as part of the challenge of responsible critical praxis. A large part of negotiating this tension means confronting and working through the pitfalls and politics of abstraction – itself one of the Enlightenment's defining tools – and its spectre within corporate academic praxis.

In their treatise on the Enlightenment's dialectic, Theodor Adorno and Max Horkheimer ([1944] 1997, p. 13) remind us of the levelling domination that abstraction implies, of how it makes everything in nature seem repeatable. It is this pretension to the universal validity of philosophic concepts that made abstraction so key to Enlightenment knowledge's own claims to mastery. We are now well aware of the partiality of all forms of knowledge, just as we are cognizant of the predicative structures and operations of (theoretical) language, and accordingly the call for critical theoretical culture to recognize itself as merely a strategic tool for achieving broader intellectual or political ends is familiar, if not standard, practice (see Spivak, 1993, pp. 1–23; Scott, 2004, pp. 1–22). But there is also a certain transcendent currency to particular theoretical debates and languages in any discipline (and across disciplines) that emerges precisely from the corporatization and transnationalism of the academy. For example, to return to my own scholarship on the 'geographies of nature' in Sri Lanka, that very formulation – 'geographies of nature' – constitutes its own relatively smooth knowledge space and community of contributing scholars that depends little on any one place in particular, least of all Sri Lanka. Nor is this knowledge space *necessarily* attendant on the politics of human relationships with the environment in Sri Lanka specifically. To put this rather more bluntly, in seeking to contribute to disciplinary knowledge spaces, the important questions we are confronted with as academics by the peer review mechanism are more frequently 'what contribution does Sri Lanka make to understanding the geographies of nature?' than 'what contribution does geographical scholarship make to understanding the politics, urgencies, necessities in the Sri Lankan context?' Sri Lanka returns as case study.

Let me be clear: in disciplinary contexts, these are important demands, necessary for a whole host of reasons that enable something like an academic 'community' to tackle some of the pressing intellectual, and indeed political, questions of our time. And, furthermore, it is important to stress that in postcolonial literary studies at least, much contemporary work has consciously sought to sensitively ground readings in and through the vagaries of place. My point then is simply that the omnipresent seductions of theory culture and their Euro-American orientations embed the *possibility* and *opportunity* of an easy turning away from place, a turning away that is constitutive of the distance that Adorno and Horkheimer remind us abstraction is dependent upon: 'The distance between subject and object, a presupposition of abstraction, [that is] grounded in the distance from the thing itself which the master achieved through the mastered' ([1944] 1997, p. 13). It not just that it is precisely this distance that can objectify, produce the object as distinct from the subject, and can thereby easily anthropologize place. It is also that this turning away can de-contextualize our theoretical languages so that they obscure more than they reveal, thus blunting their own critical potentials. In terms of postcolonial theory specifically, as Silvio Torres-Saillant (2006, pp. 40–4) has recently stressed in his work on the French and Hispanic Caribbean, postcolonialism's own Anglo-centric paradigm is precisely what displaces and obscures other regional conceptualizations on marginality and colonialism (see Martinez-San, 2009). This is to stress that theoretical languages themselves must be deployed contextually, creatively that is, in order to mobilize *new* understandings and questions that are relevant *in* place.

Returning to my own preoccupations is instructive if only to illustrate this point. For me, one of the more critically productive epistemic shifts in my explorations of the 'geographies of nature' in Sri Lanka has been unmasking the concept 'nature' itself as it can be deployed in this context. The concept 'nature' and its implicit subject–object dualisms in fact make invisible a range of ordinary and commonplace non-binary environmental encounters in the Sri Lankan context. Therefore, a key part of entering into southern Sri Lanka's very different kinds of environmental textuality means being attentive to ways of being-in-the-world wherein the subject–object dualisms implied in the very word 'nature' unravel ontologically. Unmasking 'nature' as concept-metaphor – because even constructivist approaches to 'nature' redeploy the concept precisely *by* seeking to trace 'nature's' construction – draws attention instead to an aesthetics commonly textualized as coterminous with the non-dualistic Buddhist concept dharma, which in turn raises the prospect of a racially marked (Sinhala-Buddhist) hegemony inscribed in those very taken-for-granted human relationships with the environment. The point of this too brief illustration is merely to emphasize that sometimes stepping *out*

of the theoretical space created by certain types of disciplinary episte-
mes enables new critical possibilities.

To be clear, though, posing abstraction as a frame to think through
in order to engage some of the geographies of knowledge production,
particularly in terms of knowledge's orientation, is categorically *not* to
make an argument against abstraction in any sense. Despite its politics
and pitfalls, abstraction is both necessary and unavoidable. As Alberto
Toscano (2008, p. 60) writes, some kind of 'pure abstraction' is precisely
what makes us methodologically capable of comparing two objects,
three objects, even sets of four or five objects, with confident disregard
for their tangible or phenomenological capabilities. In this respect,
abstraction is precisely what enables objects to be held apart from the
world for analysis, and therefore it is an invaluable tool in the transnational research endeavour. In choosing, for example, to employ explicitly comparative research methodologies, or to learn from a multitude
of different and variable 'field' contexts, abstracting objects from their
contingent happenings is absolutely necessary to be able to make visible
points of identification, difference, good practice, or anomaly between
and across those diverse 'case studies'.

Besides its methodological potential, though, scholars like Alfred
North Whitehead and Isabelle Stengers have variously reminded us that
some kind of abstraction is not just inevitable in cognitive activity, it
is actually a requisite for *any* kind of thought or knowledge (Toscano,
2008, pp. 60–6). Such 'real abstractions', as they might be called, occur
each time we conjure the world through the concept-metaphors particular to a language or way of thinking. Thought this way, 'real abstractions' are the *modus operandi* of any culture (including theory culture):
'A thought becoming a *thing*: here is what real abstraction is' (Paulo
Virno, quoted in Toscano, 2008, p. 71). If real abstraction enables *objects*
to be held apart from the chaos of the world, they therein also produce
that world. It seems legitimate here then to ask just how effective our
existent modes and idioms of abstraction are in seeking to adequately
convey a sense of the unfamiliar, or the different. Given the impossibility of avoiding real abstractions, what I am getting at here is a far more
uncertain and contextual process involving an invitation to a 'localized
and risky emergence of abstractions' in all their multiplicity (Toscano,
2008, p. 65). In this particular respect I take Whitehead's remarks that
'A civilization which cannot burst through its current abstractions is
doomed to sterility after a very limited period of progress' (Whitehead,
quoted in Toscano, 2008, p. 65), as entirely coterminous with Mufti's
(2005, p. 482) charge that part of the task of achieving non-repressive

and egalitarian forms of knowledge through critical praxis is to *invent* languages into which to translate practices/objects/formations that come to us already translated as text objects by the Euro centrism of global theory culture or existing epistemic space.

What these thoughts around abstraction warn against is a turning away from (social and political) context, the orienting of our knowledge production within a disciplinary constituency to the degree that it becomes disoriented from its always-already-miredness in 'field' spaces. At one level, 'abstraction' simply means 'withdrawal'. To be more precise on this particular point, it is an illusion of 'withdrawal' that thinking through the politics of abstraction signals, because as I suggest in my comments on representation below, when we write about a place/people/community we are never 'withdrawn' from accountability to context.

Negotiating the politics of abstraction is, of course, not a new challenge for social scientists and humanities scholars alike. Modern critical thought is driven by a suspicion of master narratives as well as calls for superior modes of empiricism. The Subaltern Studies project, for example, emerged precisely as a response to the abstractions of orthodox Marxist historiography. As an attempt to write the history of the Indian colonial and nation-state differently, and subsequently to provincialize the pervasiveness of Euro-American theory culture in shaping our understandings of South Asian realities and politics, the Subaltern Studies collective have worked tirelessly against the tide of universalizing scholarship that, with the best of intentions, persistently turns away from grasping politics in grounded and specific South Asian contexts. The movement is perhaps most instructive methodologically precisely because it is driven by a turning toward geographical context.

It should be evident, however, that turning toward context, toward the 'field' so to speak, is no simple and straightforward retreat from theory. A crucial dimension of intellectual freedom is the right that everyone has to read and to experiment intellectually (the institutional/ financial/digital means and resources available to do so is another question). Rather, a turning toward the 'field' involves what Said refers to as the simple ability to 'see the limits of a theory that begins as a liberating idea but can become a trap of its own' (Said, 1983, p. 238). This is to stress again that all theory is situated in some sense, and as such the seductions of Euro-American theory culture risk becoming theoretical overstatements, parodies of the situations they were originally conceived to remedy, overcome or explain. To use Said's words, as theory travels, there is a risk that should we not adapt, translate, think it in and through context – in short, turn theory toward the 'field', thereby allowing the 'field' itself to write theory over – it might 'move up into a sort of bad infinity' (ibid., p. 239). The notion of 'bad infinity' captures well the real risk of theoretical discourse spiralling away from any kind of accountability to place as it gains its own rhetorical and performative impetus within the corporate academy. In guarding against this kind of abstraction, the goal instead is for a kind of critical consciousness that emerges *from* the recognition of knowledge's always-already locatedness in the field. Turning toward the 'field' can in some sense be construed as no more than a recognition of responsibility and locatedness; it is an opening up of theory toward historical reality, toward society, toward human needs and interests, towards politics and place in a radically contextual manner. If turning toward the field recognizes that knowledge must be effectively set to work in place, it does so only because it recognizes how knowledge is always-already set-to-work in some capacity because of its representational mechanics.

Representation

In a recent meditation on memory, specifically the reconstitution of black memory from archives pieced together anew, the anthropologist David Scott remarks how:

> One way of approaching criticism is to think of it as a dimension of a community's mode of remembering, an exercise, literally and metaphorically, of *re*-membering, of putting back together aspects of our common life so as to make visible what has been excluded, what has been forgotten.
>
> (Scott, 2008, p. vi)

Drawing explicitly on Foucault's *The Archaeology of Knowledge*, Scott mobilizes an understanding of the archive as the discursive and generative condition of knowledge: the archive as constitutive of what can and cannot be said, but also a discursive artifact constituted by what is said. What interests me here is that crucial and inalienable connection between *criticism* and *community* central to Scott's very formulation. It is precisely the inseparability of criticism and community – an inevitability when knowledge is conceived of as Foucauldian 'archive' – that poses a useful insight for the pursuit of effective and responsible critical praxis in this global postcolonial moment. Specifically, Scott's remarks on memory presuppose the critic to be intractably enjoined in communion with the object of her or his analysis. Through the very performance of criticism, the critic always makes him/herself part of a community that itself is attached to the object of analysis. The critic has little choice in this, other than the choice of whether or not to pursue *that* particular research project in the first place. This is the always-already-miredness in the world of research.

Said, famously also drawing on Foucault, was also insistent that just as texts are thought worldly, criticism also is always in and of this world. Working through a miscomprehension about the secondariness of (literary) criticism to its primary object, the text being analyzed, Said was at pains to point out how criticism makes itself part of the present through its very performance:

> For if we assume ... that texts make up what Foucault calls archival facts, the archive being defined as the text's social and discursive presence in the world, then criticism too is another aspect of that present. In other words, rather than being defined by a silent past, commanded by it to speak in the present, criticism, no less than any text, is the present in the course of its articulation, its struggles for definition.
>
> (1983, p. 51)

These connections between criticism and the present conjunction necessarily engender a particular kind of attention or care to how critical praxis is performed, especially in terms of the deployment of theory. I am concerned here with a due attentiveness to the *effects* of knowledge as it is iteratively produced in the light of recognition of the representational mechanics of all critical praxis. That is to say, that if criticism makes itself part of the social, spatial and textual present, then thinking through the representational effects of critical theoretical deployments is a way of being attentive to a broader postcolonial politics of knowledge production.

Though the term 'representation' is more or less foundational for our understanding of literature and culture and though it has a complex semantic history, we can discriminate two basic meanings/understandings of the word. First, there is the constitutive sense of 'represent' as 'making present again', to re-present – *darstellen* – as in the ways the arts or literature (re)produces. Second, there is the more substitutive sense of 'represent' as 'speaking for' – *vertreten* – as in politics, specifically representative democracy (Spivak, 1999, pp. 248–66; Prendergrast, 2000, pp. 1–16). In her own critical intervention into the conversation between Deleuze and Foucault about the actions of practice and theory respectively (Foucault, 1977b, pp. 205–17), Spivak (1999, pp. 248–66) reminds us of the political necessity to recognize that intellectual work – that is, representations of the intellectual – *always* participates in both *darstellen* and *vertreten*. This is in response to Deleuze's conceit regarding the transparence of theory. She quotes him thus: 'A theory is like a box of tools. Nothing to do with the signifier' (Deleuze, quoted in Spivak, 1999, p. 256). It is precisely that transparency and disinterestedness of theory that Spivak is loath to accept in a postcolonial present where European and colonial modernities dwell so pervasively within the languages and infrastructures of transnational academic capitalism. Plainly put, Spivak's rejoinder to Deleuze's assertion that theory is non-representational (in terms of its participation in *darstellen*) is that theory cannot help but ideologically constitute the world on which it reports. Theory – invariably a component of critical praxis – is never a disinterested or transparent relay of the happenings of a world out there. Though we may search for better theoretical languages to bring aspects from our research into representation (my own search for a vocabulary that poses human relationships with the environment in southern Sri Lanka in ways not reducible to the concept-metaphor 'nature' might be one example here), we must also remember that theory also writes the world in its image.

Spivak's reminder about the two different representational mechanics at work in knowledge production's theoretical deployments is useful precisely because it displaces any sense that criticism is *not* intractably enjoined in a constitutive sense with the object of its analysis: a people/place/community. Theory, thought as part of the critic's œuvre, should never simply be thought of as a relay of a world existing 'out there'; it is sign-structure as well, participant and producer of its own system of semiotics. In terms of the space theory constructs around itself, then, the pretence that theory is untouched by representation's multiple mechanics (the pretence that it simply gives voice to the world transparently), itself participates in a violent effacement of difference within transnational academic capitalism. A one-dimensional representational understanding of theory simply as a tool positioned to reveal the world as it is (*vertreten* without *darstellen*) builds a rather too certain world around knowledge's theoretical presuppositions, once again expansively imperializing modernity's own categorizations. Spivak offers Foucault's *theorizations* of power as an example. Careful to note Foucault's own care in his empiricist and contextual deployment of his thoughts around power, she nevertheless writes how:

Because of the power of the word 'power', Foucault admits to using the 'metaphor of the point which progressively irradiates its surroundings.' Such slips become the rule rather than the exception *in less careful hands*. And that radiating point, animating an effectively heliocentric discourse, fills the empty place of the agent with the historical sun of theory, the Subject of Europe.

(1999, p. 254)

In other words, in hands less responsible and empirically inclined than Foucault's, his theory of power can acquire the dogmatism of an expansively situated explanation of the world in its entirety: Said's 'bad infinity'. The same applies to any concept-metaphors deployed in the course of our theoretical formulations: 'nature', 'postcolonial spaces', even 'abstraction' and 'representation'. All set understandings, questions, and conversations on the subjects of our knowledge production to work in some capacity. It is significant here that, in her previous work, Spivak is at pains to make a distinction between 'theory', conceived as dogmatic, exalted and relatively immovable object, and the more grounded scope and ability of 'strategy', thought and mobilized as ambivalent intellectual tools chosen conjuncturally as means of achieving broader social and political ends (1993, pp. 1–23).

The point here is that when we mobilize theory's representational effects, knowledge is always constitutive. At worst, then, in the transnational landscapes of academic capitalism, theory culture in research produces the world precisely by a 'speaking for' that 'comput[es] the national subject of the global South in this unproblematic way', with the Euro-American or indeed Euro-centric professional intellectual poised and positioned as 'the one who diagnoses the episteme' (Spivak, 1999, p. 255). At best, on the other hand, as David Scott might suggest, research performed as criticism careful of, and attentive to, our own locatedness in context holds that potential of 'putting back together aspects of our common life so as to make visible what has been obscured' (2008, p. vi), or I would add, what can be achieved.

What these thoughts around the double play of representation in theory culture gesture toward is the necessity of a due sense of responsibility in the light of such awareness about the representational mechanics of knowledge production. Responsible critical praxis must take theory culture's representational dynamics seriously, because research is always more than merely formalized curiosity. The stakes and cultural geographies of knowledge production are greater. Knowledge is in and of the world, generative precisely *because* of its representational dynamics. Such configurations of responsibility recognize that like any other text, theory is never simply a transparent window to the world, even (especially) when we suppose theory to simply be a box of tools to give voice to difference. So Spivak remarks:

> The produced 'transparency' marks the place of 'interest'; it is maintained by vehement denegation: 'Now this rôle of referee, judge and universal witness is one which I *absolutely refuse* to adopt.' One responsibility of the critic might be to read and write so that the impossibility of such interested individualistic refusals of the institutional privileges of power bestowed on the subject is taken seriously.
>
> (1999, p. 265)

If we are aware, then, that we constitute subjects and places as we produce knowledge of them, if we are aware, in other words, that *criticism* and *community* are intractably connected because of the representational mechanics of knowledge, then we must take our iterations seriously because we are always marked *inside* complex and messy spaces of immersion and involvement at the very point of knowledge production. We must, because we always do (whether we know it or not), have a stake in what we say. Even when we are enjoined to imagine our research as 'case study', or vehicle for the development of a broader contribution to a thematized 'theoretical literature', perhaps especially in these instances, we are never as academic practitioners *disconnected* from that place or that case study. In research, we constitute those objects of which we write *as* we enter into their discursive domains. In the disciplinary social sciences, this is worth remembering each time we are enjoined to frame our research within particular theoretical idioms, or even when the corporate academy demands we stretch those theoretical idioms through our own research. For those theoretical idioms are the patinas of modernity.

Conceiving of research and knowledge production this way, textually or post-empirically, is to reconfigure the geographies in which we emplace ourselves as researchers. In short, anyone who produces knowledge of a thing (people/place/community) can never be outside that thing, and thus not responsible in some way. The thing is subject as well as object, existent in and through our theoretical languages (also see Ismail, 2005, pp. xi–xiv). Knowledge is never outside power when thought about in this way, which demands an open-ness to change and dialogue, and a disposition to knowledge production as ongoing, dynamic, always unsettled and productively unsettling. Most of all, it demands a commitment to keeping at the forefront of our research endeavours questions regarding what knowledge does, who it is for, and why we are in the service of producing it.

These notes on the representational mechanics of knowledge production, thought especially through the theory cultures we employ and deploy, remind us of our own role in shaping what David Scott (1999, pp. 3–20; 2004, pp. 2–6) has elsewhere referred to as the 'problem space' *in* which critical praxis takes place. In his usage, a problem space is a context of language, discourse, and of argument. It shapes the conditions and parameters of critical inquiry, making possible only those questions and answers that it *seems* possible to ask and to answer given a discursively theoretical and, in Scott's work, historico-temporal context. But, problem spaces have geographical orientations as well, toward place and toward theory culture. The geographical orientations of problem space pose not just the parameters of intervention, but they also determine the ideological-political stakes of asking and troubling over particular questions. Given the academic's role in constituting as we produce 'knowledge of', effective criticism demands a degree of sensitivity to the geography of problem spaces in any field of enquiry. Particularly to the agency the professional academic has in orienting the problem space toward place/people/community in an unevenly global and corporatized academic landscape where we are so often enjoined to fetishize the theory object. And particularly to the possibilities of productively unsettling existent problem spaces, such that our representations can speak directly to politics in place. Attention to the representational mechanics of knowledge production might usefully engender in critical intellectual praxis, at every stage of research, due attention to some rather grounded and political introspections over 'whether and to what extent the questions [this research] is trying to answer continue to be questions worth having answers to' (Scott, 2004, p. 4).

The thoughts in this chapter attempt to speak to the cultural geographies of theory in this global postcolonial moment. In doing so, they pose just one more way of thinking about that inherent spatiality of postcolonial theory that this volume explores. To be sure, the purchase of points of critical intervention embedded in terms like *postcolonial spaces* are invaluable in a world being remade by globalization while it is caught within the frames and striations of (neo-)colonial encounter. But as I have argued, despite critical postcolonial intentionality, the inequities of a colonial present must also be traced within the cultural geographies of theory itself: in the ways we think, write and imagine the world through our research, especially the theoretical discourses we employ and deploy to do so.

Only then might we not only be able to make spatial and political critical interventions with as much humility as potential and hope, but as we do so, it may also be possible to tackle just as challenging and provocative questions like 'who is "us," who are we precisely?' (Derrida, 1993, p. 5), and what are the political implications of the ways this privileged 'we' writes the world over through our theoretical passions and preoccupations? Academic knowledge production, even postcolonial theory, is pervaded by power geometries that have real effects on the shape and actuation of knowledge produced within the contemporary corporate academy. What I have signalled in this chapter are some ways of trying to engage the inalienable connections between the geographies of theory culture and politics, especially through introspective and creative engagements with the pitfalls of abstraction and the mechanics of representation at play in critical intellectual praxis.

Finally, a very uncertain word on responsibility: I am not sure whether these thoughts move toward a postcolonial theory of responsibility. I am, in fact, more inclined to regard this chapter in the manner of something said *in* this global postcolonial moment *by* a tenured Euro-American academic subjectivized in the corporate academy. Something conjunctural that is in the manner of a response to an invitation to contribute to a collection of thoughts on the postcolonial spatial. My uncertainty to fix this as a 'theory of responsibility' is because to do so edges toward just the kind of inflexible theorization I seek to avoid. While I have persistently argued for a responsibility incumbent upon the postcolonial critic to engage the geographies of theory in the very performance of criticism, there must be no mechanical formula, or as Derrida remarked no 'ritual rule' (ibid.), for truly responsible praxis. In leaning toward the *passionate* rather than *responsibility*, Derrida usefully suggests that the experience of responsibility cannot be reduced to one of duty or debt; a gesture of responsibility would not be responsible if it were purely and simply to obey a ritual. What I take from this is a sense of the passionate as care for the effects and politics of the knowledge we produce. But passion and care also open the door for us to be wrong as well. As Doreen Massey (2008, p. 496) has recently put it in terms that capture well this dual sense of care and humility that a knowledge production attendant to the cultural geographies of theory might entail: 'It is utterly invigorating to be in a situation where ideas really matter. But also one where they are not simply taken as "truth".'

Notes

1. In this chapter, I use the term 'Euro-American' to broadly refer to institutions and researchers permanently positioned within the Global North, whereas I use Euro-centrism to refer instead to the effects of the Euro-American academy on knowledges produced from both the Global North and the Global South. I expand on this in the next section.
2. From the likes of the Subaltern Studies Collective, for example.
3. For a fuller discussion on disciplinary Geography's spatialities of theory, see Sparke (2005).
4. By '(inter)discipline bound theory culture', I mean to implicate such constellations as postcolonial theory.

Bibliography

Adam, I. (1990) 'Breaking the Chain: Anti-Saussurean Resistance in Birney, Carey and C.S. Pierce', in I. Adam and H. Tiffin (eds) *Past the Last Post: Theorizing Post-Colonialism and Post-Modernism*, Calgary: University of Calgary Press, pp. 79–93.

Adebayo, D. (1996) *Some Kind of Black*, London: Virago.

Adorno, T. W. and Horkheimer, M. ([1944] 1997) *Dialectic of Enlightenment*, trans. John Cumming, London: Verso.

Agamben, G. (2005) *State of Exception*, Chicago: University of Chicago Press.

Ahmad, A. (1992) *In Theory: Classes, Nations, Literatures*, London: Verso.

Ali, M. (2003) *Brick Lane*, London: Doubleday.

Allen, J. (2003) 'A Question of Language', in M. Pryke, G. Rose and S. Whatmore (eds) *Using Social Theory: Thinking Through Research*, London: Sage, pp.11–27.

AmazonGISnet (2008) 'Como acertar, recuperar y crear espacios y planes de vida dentro de nuestra geografía del Ecuador – La gestión colectiva y planes de planificación territorial AmazonGISnet y GISciudadano', presentation at Workshop 'El uso de la geografía en el Ecuador' by R. Resl, N. Wampankit, P. Ankuash, and J.C. Unkuch. 11 April, Quito: FLACSO.

AmazonGISnet (2010) *AmazonGISnet website*, www.amazongisnet.net (accessed 22 June 2010).

Anderson, B. (1991) *Imagined Communities*, London: Verso.

Andolina, R., Laurie, N. and Radcliffe, S. (2009) *Indigenous Development in the Andes: Culture, Power and Transnationalism*, Durham, NC: Duke University Press.

Anvari, H. (nd) Haleh Anvari website, available at: www.halehanvari.com (accessed 29 July 2010).

Anzaldúa, G. (1987) *Borderlands/La Frontera: The New Mestiza*, 2nd edn, San Francisco: Aunt Lute Books.

Appadurai, A. (1996) *Modernity at Large: Cultural Dimensions of Globalization*, Minneapolis: University of Minnesota Press.

Appadurai, A. (2000a) 'Spectral Housing and Urban Cleansing: Notes on Millennial Mumbai', *Public Culture*, 12(3): 627–51.

Appadurai, A. (2000b) 'Grassroots Globalization and the Research Imagination', *Public Culture*, 12(1): 1–19.

Appadurai, A. (2002) 'Deep Democracy: Urban Governmentality and the Horizon of Politics', *Public Culture*, 14(1): 21–47.

Appadurai, A. and Breckenridge, C. A. (1995) 'Public Modernity in India', in C. Breckenridge (ed.) *Consuming Modernity: Public Culture in a South Asian World*, Minneapolis: University of Minnesota Press, pp. 1–20.

Appiah, K. A. (2006) *Cosmopolitanism: Ethics in a World of Strangers*, London: Allen Lane.

Aronowitz, S. (2000) *The Knowledge Factory: Dismantling the Corporate University and Creating True Higher Learning*, Boston: Beacon Press.

Ashcroft, B., Griffiths, G. and Tiffin, H. (1989) *The Empire Writes Back*, London: Routledge.

Ashcroft, B, Griffiths, G. and Tiffin, H. (eds) (1994) *The Post-Colonial Studies Reader*, London: Routledge.

Aspden, K. (2007) *Nationality: Wog: The Hounding of David Oluwale*, London: Jonathan Cape.

Augé, M. (1995) *Non-Places: Introduction to an Anthropology of Supermodernity*, London: Verso.

Azima, R. (2006/2007) '"Not-the-Native": Self-Transplantation, Ecocriticism, and Postcolonialism in Jamaica Kincaid's *My Garden (Book):*', *Journal of Commonwealth and Postcolonial Studies*, 13(2)– 4 (1): 101–19.

Baker, P. (1995) *Deconstruction and the Ethical Turn*, Florida: University Press of Florida.

Ballard, J. G. (2000) *Super-Cannes*, London: HarperCollins.

Balutansky, K. M. and Kincaid, J. (2002) 'On Gardening', *Callaloo*, 25(3): 790–800.

Barnes, T. and Duncan, J. (1992) 'Writing Worlds: Introduction', in T. Barnes and J. Duncan (eds) *Writing Worlds: Discourse, Texts and Metaphors in the Representation of Landscape*, London: Routledge, pp.1–17.

Barnett, C. (1997) '"Sing Along with the Common People": Politics, Postcolonialism, and Other Figures', *Environment and Planning D*, 15: 137–54.

Barry, A., Osbourne, T. and Rose, N. (1996) *Foucault and Political Reason: Liberalism, Neo-Liberalism and Rationalities of Government*, London: University College London Press.

Baucom, I. (1999) *Out of Place: Englishness, Empire and the Locations of Identity*, Princeton, NJ: Princeton University Press.

Baudrillard, J. (1992) *Selected Writings*, ed. M. Poster, Cambridge: Polity Press.

Baudrillard, J. (1997) *Simulacra and Simulation*, trans. S. Glaser, Ann Arbor, MI: University of Michigan Press.

Bell, M., *et al.* (eds) (1995) *Geography and Imperialism, 1820–1940*, Manchester: Manchester University Press.

Bender, D. E. (2004) *Sweated Work, Weak Bodies: Anti-Sweatshop Campaigns and Languages of Labor*, New Brunswick, NJ: Rutgers University Press.

Bhabha, H. (1986) 'Foreword: Remembering Fanon: Self, Psyche and the Colonial Condition', in F. Fanon, *Black Skin, White Masks*, London: Pluto.

Bhabha, H. (1989) 'The Commitment to Theory', in J. Pines and P. Willemen (eds) *Questions of Third Cinema*, London: British Film Institute, pp. 111–32.

Bhabha, H. (1990a) 'Narrating the Nation', in H. Bhabha (ed.) *Nation and Narration*, London: Routledge, pp. 1–7.

Bhabha, H. (1990b) 'DissemiNation: Time, Narrative and the Margins of the Modern Nation', in H. Bhabha (ed.) *Nation and Narration*, London: Routledge, pp. 291–322.

Bhabha, H. (1990c) 'The Third Space: Interview with Homi Bhabha', in J. Rutherford (ed.) *Identity: Community, Culture, Difference*, London: Lawrence & Wishart.

Bhabha, H. (1994) *The Location of Culture*, London: Routledge.

Black, J. (1997) *Maps and Politics*, London: Reaktion Books.

Blunt, A. (1999) *Travel, Gender and Imperialism: Mary Kingsley and West Africa*, New York: Guildford.

Blunt, A. (2005) *Domicile and Diaspora: Anglo-Indian Women and the Spatial Politics of Home*, Cambridge, MA: Blackwell.

Blunt, A. and McEwan, C. (eds) (2002a) *Postcolonial Geographies*, New York: Continuum.

Blunt, A. and McEwan, C. (2002b) 'Introduction', in A. Blunt and C. McEwan (eds) *Postcolonial Geographies*, New York: Continuum, pp. 1–6.

Blunt, A. and Rose, G. (1994) *Writing Women and Space: Colonial and Postcolonial Geographies*, London: Guildford Press.

Blunt, A. and Wills, J. (2000) 'Decolonizing Geography: Postcolonial Perspectives', in A. Blunt and J. Wills (eds) *Dissident Geographies: An Introduction to Radical Ideas and Practice*, Harlow: Longman, pp. 167–207.

Boehmer, E. (2005) *Stories of Women: Gender and Narrative in the Postcolonial Nation*, Manchester: Manchester University Press.

Bonta, M. and Proveti, J. (2004) *Deleuze and Geophilosophy: A Guide and Glossary*, Edinburgh: Edinburgh University Press.

Borges, J. L. ([1946] 1998) 'On Exactitude in Science', in *Collected Fictions*, trans. A. Hurley, London: Penguin Press.

Bradshaw, P. (2007) 'Eastern Promises', *The Guardian*, 17 October, available at: http://www.guardian.co.uk/film/2007/oct/17/londonfilmfestival2007.london-filmfestival, (accessed 13 July, 2010).

Brah, A. (1996) *Cartographies of Diaspora: Contesting Identities*, London: Routledge.

Braun, B. (2000) 'Producing Vertical Territory: Geology and Governmentality in Late Victorian Canada', *Ecumene*, 7: 7–46.

Breckenridge, C. A. (ed.) (1995) *Consuming Modernity: Public Culture in a South Asian World*, Minneapolis: University of Minnesota Press.

Brennan, T. (1989) *Salman Rushdie and the Third World: Myths of the Nation*, London: Macmillan.

Brookes, E. C. (2007) *Unraveling the Garment Industry: Transnational Organizing and Women's Work*, Minneapolis: University of Minnesota Press.

Brown, M. and Knopp, L. (2006) 'Places of Polygons? Governmentality, Scale and the Census in *The Gay and Lesbian Atlas*', *Population, Space and Place*, 12: 223–42.

Browne, A. (2006) 'I Would Prefer Women Not to Wear the Veil at All, Says Straw', *The Times*, 7 October, p. 6.

Brownmiller, S. (1984) *Femininity*, New York: Simon and Schuster.

Brunsdon, C. (2007) *London in Cinema: The Cinematic City since 1945*, London: British Film Institute.

Buchanan, I. and Lambert, G (eds) (2005) *Deleuze and Space*, Edinburgh: Edinburgh University Press.

Budhos, M. (2006) *Ask Me No Questions*, New York: Atheneum Books for Young Readers.

Burchell, G., Gordon, C. and Miller, P. (1991) *The Foucault Effect: Studies in Governmentality*, London: Harvester Wheatsheaf.

Burnett, D. G. (2000) *Masters of All They Surveyed: Explorations, Geography, and a British El Dorado*, Chicago: University of Chicago Press.

Butt, R. (2006) 'Rushdie Backs Straw in Row over Muslim Veils', *The Guardian*, 11 October, available at: http://www.guardian.co.uk/uk/2006/oct/11/religion.immigrationpolicy (accessed 29 July 2010).

Campbell, C. and Somerville, E. (eds) (2007) *'What is the Earthly Paradise?' Ecocritical Responses to the Caribbean*, Newcastle: Cambridge Scholars Publishing.

Carey, P. (1994) *Collected Stories*, London: Faber.

Carter, P. (1987) *The Road to Botany Bay: An Essay in Spatial History*, London: Faber.

Castells, M. (2000) *The Information Age: Economy, Society and Culture*, Vol. I, *The Rise of the Network Society*, 2nd edn, Malden, MA: Blackwell Publishing.

Castles, S. and Miller, M. J. (2003) *The Age of Migration: International Population Movements in the Modern World*, London: Palgrave.

Castro Gómez, S. (1999) 'Introducción: Poscolonialismo, o la crítica cultural del capitalismo tardío', in S. Castro Gómez *et al.* (eds) *Pensar (en) los intersticios: teoría y práctica de la crítica poscolonial*, Bogota: CEJA, pp. 9–19.

Castro Gómez, S., Guardiola Rivera, O. and Millán de Benavides, C. (eds) (1999) *Pensar (en) los intersticios: teoría y práctica de la crítica poscolonial*, Bogota: CEJA.

Çelik, Z. (1997) *Urban Forms and Colonial Confrontations: Algiers under French Rule*, Berkeley, CA: University of California Press.

Chakrabarty, D. (2002) *Habitations of Modernity: Essays in the Wake of Subaltern Studies*, Chicago: University of Chicago Press.

Chambers, I. and Curti, L. (1996) *The Post-colonial Question: Common Skies, Divided Horizons*, London: Routledge.

Chatterjee, M. (2005) 'LK to Step Down in December', *Times of India*, 18 September, available at: http://timesofindia.indiatimes.com/articleshow/msid-1235052,prtpage-1.cms (accessed 21 July 2008).

Chatterjee, M. and Tohid, O. (2005) 'Jinnah Secular: Advani Upsets Sangh Parivar', *Times of India*, 5 June, available at: http://timesofindia.indiatimes.com/articleshow/1132824.cms (accessed 7 October 2008).

Chrisman, L. (2003) *Postcolonial Contraventions: Cultural Readings of Race, Imperialism and Transnationalism*, Manchester: Manchester University Press.

Clark, S. (ed.) (1999) *Travel Writing and Empire*, London: Zed.

Clayton, D. W. (2000) *Islands of Truth: The Imperial Fashioning of Vancouver Island*, Vancouver: UBC Press.

Clayton, D. W. (2003) 'Critical Imperial and Colonial Geographies', in K. Anderson *et al.*, *Handbook of Cultural Geography*, London: Sage, pp. 354–68.

Clingman, S. (2007) '"England Has Changed": Questions of National Form in *A Distant Shore*', *Moving Worlds: Journal of Transcultural Writings*, 7(1): 46–58.

Clingman, S. (2009) 'Other Voices: An Interview with Caryl Phillips', in R. T. Schatteman (ed.) *Conversations with Caryl Phillips*, Jackson, MO: University Press of Mississippi, pp. 95–117.

Collett, A. (2006) 'Boots and Bare-Feet in Jamaica Kincaid's "Garden (Book)"', *Wasafiri: The Transnational Journal of International Writing*, 21(2): 58–63.

Cooper, D. E. (2006) *A Philosophy of Gardens*, Oxford: Oxford University Press.

Cooper, M. (2004) 'Insecure Times, Tough Decisions: The Nomos of Liberalism', *Alternatives*, 29: 515–33.

Coronil, F. (2006) 'Latin American Postcolonial Studies and Global Decolonization', in N. Lazarus (ed.) *Cambridge Companion to Postcolonial Studies*, Cambridge: Cambridge University Press, pp. 221–40.

Craib, R (2004) *Cartographic Mexico: A History of State Fixations and Fugitive Landscapes*, Durham, NC: Duke University Press.

Crampton, J. W. and Elden, S. (2006) 'Space, Politics, Calculation: An Introduction', *Social and Cultural Geographies*, 7: 681–5.

Crampton, J. W. and Elden, S. (eds) (2007) *Space, Knowledge and Power: Foucault and Geography*, Aldershot: Ashgate.

Crosby, A. W. (1986) *Ecological Imperialism: The Biological Expansion of Europe, 900–1900*, Cambridge: Cambridge University Press.

Crush, J. (1994) 'Post-colonialism, De-colonization, and Geography', in A. Godlewska and N. Smith (eds) *Geography and Empire*, Oxford: Blackwell, pp. 333–50.

D'Amore, A. (2005) 'Kincaid's Garden: A Fourth Garden of Self-Awareness', *MaComère: Journal of the Association of Caribbean Women Writers and Scholars*, 7: 150–66.

Davis, E. S. (2006) 'The Intimacies of Globalization: Bodies and Borders on-Screen', *Camera Obscura*, 21(2): 32–73.

Davis, T. F. and Womack, K. (2001) 'Preface: Reading Literature and the Ethics of Criticism', in T. F. Davis and K. Womack (eds) *Mapping the Ethical Turn: A Reader in Ethics, Culture, and Literary Theory*, Charlottesville, VA: University Press of Virginia, pp. ix–xiv.

Dean, M. (1999) *Governmentality: Power and Rule in Modern Society*, London: Sage.

Dean, M. (2002) '"Demonic Societies": Liberalism, Biopolitics, and Sovereignty', in T. Blom Hansen and F. Stepputat (eds) *States of Imagination: Ethnographic Explorations of the Postcolonial State*, Durham, NC: Duke University Press, pp. 41–64.

Deler, J. P. (1981) *Genèse de l'espace equatorien: Essai sur le territoire et la formation de l'état national*, Paris: IFEA.

DeLoughrey, E. (2004) 'Island Ecologies and Caribbean Literatures', *Tijdschrift voor Economische en Sociale Geografie*, 95(3): 298–310.

DeLoughrey, E., Gosson, R. K. and Handley, G. B. (eds) (2005) *Caribbean Literature and the Environment: Between Nature and Culture*, Charlottesville, VA: University of Virginia Press.

Derrida, J. (1978) 'Structure, Sign and Play in the Discourse of the Human Sciences', in *Writing and Difference*, Chicago: University of Chicago Press, pp. 279–93.

Derrida, J. (1993) *On the Name*, ed. T. Dutoit, trans. D. Wood, J. P. Leavey Jr., and I. McLeod, Stanford, CA: Stanford University Press.

Desai, A. (1963) *Cry, the Peacock*, Delhi: Orient.

Desai, A. (1975) *Where Shall We Go This Summer?* Delhi: Orient.

Desai, A. (1977) *Fire on the Mountain*, London: Vintage.

Desai, A. (1980) *Clear Light of Day*, London: Vintage.

Desai, A. (1984) *In Custody*, London: Heinemann.

Desai, A. (1988) *Baumgartner's Bombay*, London: Heinemann.

Desai, A. (1995) *Journey to Ithaca*, London: Heinemann.

Desai, A. (1999) *Fasting, Feasting*, London: Vintage.

Desai Hidier, Tanuja (2002) *Born Confused*, London: Scholastic Children's Book.

Deshpande, Shashi. (1980) *The Dark Holds No Terrors*, New Delhi: Penguin.

Deshpande, Shashi. (1983) *Roots and Shadows*, Hyderabad: Disha.

Deshpande, Shashi. (1993) *The Binding Vine*, New Delhi: Penguin.

Deshpande, Shashi. (2000) *Small Remedies*, New Delhi: Penguin.

Deshpande, Satish. (2001) 'Hegemonic Spatial Strategies: The Nation-Space and Hindu Communalism in Twentieth-century India', in P. Chatterjee and P. Jaganathan (eds) *Subaltern Studies XI: Community, Gender and Violence*, London: Hurst, pp. 167–211.

Dickey, S. (1995) 'Consuming Utopia: Film Watching in Tamil Nadu', in C. A. Breckenridge (ed.) *Consuming Modernity: Public Culture in a South Asian World*, Minneapolis: University of Minnesota Press, pp. 131–56.

Dirlik, A. (1994) 'The Post-Colonial Aura: Third World Criticism in the Age of Global Capitalism', *Critical Inquiry*, 20: 328–56.

Doel, M. (1999) *Poststructuralist Geographies*, Edinburgh: Edinburgh University Press.

Driver, F. (1985) 'Power, Space, and the Body – A Critical-Assessment of Foucault's *Discipline and Punish*', *Environment and Planning D*, 3: 425–46.

Driver, F. (1992) 'Geography's Empire: Histories of Geographical Knowledge', *Environment and Planning D*, 10: 23–40.

Driver, F. (1993) *Power and Pauperism: The Workhouse System, 1834–1884*, Cambridge: Cambridge University Press.

Driver, F. (2001) *Geography Militant: Cultures of Exploration and Empire*, Oxford: Blackwell.

Driver, F. and Gilbert, D. (eds) (1999) *Imperial Cities: Landscape, Display and Identity*, Manchester: Manchester University Press.

Du Bois, W. W. B. (1989) *The Souls of Black Folk*, New York: Penguin Books.

During, S. (2000) 'Postcolonialism and Globalization', *Cultural Studies*, 14(3/4): 385–404.

Dwyer, R. (2000) *All You Want Is Money, All You Need Is Love: Sexuality and Romance in Modern India*, London: Cassell.

Edney, M. (1997) *Mapping an Empire: The Geographical Construction of British India, 1765–1843*, Chicago: University of Chicago Press.

Elden, S. (2001) *Mapping the Present: Heidegger, Foucault and the Project of Spatial History*, London: Continuum.

Elden, S. (2005) 'Missing the Point: Globalization, Deterritorialization and the Space of the World', *Transactions of the Institute of British Geographers*, 30: 8–19.

Elden, S. (2007a) 'Governmentality, Calculation, Territory', *Environment and Planning D*, 25: 562–80.

Elden, S. (2007b) 'Rethinking Governmentality', *Political Geography*, 27: 29–33.

Elden, S. (2008) 'Strategies for Waging Peace: Foucault as *Collaborateur*', in M. Dillon and A. Neal (eds) *Foucault on Politics, Security and War*, London: Palgrave Macmillan, pp. 21–39.

Elsaesser, T. (2006) 'Space, Place and Identity in European Cinema of the 1990s', *Third Text*, 20(6): 647–58.

Ewert, J. C. (2007) '"Great Plant Appropriators" and Acquisitive Gardeners: Jamaica Kincaid's Ambivalent Garden', in L. Lang-Peralta (ed.) *Jamaica Kincaid and Caribbean Double Crossings*, Newark: University of Delaware Press, pp. 113–26.

Fakhri, A. R. (2008) 'Photos: Village Women Making Niqab in Hormozgan, Iran', *Payvand Iran News*, 10 May, available at: http://www.payvand.com/news/08/oct/1048.html (accessed 29 July 2010).

Fanon, F. ([1952] 1986) *Black Skin, White Masks*, trans. C. Lam Markmann, London: Pluto Press.

Farrar, M. (2009) 'Why We Still Need a Memorial to the Ordeal of David Oluwale', *Yorkshire Post*, available at: http://www.yorkshirepost.co.uk/features/Why-we-still-need-a.4892810.jp (accessed 14 August 2010).

Ferguson, M. and Kincaid, J. (1994) 'A Lot of Memory: An Interview with Jamaica Kincaid', *The Kenyon Review*, 16(1):163–88.

Fidecaro, A. (2006a) '"To Name Is to Possess": La Critique de la botanique dans *My Garden(Book)* de Jamaica Kincaid', *Colloquium Helveticum: Cahiers Suisses de Littérature Comparée/Schweizer Hefte für Allgemeine und Vergleichende Literaturwissenschaft/Quaderni Svizzeri di Letteratura Generale e Comparata*, 37: 73–93.

Fidecaro, A. (2006b) 'Jamaica Kincaid's Practical Politics of the Intimate in *My Garden (Book):*', *WSQ*, Special Issue: 'The Global and the Intimate', 34(1/2): 250–71.

Foster, K. (2006) 'Migrants, Asylum Seekers and British Identity', *Third Text*, 20(6): 683–91.

Foucault, M. (1961) *Folie et déraison: histoire de la folie à l'âge classique*, Paris: Plon.

Foucault, M. (1972) *The Archaeology of Knowledge*, London: Tavistock.

Foucault, M. ([1975–6] 2003) *Society Must Be Defended: Lectures at the Collège de France 1975–6*, London: Penguin.

Foucault, M. ([1976] 1980) 'Questions on Geography', in C. Gordon (ed.) *Power/ Knowledge: Selected Interviews and Other Writings, 1972–1977*, Brighton: Harvester Press, pp. 63–77.

Foucault, M. (1977a) *Discipline and Punish: The Birth of the Prison*, Harmondsworth: Penguin.

Foucault, M. (1977b) *Language, Counter-memory, Practice: Selected Essays and Interviews*, trans. D. Bouchard and S. Simon, Ithaca, NY: Cornell University Press.

Foucault, M. ([1978a] 2001) 'Governmentality', in J. D. Faubion (ed.) *Essential Works of Foucault, 1954–1984*, Vol. 3: *Power*, London: Penguin, pp. 201–22.

Foucault, M. ([1978b] 2007) *Security, Territory, Population: Lectures at the Collège de France, 1977–1978*, Basingstoke: Palgrave Macmillan.

Foucault, M. ([1978–9] 2008) *The Birth of Biopolitics: Lectures at the Collège de France 1978–1979*, Basingstoke: Palgrave Macmillan.

Foucault, M. (1979a) *The History of Sexuality*, Vol. 1: *An Introduction*, London: Allen Lane.

Foucault, M. ([1979b] 2008) *The Birth of Biopolitics: Lectures at the Collège de France, 1978–1979*, Basingstoke: Palgrave Macmillan.

Foucault, M. (1980) *Power/Knowledge: Selected Interviews and Other Writings, 1972–1977*, Brighton: Harvester Press.

Foucault, M. ([1982a] 2001) 'Space, Knowledge and Power', in J. D. Faubion (ed.) *Essential Works of Foucault, 1954–1984*, Vol. 3: *Power*, London: Penguin, pp. 349– 64.

Foucault, M. ([1982b] 2001) 'The Subject and Power', in J. D. Faubion (ed.) *Essential Works of Foucault, 1954–1984*, Vol. 3: *Power*, London: Penguin, pp. 326–48.

Foucault, M. (1986) 'Of Other Spaces', trans., J. Miskoweic, *Diacritics*, 16(1): 22–7.

Foucault, M. (2000) *Essential Works of Foucault, 1954–1984*, Vol. 1: *Ethics*, London: Penguin.

Foucault, M. (2001) 'The Politics of Health in the Eighteenth Century', in J. D. Faubion (ed.) *Essential Works of Foucault, 1954–1984*, Vol. 3: *Power*, London: Penguin, pp. 90–105.

Foucault, M. (2006) *Psychiatric Power: Lectures at the Collège de France, 1973–1974*, Basingstoke: Palgrave Macmillan.

Foucault, M. (2007) 'Spaces of Security: The Example of the Town. Lecture of 11th January 1978', *Political Geography*, 27: 48–56.

Francis, M. and Hester, Jr., R.T. (eds) (1990) *The Meaning of Gardens*, Cambridge, MA: MIT Press.

French, P. (2002) 'Frears Finds the Heart of London's Underground', *The Observer*, 15 December, http://film.guardian.co.uk/News_Story/Critic_Review/Observer_review/0,,860195,00.htm (accessed 13 July 2010).

Fryer, P. (1984) *Staying Power: The History of Black People in Britain*, London: Pluto Press.

Fuss, D. (1995) *Identification Papers*, London: Routledge.

Gangar, A. (1995) 'Films from the City of Dreams', in Patel, S. and A. Thorner (eds) *Bombay: Metaphor for Modern India*, New Delhi: Oxford University Press, pp. 210–24.

Gaonkar, D. P (ed.) (2001) *Alternative Modernities*, Durham, NC: Duke University Press.

Garis, L. (1990) 'Through West Indian Eyes', *New York Times Magazine*, 7 October, p. 80.

George, R.M. (1996) *The Politics of Home: Postcolonial Relocations and Twentieth-Century Fiction*, Cambridge: Cambridge University Press.

Gibson, S. (2003) 'Accommodating Strangers: British Hospitality and the Asylum Hotel Debate', *Journal for Cultural Research*, 7(4): 367–86.

Gibson, S. (2006) '"The Hotel Business Is About Strangers": Border Politics and Hospitable Spaces in Stephen Frears's *Dirty Pretty Things*', *Third Text*, 20(6): 693–701.

Giddens, A. (1990) *The Consequences of Modernity*, Oxford: Blackwell.

Gikandi, S. (1996) *Maps of Englishness: Writing Identity in the Culture of Colonialism*, New York: Columbia University Press.

Gikandi, S. (2001) 'Globalization and the Claims of Postcoloniality', *South Atlantic Quarterly*, 100(3): 627–58.

Gilroy, P. (2004) *After Empire: Melancholia or Convivial Culture?*, London: Routledge.

Gilroy, P. (2005) *Postcolonial Melancholia*, New York: Columbia University Press.

Glissant, É. (1997) *Poetics of Relation*, trans. B. Wing, Ann Arbor, MI: The University of Michigan Press.

Glover, W. J. (2008) *Making Lahore Modern: Constructing and Imagining a Colonial City*, Minneapolis: University of Minnesota Press.

Godlewska, A. and Smith, N. (eds) (1994a) *Geography and Empire*, Oxford: Blackwell.

Godlewska, A. and Smith, N. (1994b) 'Introduction: Critical Histories of Geographies', in A. Godlewska and N. Smith (eds) *Geography and Empire*, Oxford: Blackwell, pp. 1–12.

Gopalan, L. (2002) *Cinema of Interruptions: Action Genres in Contemporary Indian Cinema*, London: British Film Institute.

Gowans, G (2001) 'Gender, Imperialism and Domesticity: British Women Repatriated from India, 1940–47', *Gender, Place and Culture*, 8(3): 255–69.

Graham-Brown, S. (1988) 'The Seen, the Unseen and the Imagined: Private and Public Lives', in S. Graham-Brown, *Images of Women: The Portrayal of Women in Photography of the Middle-East, 1860–1950*, New York: Columbia University Press, pp. 70–91, reprinted in R. Lewis and S. Mills (eds) *Feminist Postcolonial Theory: A Reader*, Edinburgh: Edinburgh University Press, pp. 502–19.

Graves, R. (1974) *The Greek Myths*, vol. II, Harmondsworth: Penguin.

Greer, G. (2006) 'Reality Bites', *The Guardian*, 24 July, available at: http://www.guardian.co.uk/film/2006/jul/24/culture.books (accessed 29 July 2010).

Gregory, D. (2004) *The Colonial Present*, Oxford: Blackwell.

Grossberg, L. (1996) 'The Space of Culture, the Power of Space', in I. Chambers and L. Curti (eds) *The Post-colonial Question: Common Skies, Divided Horizons*, London: Routledge, pp. 169–88.

Guha, R. (ed.) (1982) *Subaltern Studies I: Writings on South Asian History and Society*, Delhi: Oxford University Press.

Guha, R. ([1983] 1999) *Elementary Aspects of Peasant Insurgency in Colonial India*, Durham, NC: Duke University Press.

Hall, C. (2000) 'Introduction: Thinking the Postcolonial, Thinking the Empire', in C. Hall, *Cultures of Empire: Colonizers in Britain and the Empire in the Nineteenth and Twentieth Centuries: A Reader*, Manchester: Manchester University Press, pp. 1–33.

Hall, C. (2002) *Civilising Subjects: Metropole and Colony in the English Imagination, 1830–1867*, Cambridge: Polity.

Hall, K. (1995) '"There's a Time to Act English and a Time to Act Indian": The Politics of Identity among British-Sikh Teenagers', in S. Stephens (ed.) *Children and the Politics of Culture*, Princeton, NJ: Princeton University Press, pp. 243–64.

Hall, S. (1991a) 'Cultural Identity and Diaspora', in J. Rutherford (ed.) *Identity: Community, Culture, Difference*, London: Lawrence & Wishart, pp. 223–37.

Hall, S. (1991b) 'Old and New Identities, Old and New Ethnicities', in A. D. King (ed.) *Culture Globalization and the World-System*, London: Macmillan, pp. 31–68.

Hall, S. (1996) 'The Question of Cultural Identity', in S. Hall *et al.* (eds) *Modernity and its Futures*, Cambridge: Polity Press, pp. 274–316.

Hall, T. (2005) *Salaam Brick Lane: A Year in the New East End*, London: John Murray.

Hamnett, C. (2003) *Unequal City: London in the Global Arena*, London: Routledge.

Hanman, N. (2008) 'Photographer Haleh Anvari: More than Meets the Eye', *The Guardian*, 6 December 2008, available at: http://www.guardian.co.uk/artanddesign/2008/dec/06/photography-halehanvari-iran (accessed 29 July 2010).

Hannah, M. (2000) *Governmentality and the Mastery of Territory in Nineteenth-century America*, Cambridge: Cambridge University Press.

Hansen, T. B. (2001a) *Wages of Violence: Naming and Identity in Postcolonial Bombay*, Princeton, NJ: Princeton University Press.

Hansen, T. B. (2001b) 'The Ethics of Hindutva and the Spirit of Capitalism', in T. B. Hansen and C. Jaffrelot (eds) *The BJP and the Compulsions of Politics in India*, New Delhi: Oxford University Press, pp. 291–314.

Hapke, L. (2004) *Sweatshop: The History of an American Idea*, New Brunswick, NJ: Rutgers University Press.

Hardt, M. and Negri, A. (2001) *Empire*, Cambridge, MA: Harvard University Press.

Harley B. (1992) 'Rereading the Maps of the Columbian Encounter', *Annals of the Association of American Geographers*, 82(3): 522–35.

Harley B. (2001) *The New Nature of Maps: Essays in the History of Cartography*, London: Johns Hopkins University Press.

Harris, J. R. (1995) 'Where Is the Child's Environment? A Group Socialization Theory of Development', *Psychological Review*, 102: 458–89.

Harrison, R. P. (2008) *Gardens: An Essay on the Human Condition*, Chicago: University of Chicago Press.

Harvey, D. (2003) *The New Imperialism*, Oxford: Oxford University Press.

Hassall, A. J. (1994) *Dancing on Hot Macadam: Peter Carey's Fiction*, St. Lucia: University of Queensland Press.

Hazareesingh, S. (2007) *The Colonial City and the Challenge of Modernity: Urban Hegemonies and Civic Contestations in Bombay City, 1900–1925*, Hyderabad: Orient Longman.

Head, D. (2008) *The State of the Novel: Britain and Beyond*, Oxford: Wiley-Blackwell.

Held, D., McGrew, A., Goldblatt, D. and Perraton, J. (eds) (1999) *Global Transformations: Politics, Economics, and Culture*, Cambridge: Polity Press.

Hetherington, K. (1997) *The Badlands of Modernity: Heterotopia and Social Ordering*, London: Routledge.

Horrocks, C. and Jevtic, Z. (1999) *Introducing Baudrillard*, Cambridge: Icon Books.

Hovet, T. (2006) 'The Invisible London of *Dirty Pretty Things*; or, Dickens, Frears and Film Today', *Literary London*, 4(2), available at: www.literarylondon.org/londonjournal/september2006/hovet.html (accessed 4 January 2007).

Hoving, I. (2002) 'Remaining Where You Are: Kincaid and Glissant on Space and Knowledge', in G. Verstraete and T. Cresswell (eds) *Mobilizing Place, Placing Mobility: The Politics of Representation in a Globalized World*, Amsterdam: Rodopi, pp. 125–40.

Hoving, I. (2005) 'Moving the Caribbean Landscape: *Cereus Blooms at Night* as a Re-imagination of the Caribbean Environment', in E. DeLoughrey, R. K. Gosson and G. B. Handley (eds) *Caribbean Literature and the Environment: Between Nature and Culture*, Charlottesville, VA: University of Virginia Press, pp. 154–68.

Howell, P. (2000a) 'A Private Contagious Diseases Act: Prostitution and Public Space in Victorian Cambridge', *Journal of Historical Geography*, 26: 376–402.

Howell, P. (2000b) 'Prostitution and Racialised Sexuality: The Regulation of Prostitution in Britain and the British Empire before the Contagious Diseases Acts', *Environment and Planning D*, 18: 321–39.

Hubbard, P. (2000) 'Desire/Disgust: Moral Geographies of Heterosexuality', *Progress in Human Geography*, 24: 191–217.

Hudson, B. (1977) 'The New Geography and the New Imperialism', *Antipode*, 9(2): 12–19.

Huggan, G. (1990) 'Decolonising the Map: Post-Colonialism, Post-Structuralism and the Cartographic Connection', in I. Adam and H. Tiffin (eds) *Past the Last Post: Theorizing Post-Colonialism and Post-Modernism*, Calgary: University of Calgary Press, pp. 125–38.

Huggan, G. (1994) *Territorial Disputes: Maps and Mapping Strategies in Contemporary Canadian and Australian Fiction*, Toronto: University of Toronto Press.

Huggan, G. (1996) *Peter Carey*, Melbourne: Oxford University Press.

Huggan, G. (2002) 'Postcolonial Studies and the Anxiety of Interdisciplinarity', *Postcolonial Studies*, 5(3): 245–75.

Huggan, G. (2008) *Interdisciplinary Measures: Literature and the Future of Postcolonial Studies*, Liverpool: Liverpool University Press.

Hulme, P. (1986) *Colonial Encounters: Europe and the Native Caribbean, 1492–1797*, London: Methuen.

Hussain, Y. (2005) *Writing Diaspora: South Asian Women, Culture and Ethnicity*, Aldershot: Ashgate.

Huxley, M. (2007) 'Geographies of Governmentality', in J. Crampton and S. Elden (eds) *Space, Knowledge and Power: Foucault and Geography*, Aldershot: Ashgate, pp. 185–204.

Huxley, M. (2008) 'Space and Government: Governmentality and Geography', *Geography Compass*, 2: 1635–58.

Hyam, R. (1990) *Empire and Sexuality: The British Experience*, Manchester: Manchester University Press.

Islam, S. M. (1996) *The Ethics of Travel: From Marco Polo to Kafka*, Manchester: Manchester University Press.

Ismail, Q. (2005) *Abiding by Sri Lanka: On Peace, Place and Postcoloniality*, Minneapolis: University of Minnesota Press.

Jacobs, J. M. (1996) *Edge of Empire: Postcolonialism and the City*, London: Routledge.

Jacobs, S. (1996) 'Don't Mess with Jamaica Kincaid', *Boston Globe*, 20 June, 57.

Jaggi, M. (2000) '*The Final Passage*: An Interview with Writer Caryl Phillips', in K. Owusu (ed.) *Black British Culture and Society: A Text Reader*, London: Routledge.

Jameson, F. (1991) 'Secondary Elaborations', in *Postmodernism, or the Cultural Logic of Late Capitalism*, Durham, NC: Duke University Press, pp. 297–418.

Jazeel, T. (2005) '"Nature", Nationhood and the Poetics of Meaning in Ruhuna National Park, Sri Lanka', *Cultural Geographies*, 12, 199–227.

Jazeel, T. (2009) 'Governmentality', *Social Text*, 100: 136–40.

Johnson, A. (2007) 'Everydayness and Subalternity', *South Atlantic Quarterly*, 106: 21–38.

Jones, R. and Phillips, R. (2005) 'Unsettling Geographical Horizons: Exploring Premodern and Non-European Imperialism', *Annals of the Association of American Geographers*, 95: 141–61.

Joyce, P. (2003) *The Rule of Freedom: Liberalism and the Modern City*, London: Verso.

Kabeer, N. (2000) *The Power to Choose: Bangladeshi Women and Labour Market Decisions in London and Dhaka*, London: Verso.

Kidambi, P. (2007) *The Making of an Indian Metropolis: Colonial Governance and Public Culture in Bombay, 1890–1920*, Aldershot: Ashgate.

Kincaid, J. (2000) *My Garden (Book):*, London: Vintage.

Kincaid, J. (2005) *Among Flowers: A Walk in the Himalaya*, Washington, DC: National Geographic.

Kincaid, J. (2007) 'Dances with Daffodils', *Architectural Digest*, available at: http://www.architecturaldigest.com/homes/spaces/2007/04/gardens_article (accessed 5 February 2009).

King, A. (1990) *Global Cities: Post-Imperialism and the Internationalization of London*, London: Routledge.

Koolhaas, R. (2002) 'Junkspace', in C. J. Chung, J. Inaba *et al.* (eds) *Harvard School of Design Guide to Shopping*, Los Angeles: Taschen.

Kristeva, J. (1982) *Powers of Horror: An Essay on Abjection*, trans. L. Samuel Roudiez, New York: Columbia University Press.

Lamming, G. ([1953] 2003) *In the Castle of My Skin*, Harlow: Longman Group.

Landry, J. M. (2009) 'Confession, Obedience, and Subjectivity: Michel Foucault's Unpublished Lectures on the Government of the Living', *Telos*, 2009: 111–23.

Larsen, N. (2000) 'DetermiNation: Postcolonialism, Poststructuralism, and the Problem of Ideology', in F. Afzal-Khan and K. Seshadri-Crooks (eds) *The Pre-Occupation of Postcolonial Studies*, Durham, NC: Duke University Press, pp. 140–56.

Legg, S. (2005) 'Foucault's Population Geographies: Classifications, Biopolitics and Governmental Spaces', *Population, Space and Place*, 11: 137–56.

Legg, S. (2007a) 'Beyond the European Province: Foucault and Postcolonialism', in Crampton, J. W. and Elden, S. (eds) *Space, Knowledge and Power: Foucault and Geography*, Aldershot: Ashgate, pp. 265–88.

Legg, S. (2007b) *Spaces of Colonialism: Delhi's Urban Governmentalities*, Oxford: Blackwell.

Legg, S. (2009a) 'Governing Prostitution in Colonial Delhi: From Cantonment Regulations to International Hygiene (1864–1939)', *Social History*, 34: 447–67.

Legg, S. (2009b) 'An "Indispensable Hypodermis"? The Role of Scale in *The Birth of Biopolitics*', *Journal of Cultural Economy*, 2: 219–25.

Legg, S. (ed.) (2011) *Sovereignty, Spatiality, and Carl Schmitt: Geographies of the Nomos*, London: Routledge.

Levine, P. (2004) 'Sexuality, Gender and Empire', in P. Levine (ed.) *Gender and Empire*, Oxford: Oxford University Press, pp. 134–55.

Levy, A. (2006) *Small Island*, London: Headline Review.

Lewis, P. (2006) 'Brick Lane Protests Force Film Company to Beat Retreat', *The Guardian*, 27 July, available at: www.guardian.co.uk/uk/2006/jul/27/film.books (accessed 29 July 2010).

Lewis, R. and Mills, S. (eds) (2003) *Feminist Postcolonial Theory: A Reader*, Edinburgh: Edinburgh University Press.

Lindridge, A. *et al.* (2004) 'Imagined Multiple Worlds: How South Asian Women in Britain Use Family and Friends to Navigate the "Border Crossings" Between Household and Societal Contexts', *Consumption Markets*, 7: 211–39.

Linton, R. (1961) *The Tree of Culture*, New York: Alfred A. Knopf.

Litvack, L. (1999) 'Dickens, Australia and Magwitch: The Colonial Context', *Dickensian*, 95: 7–32.

Loomba, A. (1993) 'Overworlding the "Third World"', in P. Williams and L. Chrisman (eds) *Colonial Discourse and Post-colonial Theory: A Reader*, New York: Harvester Wheatsheaf, New York, pp. 305–23.

Loshitzky, J. (2006) 'Journeys of Hope to Fortress Europe', *Third Text*, 20(6): 745–54.

McClintock, A. (1995) *Imperial Leather: Race, Gender and Sexuality in the Colonial Context*, London: Routledge.

McFarlane, C. (2008) 'Postcolonial Bombay: Decline of a Cosmopolitan City?', *Environment and Planning D*, 26: 480–99.

McLaughlin, Joseph (2000) *Writing the Urban Jungle: Reading Empire in London from Doyle to Eliot*, Charlottesville, VA: University Press of Virginia.

McLeod, J. (2009) '*Dancing in the Dark*: Caryl Phillips in Conversation with John McLeod', in R. T. Schatteman (ed.) *Conversations with Caryl Phillips*, Jackson, MO: University Press of Mississippi, pp. 143–50.

Maes-Jelinek, H. (ed.) (1991) *Wilson Harris: The Uncompromising Imagination*, Liège: Dangaroo Press.

Maira, S. (1996) 'Ethnic Identity Development of Second-Generation Indian American Adolescents', paper presented at Annual Meeting of the American Educational Research Association, New York, 8–12 April.

Maira, S. (1999) 'Identity Dub: The Paradoxes of an Indian American Youth Subculture (New York Mix)', *Cultural Anthropology*, 14: 29–60.

Martinez-San, M. Y. (2009) 'Postcolonialism', *Social Text*, 100: 188–94.

Marzec, R. P. (2007) *An Ecological and Postcolonial Study of Literature: From Daniel Defoe to Salman Rushdie*, Basingstoke: Palgrave Macmillan.

Massey, D. (2008) 'When Theory Meets Politics', *Antipode*, 40(3): 492–7.

Mathess, D. (1992) 'An Occasion for Geography: Landscape, Representation and Foucault's Corpus', *Environment and Planning D*, 10: 41–56.

Mazumdar, R. (2007) *Bombay Cinema: An Archive of the City*, Minneapolis: University of Minnesota Press.

Mernissi, F. (1975) 'The Meaning of Spatial Boundaries', in F. Mernissi, *Beyond the Veil: Male-Female Dynamics in Muslim Society*, London: Al Saqi Books, reprinted in R. Lewis and S. Mills (eds) *Feminist Postcolonial Theory: A Reader*, Edinburgh: Edinburgh University Press, pp. 489–501.

Mignolo, W. (1992a) 'Putting the Americas on the Map (Geography and the Colonization of Space)', *Colonial Latin American Review*, 1(1): 25–63.

Mignolo, W. (1992b) 'The Darker Side of the Renaissance: Colonization and the Discontinuity of the Classical Tradition', *Renaissance Quarterly*, 45(4): 808–28.

Mignolo, W. (2000) *Local Histories/Global Designs*, Princeton, NJ: Princeton University Press.

Mignolo, W. (2005) *The Idea of Latin America*, Oxford: Blackwell.

Miller, D. P. and Reill, P.H. (1996) *Visions of Empire: Voyages, Botany, and Representations of Nature*, New York: Cambridge University Press.

Mills, S. (2005) *Gender and Colonial Space*, Manchester: Manchester University Press.

Mishra, P. (2006) *Temptations of the West: How to Be Modern in India, Pakistan, Tibet and Beyond*, New York: Farrar, Straus and Giroux.

Mitchell, K. (1997) 'Different Diasporas and the Hype of Hybridity', *Environment and Planning D*, 15: 533–53.

Miyoshi, M. and Harootunian, H. D. (eds) (2002) *Learning Places: The Afterlives of Area Studies*, Durham, NC: Duke University Press.

Mohanty, C. T. (2003) *Feminism Without Borders: Decolonizing Theory, Practicing Solidarity*, Durham, NC: Duke University Press.

Monaco, J. (2000) *How to Read a Film: Movies, Media, Multimedia*, New York: Oxford University Press.

Monmonier, M. (1991) *How to Lie With Maps*, Chicago: University of Chicago Press.

Mootoo, S. (1996) *Cereus Blooms at Night*, Vancouver: Press Gang Publishers.

Moss, J. (1998) 'The Later Foucault', in J. Moss (ed.) *The Later Foucault*, London: Sage, pp. 1–17.

Moya, A. (1998) *Ethnos: Atlas etnográfico del Ecuador*, Quito: EBI Proyecto de Educación Bilingue Intercultural.

Mufti, M. (2005) 'Global Comparativism', *Critical Inquiry*, 31: 472–87.

Murphy, R. (2001) 'CityLife: Urban Fairy-Tales in Late 90s British Cinema', in R. Murphy (ed.) *The British Cinema Book*, London: BFI, pp. 292–300.

Murray, M. A. (2001) 'Shifting Identities and Locations in Jamaica Kincaid's *My Garden (Book):* and *A Small Place*', *World Literature Written in English*, 39(1): 116–26.

Noyes, J. K. (1992) *Colonial Space: Spatiality in the Discourse of German South West Africa 1884–1915*, Chur: Harwood.

O'Brien, S. (2002) 'The Garden and the World: Jamaica Kincaid and the Cultural Borders of Ecocriticism', *Mosaic*, 35(2): 167–84.

Ogborn, M. (1993) 'Law and Discipline in Nineteenth Century English State Formation: The Contagious Diseases Acts of 1864, 1866 and 1869', *Journal of Historical Sociology*, 6: 28–55.

Oswald, L. R. (1999) 'Culture Swapping: Consumption and the Ethnogenesis of Middle-Class Haitian Immigrants', *Journal of Consumer Research*, 25: 303–18.

Panayi, P. (1999) *The Impact of Immigration: A Documentary History of the Effects and Experiences of Immigrants in Britain since 1945*, Manchester: Manchester University Press.

Parry, B. (2004) *Postcolonial Studies: A Materialist Critique*, London: Routledge.

Patel, S. and Masselos, J. (eds) (2003) *Bombay and Mumbai: The City in Transition*, New Delhi: Oxford University Press.

Patel, S. and Thorner, A. (eds) (1995a) *Bombay: Metaphor for Modern India*, New Delhi: Oxford University Press.

Patel, S. and Thorner, A. (1995b) *Bombay: Mosaic of Modern Culture*, New Delhi: Oxford University Press.

Phillips, A. A. (1950) 'The Cultural Cringe', *Meanjin*, 9: 299–302.

Phillips, C. (1993) *Crossing the River*, London: Bloomsbury.

Phillips, C. (2000) *The Atlantic Sound*, London: Faber and Faber.

Phillips, C. (2001) *A New World Order: Essays*, London: Secker and Warburg.

Phillips, C. (2003) *A Distant Shore*, London: Secker and Warburg.

Phillips, C. (2005) 'Growing Pains', *Guardian*, 20 August, available at: http://www.guardian.co.uk/books/2005/aug/20/featuresreviews.guardianreview18 (accessed 14 August 2010).

Phillips, C. (2007) *Foreigners: Three English Lives*, London: Harvill Secker.

Phillips, C. (2009) *In the Falling Snow*, London: Harvill Secker.

Philo, C. (2000) 'The Birth of the Clinic: An Unknown Work of Medical Geography', *Area*, 32: 11–19.

Philo, C. (2004) *A Geographical History of Institutional Provision for the Insane from Medieval Times to the 1860s in England and Wales: The Space Reserved for Insanity*, Lewiston: The Edwin Mellen Press.

Pinney, Christopher (2001) 'Introduction: Public, Popular, and Other Cultures', in R. Dwyer and C. Pinney (eds.) *Pleasure and the Nation: The History, Politics and Consumption of Public Culture in India* (New Delhi: Oxford University Press) pp. 1–34.

Porter, T. (1986) *The Rise of Statistical Thinking, 1820–1900*, Princeton, NJ: Princeton University Press.

Portes, A. and Rumbaut, R. G. (2001) *Legacies: The Story of the Immigrant Second Generation*, Berkeley, CA: University of California Press.

Prasad, M. M. (1998) *Ideology of the Hindi Film: A Historical Construction*, New Delhi: Oxford University Press.

Prasad, M. M. (2004) 'Realism and Fantasy in Representations of Metropolitan Life in Indian Cinema', in P. Kaarsholm (ed.) *City Flicks: Indian Cinema and the Urban Experience*, New Delhi: Seagull Books, pp. 83–99.

Pratt, G. (1992) 'Spatial Metaphors and Speaking Positions', *Environment and Planning D*, 10: 241–4.

Pratt, M. L. (1992) *Imperial Eyes: Travel Writing and Transculturation*, London: Routledge.

Prendergrast, C. (2000) *The Triangle of Representation*, New York: Columbia University Press.

Prescott, W. H. (1867) *History of the Conquest of Mexico, with a Preliminary View of Ancient Mexican Civilization, and the Life of the Conqueror, Hernando Cortes*, Philadelphia, PA: J.B. Lippincott and Co.

Procter, J. (2003) *Dwelling Places: Postwar Black British Writing*, New York: Palgrave Macmillan.

Rabasa, J. (1993) *Inventing America: Spanish Historiography and the Formation of Eurocentrism*, London: University of Oklahoma Press.

Rabinow, P. (1982) 'Ordonnance, Discipline, Regulation: Some Reflections on Urbanism', *Humanities in Society*, 5: 267–78.

Radcliffe S. A. (1996) 'Imaginative Geographies, Post-colonialism and National Identities: Contemporary Discourses of the Nation in Ecuador', *Ecumene*, 3(1): 21–42.

Radcliffe, S. A. (2001) 'Imagining the State as a Space: Territoriality and the Formation of the State in Ecuador', in T. Blom Hanson and F. Stepputat (eds) *States of Imagination*, Durham, NC: Duke University Press, pp. 123–45.

Radcliffe, S. A. (2009) 'National Maps, Digitalisation and Neoliberal Cartographies: Transforming Nation-state Practices and Symbols in Postcolonial Ecuador', *Transactions of the Institute of British Geographers*, 34(4): 426–44.

Radcliffe, S. A. (2010a) 'Re-Mapping the Nation: Cartography, Geographical Knowledge and Ecuadorian Multiculturalism', *Journal of Latin American Studies*, 42(2): 293–323.

Radcliffe, S. A. (2010b) 'Diversity and Development: Post-liberal Rights, Interculturalism and *Sumak Kawsay* in Ecuador', paper presented at Royal Geographical Society with Institute of British Geographers, September.

Rajagopal, A. (2001) *Politics After Television: Hindu Nationalism and the Reshaping of the Public in India*, Cambridge: Cambridge University Press.

Ram, A. (1983) *Interviews with Indian English Writers*, Calcutta: Calcutta Writers' Workshop.

Ransom, J. S. (1997) *Foucault's Discipline: The Politics of Subjectivity*, Durham, NC: Duke University Press.

Ray, S. (2000) *En-Gendering India: Woman and Nation in Colonial and Postcolonial Narratives*, Durham, NC: Duke University Press.

Rennie-Short, J. (2002) 'The Disturbing Case of the Concentration of Power in Human Geography', *Area*, 34(3): 323–4.

Reynolds, R. (2008) *On Guerrilla Gardening: A Handbook for Gardening without Boundaries*, London: Bloomsbury.

Rhys, J. ([1966] 1982) *Wide Sargasso Sea*, New York: W. W. Norton.

Robinson, J. (2003) 'Postcolonialising Geography: Tactics and Pitfalls', *Singapore Journal of Tropical Geography*, 24(3): 274.

Rogers, A. (1992) 'The Boundaries of Reason: The World, the Homeland, and Edward Said', *Environment and Planning D*, 10: 511–26.

Rose, N. (1999) *Powers of Freedom: Reframing Political Thought*, Cambridge: Cambridge University Press.

Rosenau, J. (2003) *Distant Proximities: Dynamics beyond Globalization*, Princeton, NJ: Princeton University Press.

Rose-Redwood, R. (2006) 'Governmentality, Geography and the Geo-coded World', *Progress in Human Geography*, 30: 469–86.

Routledge, P. (2009) 'Third Space', in D. Gregory, R. Johnston, G. Pratt, M. Watts and S. Whatmore (eds) *The Dictionary of Human Geography*, 5th edn, Oxford: Blackwell.

Rushdie, S. ([1988] 1992) *The Satanic Verses*, Delaware: Consortium.

Rushdie, S. (1991) *Imaginary Homelands: Essays and Criticism, 1981–1991*, London: Granta Books.

Rushdie, S. (1992) *The Wizard of Oz*, London: The British Film Institute.

Rushdie, S. (2006) 'Brickbats Fly over Brick Lane', *The Guardian*, Letters, 29 July, available at: http://www.guardian.co.uk/books/2006/jul/29/comment.letters (accessed 29 July 2010).

Russell, D. (2004) *Looking North: Northern England and the National Imagination*, Manchester: Manchester University Press.

Rutherford, J. (1991) 'The Third Space: Interview with Homi K. Bhabha', in J. Rutherford (ed.) *Identity: Community, Culture, Difference*, London: Lawrence & Wishart.

Ryan, S. (1996) *The Cartographic Eye: How Explorers Saw Australia*, Cambridge: Cambridge University Press.

Sackville-West, V. (2004a) *In Your Garden*, London: Frances-Lincoln.

Sackville-West, V. (2004b) *The Garden*, London: Frances-Lincoln.

Said, E. ([1978] 1995) *Orientalism*, Harmondsworth: Penguin.

Said, E. (1983) *The World, the Text, and the Critic*, Cambridge, MA: Harvard University Press.

Said, E. (1990) 'Geography, Narrative, Interpretation', *New Left Review*, 180: 81–97.

Said, E. (1993) *Culture and Imperialism*, London: Vintage.

Said, E. (1994) *Representations of the Intellectual*, New York: Vintage.

Said, E. (1997) *Covering Islam: How the Media and the Experts Determine How We See the Rest of the World*, London: Vintage.

Salih, T. (1969) *Season of Migration to the North*, New Hampshire: Heinemann.

Schmitt, C. ([1950] 2003) *The Nomos of the Earth in the International Law of the Jus Publicum Europaeum*, New York: Telos Press Ltd.

Scott, D. (1999) *Refashioning Futures: Criticism after Postcoloniality*, Princeton, NJ: Princeton University Press.

Scott, D. (2004) *Conscripts of Modernity: The Tragedy of Colonial Enlightenment*, Durham, NC: Duke University Press.

Scott, D. (2008) 'Introduction: On the Archaeologies of Black Memory', *Small Axe*, 26: v–xvi.

Scott, H. (2006) *Caribbean Women Writers and Globalization: Fictions of Independence*, Aldershot: Ashgate.

Scott, H.V. (2009) *Contested Territory: Mapping Peru in the Sixteenth and Seventeenth Centuries*, Notre Dame, IN: University of Notre Dame.

Sekhon, Y. K. and Szmigin, I. (2005) 'Conceptualizing Ethnicity and Acculturation of Second Generation Asian Indians in Britain', *Academy of Marketing Science Review*, 3: 1–18.

Selvon, S. ([1956] 2006) *The Lonely Londoners*, London, Penguin.

Shands, K. (1999) *Embracing Space: Spatial Metaphors in Feminist Discourse*, Westport, CT: Greenwood Press.

Sharma, S. (2009) 'Baring Life and Lifestyle in the Non-Place', *Cultural Studies*, 23(1): 129–48.

Sharp, J. (1996) 'Locating Imaginary Homelands: Literature, Geography, and Salman Rushdie', *Geojournal*, 38(1): 119–27.

Sharp, J. (2008) *Geographies of Postcolonialism*, London: Sage.

Sharp, J. P., Routledge, P., Philo, C. and Paddison, R. (2000) 'Entanglements of Power: Geographies of Domination/Resistance', in R. Paddison, C. Philo, P. Routledge and J. P. Sharp (eds) *Entanglements of Power: Geographies of Domination and Resistance*, London: Routledge, pp. 1–42.

Shohat, E. (2000) 'Notes on the "Post-Colonial"', in F. Afzal-Khan and K. Seshadri-Crooks (eds) *The Pre-Occupation of Postcolonial Studies*, Durham, NC: Duke University Press, 2000, pp. 126–39.

Simmons, D. (1994) *Jamaica Kincaid*, New York: Twayne.

Slemon, S. (1990) 'Unsettling the Empire: Resistance Theory for the Second World', *World Literatures Written in English*, 30: 30–41.

Smith, A. (2004) 'Migrancy, Hybridity, and Postcolonial Literary Studies', in N. Lazarus (ed.) *The Cambridge Companion to Postcolonial Literary Studies*, Cambridge: Cambridge University Press, pp. 241–61.

Smith, N. (1994) 'Geography, Empire and Social Theory', *Progress in Human Geography*, 18(4): 491–500.

Smith, N. and Katz, C. (1993) 'Grounding Metaphor: Towards a Spatialised Politics,' in M. Keith and S. Pile (eds) *Place and the Politics of Identity*, London: Routledge, pp. 67–83.

Smith, Z. (2000) *White Teeth*, London: Hamish Hamilton.

Soja, E. W. (1996) *Thirdspace: Journeys to Los Angeles and Other Real-and-Imagined Places*, Oxford: Blackwell.

Soto-Crespo, R. E. (2002) 'Death and the Diaspora Writer: Hybridity and Mourning in the Work of Jamaica Kincaid', *Contemporary Literature*, 43(2): 342–76.

Sparke, M. (2005) *In the Space of Theory: Postfoundational Geographies of the Nation-state*, Minneapolis: University of Minnesota Press.

Spivak, G. (1993) *Outside in the Teaching Machine*, London: Routledge.

Spivak, G. (1999) *A Critique of Postcolonial Reason: Toward a History of the Vanishing Present*, Cambridge, MA: Harvard University Press.

Spivak, G. (2003) *Death of a Discipline*, New York: Columbia University Press.

Spurr, D. (1993) *The Rhetoric of Empire: Colonial Discourse in Journalism, Travel Writing, and Imperial Administration*, Durham, NC: Duke University Press.

Stoler, A. L. (1995) *Race and the Education of Desire: Foucault's History of Sexuality and the Colonial Order of Things*, Durham, NC: Duke University Press.

Stoler, A. L. (1997) 'Educating Desire in Colonial South-East Asia: Foucault, Freud, and Imperial Sexualities', in L. Manderson and M. Jolly (eds) *Sites of Desire, Economies of Pleasure: Sexualities in Asia and the Pacific*, Chicago: University of Chicago Press, pp. 27–47.

Szeman, I. (2003) *Zones of Instability: Literature, Postcolonialism, and the Nation*, Baltimore, MD: Johns Hopkins University Press.

Tiffin, H. (2000) '"Replanted in this Arboreal Place": Gardens and Flowers in Contemporary Caribbean Writing', in H. Antor and K. Stierstorfer (eds) *English Literatures in International Contexts*, Heidelberg: Carl Winter Universitätsverlag, pp. 149–63.

Torres-Saillant, S. (2006) *An Intellectual History of the Caribbean*, New York: Palgrave Macmillan.

Toscano, A. (2008) 'The Culture of Abstraction', *Theory, Culture & Society*, 25: 57–75.

Upstone, S. (2009) *Spatial Politics in the Postcolonial Novel*, Aldershot: Ashgate.

Varma, R. (2004) 'Provincializing the Global City: From Bombay to Mumbai', *Social Text*, 22(4): 65–89.

Venn, C. (2009) 'Neoliberal Political Economy, Biopolitics and Colonialism: A Transcolonial Genealogy of Inequality', *Theory, Culture & Society*, 26: 206–33.

Virdi, J. (2003) *The Cinematic ImagiNation: Indian Popular Films as Social History*, New Brunswick, NJ: Rutgers University Press.

Viswanath, K. (1997) 'Shame and Control: Sexuality and Power in Feminist Discourse', in M. Thapan (ed.) *Embodiment: Essays on Gender and Identity*, Delhi: Oxford University Press.

Walcott, D. (1990) *Omeros*, New York: Farrar, Straus and Giroux.

Walsh, C. (ed.) (2009) *Interculturalidad, estado, sociedad: Luchas (de) coloniales de nuestra época*, Quito: Universidad Andina Simón Bolívar.

Warner, M. (2006) '"Among Flowers": Jamaica Kincaid in Conversation', *Wasafiri: The Transnational Journal of International Writing*, 21(2): 52–7.

Warnes, A. (2007) 'Enemies Within: Diaspora and Democracy in *Crossing the River* and *A Distant Shore*', *Moving Worlds: Journal of Transcultural Writings*, 7(1): 33–45.

White, C. C. R. (1998) 'Hussein Chalayan's High-Wire Act'. *The New York Times*, 21 April, available at: http://www.nytimes.com/1998/04/21/style/hussein-chalayan-s-high-wire-act.html (accessed 29 July 2010).

Wilson, K. (2004) 'Introduction: Histories, Empires, Modernities', in K. Wilson (ed.) *A New Imperial History: Culture, Identity and Modernity in Britain and the Empire, 1660–1840*, Cambridge: Cambridge University Press, pp. 1–26.

Woolf, V. (1929) *A Room of One's Own*, London: Hogarth Press.

Wyatt, A. (2005) 'Building the Temples of Postmodern India: Economic Constructions of National Identity', *Contemporary South Asia*, 14(4): 465–80.

Yeoh, B. S. A. (1996) *Contesting Space: Power Relations and the Urban Built Environment in Colonial Singapore*, New York: Oxford University Press.

Young, R. C. (1995) *Colonial Desire: Hybridity in Culture, Theory and Race*, London: Routledge.

Young, R. C. (2001) *Postcolonialism: An Historical Introduction*, Oxford: Blackwell.

Youngs, Tim (1994) *Travellers in Africa: British Travelogues, 1850–1900*, Manchester: Manchester University Press.

Zylinska, J. (2004) 'The Universal Acts: Judith Butler and the Biopolitics of Immigration', *Cultural Studies*, 18(4): 523–37.

Filmography

Beautiful People (1999) dir. J. Dizdar (Arts Council of England).

Closer (2004) dir. M. Nichols (Icarus Productions).

Eastern Promises (2007) dir. D. Cronenberg (Serendipity Point Films).

In This World (2003) dir. M. Winterbottom (The Film Consortium).

Last Resort (2000) dir. P. Pawlikowski (BBC).

Love Actually (2003) dir. R. Curtis (Universal Pictures).

My Beautiful Launderette (1985) dir. S. Frears (Channel Four Films).

Notting Hill (1999) dir. R. Michell (Polygram).

Pressure (1976) dir. H. Ové (BFI).

Sliding Doors (1997) dir. P. Howitt (Intermedia Films).

Taxi 9 2 11 (2006) dir M. Luthria (UTV Communications).

Wimbledon (2004) dir. R. Loncraine (Inside Track Films).

The Wizard of Oz (1939) dir. V. Fleming (Metro-Goldwyn-Mayer).

Index

Note: Titles of books are listed under the names of authors. Titles of films are listed separately. An 'n.' after a page reference indicates a note on that page.

CPI Antony Rowe

Chippenham, UK

2017-11-02 12:28